Stephan Kessler (ed.)
Contributions to Baltic-Slavonic Relations in Literature and Languages

Contributions to Baltic-Slavonic Relations in Literature and Languages

An Interdisciplinary Collection of Essays

edited by
Stephan Kessler

Logos Verlag Berlin
2022

About the editor
Stephan Kessler holds the chair of Baltic Studies at the University of Greifswald. His research topics are in linguistics as well as in literary studies.

The contributions to this collection have been one-time blind peer-reviewed

We acknowledge support for the open access publication
from the University of Greifswald

Kyrillica is transliterated according to ISO 9:1995. Therefore, inconsistencies in the transliteration of proper names can occur if the proper names' spelling is based on published titles applying rules different from ISO 9.

Typeset in FS Irwin

Bibliographic information published by the Deutsche Nationalbibliothek

The Deutsche Nationalbibliothek lists this publication in the Deutsche Nationalbibliografie; detailed bibliographic data are available on the Internet at http://dnb.d-nb.de.

This work is licensed under a Creative Commons Attribution 4.0 International
(https://creativecommons.org/licenses/by/4.0/).
The Creative Commons license and its terms do not apply to any content (such as graphs, figures, photos, excerpts, etc.) that does not originate from the authors. Further distribution permission of content from other sources may be required from the original rights holder.

ISBN 978-3-8325-5497-2
DOI 10.30819/5497

Logos Verlag Berlin GmbH
Georg-Knorr-Str. 4, Geb. 10
D-12681 Berlin
Tel.: +49 (0)30 42 85 10 90
Fax: +49 (0)30 42 85 10 92
https://www.logos-verlag.com

Contents

Preface 7

① Teresa Dalecka (Vilnius)
Die polnischsprachige Literatur Litauens seit 1990 9

② Stephan Kessler (Greifswald)
The Culture of Happy Endings, the Basic Structure of Narration, and
Maks Fraj's *Skazki starogo Vil'nûsa* 27

③ Anna Stankeviča / Inna Dvorecka / Jekaterina Gusakova (Daugavpils)
Russophone Literature in Latvia: Its Sociocultural Dimension and
Vadim Vernik's *Gorlica* 49

④ Sergei Kruk (Rīga)
Latvian Concept of Linguistic Integration 69

⑤ Nicole Nau (Poznań)
Zur Integration slawischer Verben und verbaler
Wortbildungselemente im Lettgallischen 87

⑥ Anastasija Kostiučenko (Greifswald)
Der Südosten Litauens als hybrider Sprachraum? Überlegungen mit Blick auf
Polszczyzna Wileńska und Po Prostu 111

Preface

This collection of essays follows two lines. The first line is the Proceedings of the Institute of Baltic Studies at the University of Greifswald, the last of which, *Contributions to Morphology and Syntax*, was published by Logos in Berlin in 2013. The Institute of Baltic Studies also originally wanted to organise a conference on Baltic and Slavonic relations in literature and culture. However, this idea had to be dropped because of the then devastating Covid-19 pandemic. Instead, it was envisaged to bring together a special issue for the venerable *Zeitschrift für Slawisik*. After the work on the special issue had already begun, unforeseen problems arose again, so it became obvious to turn the contributions already at hand into an independent publication. I want to take this opportunity to thank Logos Verlag Berlin and, in particular, its publisher, Mr Buchholtz, for making it possible to release the six interdisciplinary contributions of outstanding experts in a book and digital format!

The second line which this collection of essays follows arises from the book topic itself. As much as scholars of Baltic Studies have always emphasised the discipline's independence in the circle of philologies in — roughly estimated — the last one hundred fifty years and also claim independence for the languages and literature it involves, it is evident that the Baltic and Slavic languages and literature have been and still are in latent contact and exchange. In these last one hundred fifty years, scholars have repeatedly set out to document the relations, and they have published their discoveries and insights in corresponding collections of essays. There are, to name only a few newer titles: the *Балто-славянские исследования* [Balto-Slavonic research], in fact a book series published since 1972 by the Institut Slavânovedeniâ i Balkanistiki in Moscow and still published today; *Deutsche, Slawen und Balten: Aspekte des Zusammenlebens im Osten des Deutschen Reiches und in Ostmitteleuropa* [Germans, Slavs and Balts: aspects of living together in the East of the German Empire and in East Central Europe] edited by Hans Hecker and Silke Spieler (Bonn 1989); *Balten – Slaven – Deutsche: Aspekte und Perspektiven kultureller Kontakte* [Balts – Slavs – Germans: aspects and perspectives of cultural contacts] edited by Ulrich Obst (München 2000); *Tożsamość – język – rodzina: z badań na pograniczu słowiańsko-bałtyckim* [Identity – language – homeland: research in the Slavic-Baltic border region] edited by Anna Engelking (Warszawa 2008); and the consistently bilingual *Baltu un slāvu kultūrkontakti / Балто-славянские культурные связи* [Cultural contacts of the Balts and Slavs] edited by Janīna Kursīte (Rīga 2009). This abbreviated list is joined by several collections and monographs that already focus on more specific spheres of Slavic-Baltic language and literary relations, including research in the common language history, certain isoglosses, and individual aspects of folklore. One such example is *Исследования в области балто-славянской духовной культуры: загадка как текст* [Research in the field of Balto-Slavic immaterial culture: the enigma as text] edited by T. M. Nikolaeva (Москва 1999). There are many publications, therefore, not all of these titles can be listed individually at this point.

To present certain aspects in literature and language as something that exists in a common realm, or at least in a shared field of tension has neither been nor will ever be free of political animosities in particular or of world politics in general. The aforementioned titles bear witness to this in the best possible way. Moreover, they bear witness to the fact that scholars, regardless of the political circumstances, have chosen the path to recognise the interdependencies of all humans — what are cultures or nations? — and scrutinise corresponding relationships in their respective disciplines. The present collection of essays does not see itself in any other situation: after 24/02/22, the world's look at certain Slavic states is a different one; and yet the relationships of the humans who interact with each other — those who look and those who are looked at differently — are much more complex.

I would like to thank all those who provided helpful corrections, especially Cathy DeLibero who was an incredible help with the English version of my contribution.

Greifswald, March 2022   Stephan Kessler

Die polnischsprachige Literatur Litauens seit 1990

Ein Überblick
von Teresa Dalecka (Vilnius)

Outline

The article describes the Polish literature in Lithuania since 1990 and the environment that created it. By presenting Polish poets from different generations, the topics of their poems were discussed. The reasons for the weakness of Polish culture in Lithuania were also diagnosed; they lie in a lack of Polish scholars ('intelligentsia') after World War II or in the poor economic situation of the region where the vast majority of Poles live. Nevertheless, the Polish community has attempted to break out of the existing limitations in recent years. For instance, the poetry group *Nowa Awangarda Wileńska* [New Vilnius Avant-garde] was founded, the novel *Cień słońca* [The shadow of the sun] and the collection of short stories *Thriller po wileńsku* [Thriller Vilnius style] were published. These events led to a different representation of Polishness in Lithuania than before.

Gliederung

1	Allgemeine Situation	11
2	Die Lyrik	14
3	Die Prosa	19
4	Zusammenfassung	22
5	Nachweise	23
5.1	Primärliteratur	23
5.2	Sekundärliteratur	24
	5.2.1 Gedruckte Titel … 24 — 5.2.2 Digitale Titel … 26	

1 Allgemeine Situation

Die polonofone Literatur, die seit 1990 in Litauen entstanden ist, ist bisher unter Forschern, Literaturhistorikern und Kulturschaffenden auf ein recht breites Interesse gestoßen. Den bisher wohl wichtigsten Beitrag, durch den die Werke litauenpolnischer Schriftsteller einem größeren Publikum bekannt gemacht wurden, leistete 1985 Krzysztof Woźniakowski, Autor von *Polska Literatura Wileńszczyzny 1944–1984* [Die polnische Literatur der Region Vilnius 1944–1984]. Woźniakowski widmete auch spätere Aufsätze der Lage der polnischen Schriftsteller in Litauen; zu erwähnen wäre hier besonders Woźniakowski (2000). Ebenfalls ein Meilenstein ist der 1995 in Zielona Góra erschienene *Słownik polskich pisarzy współczesnych Wileńszczyzny* [Lexikon der polnischen Gegenwartsschriftsteller der Region Vilnius], das 28 Personen aufführt und vom Dichter, Herausgeber und Spiritus Rector Eugeniusz Kurzawa stammt. Da seit dem Erscheinen des *Słownik* mehr als 25 Jahre vergangen sind, müsste man dieses Lexikon sicherlich um eine Reihe neuer Namen ergänzen. Auch bekannte Professoren und Literaturwissenschaftler wie Wojciech Podgórski (1994) und Tadeusz Bujnicki (2002, 2013) richteten inzwischen ihre Aufmerksamkeit auf die polnischsprachige Literatur Litauens. Neuere Werke polnischsprachiger Schriftsteller aus Vilnius und Umgebung werden außerdem von Halina Turkiewicz (1995, 1996, 2005 und später) besprochen, die außerdem Autorin einiger Aufsätze zur polnischsprachigen Lyrik in Litauen und verschiedener Einführungen zu einschlägigen Anthologien ist.

Einen wichtigen Platz unter den Initiativen, die Vilnius' literarisches Milieu zugunsten der Lyrik geprägt haben, nimmt die Arbeit der Mäzene und Tutoren litauenpolnischer Dichter ein. Zu dieser Gruppe gehört vor allem der Dichter Henryk Szylkin, der 1928 in der Nähe von Vilnius geboren wurde und heute in Zielona Góra lebt und der mithilfe der dortigen *Towarzystwa Miłośników Wilna i Ziemi Wileńskiej* [Gesellschaft der Freunde von Vilnius und seines Umlands] eine Reihe von litauenpolnischen Autoren herausgab. Zwischen 1990 und 1998 erschienen dort elf Gedichtsammlungen von zehn Autorinnen und Autoren (Sokołowski 1990, 1993a; Komaiszko 1992; Lassota 1992; Śnieżko 1993; Bukowska 1994; Wierbajtis 1995; Mieczkowski 1996; Pszczołowska 1996; Kuncewicz 1997; Piotrowicz 1998). Szylkin ist auch selbst Autor eines bibliografischen Werkes zum literarischen Milieu der Region Vilnius (PPzW 2001). Lyrik von litauenpolnischen Dichtern erschienen auch in der Warschauer *Biblioteka Wileńska* [Wilnaer Bibliothek] (so Mieczkowski 1992, 1994; Piotrowicz 1992; Rybałko 1992; Szostakowski 1992; Sokołowski 1993b), die der Verlag *Oficyna Literatów i Dziennikarzy »Pod Wiatr«* [Verlagshaus der Schriftsteller und Journalisten »Gegen den Wind«] unter Leitung des Lyrikers und Journalisten Romuald Karaś herausgab. Eine wichtige Rolle spielen auch lokale Initiativen wie zum Beispiel das Dichterfestival »Maj nad Wilią« [Der Mai an der Neris; s. unten Anm. 3], das seit über zwei Jahrzehnten von Romuald Mieczkowski, einem jetzt in Warschau lebenden Dichter, organisiert wird, der auch der Herausgeber der Vierteljahreszeitschrift *Znad Wilii* [Von der Neris her; s. Anm. 3] ist. Auf diesen Lyrikertreffen begegnen den lokalen polnischschreibenden Dichtern Kreative aus vielen anderen Länder der Welt. Die Reihe *Biblioteka »Magazynu Wileński«* [Die Bibliothek des »Wilnaer Magazins«] ist in der Region Vilnius ebenfalls zu einem wichtigen Ort für die Veröffentlichung von Gedichtbänden geworden. In ihr erschienen 1991 Alicja

Rybałkos *Listy z Arki Noego* [Briefe aus der Arche Noah], Henryk Mażuls *Doszukać się orła* [Den Adler finden] und 1992 Aleksander Sokołowskis *Kolce losu* [Schicksalsspikes].

Derzeit bedienen in Litauen einige Dutzend Personen aktiv verschiedene literarische Formen auf Polnisch. Etliche Personen gehen auch darüber hinaus und arbeiten für die polnischsprachige Literatur als Herausgeber, Korrektoren oder Rezensenten. Etwa zehn Namen gehören dem 2009 gegründeten *Krajowe Stowarzyszenie Literatów Polskich* [Nationalverband Polnischer Schriftsteller] an, die übrigen sind freie Künstler (Krupka 2021: 477–478).

Bei den genannten Namen ist zu berücksichtigen, dass es sich um Autoren verschiedener Generationen handelt. Michał Wołosewicz (1925–2004) gilt als Nestor der litauenpolnischen Lyrik des 20. Jahrhunderts und er widmete seine Gedichte zum überwiegenden Teil Adam Mickiewiczs Verbindung zu Litauen.[1] Das wurde dadurch begünstigt, dass Wołosewicz mehrere Jahrzehnte seines Lebens in Bieniakonie (heute Weißrussland) verbrachte, wo sich das Grab von Maryla Wereszczakówna, Mickiewiczs Geliebter, befindet. Gegenwärtig wird die älteste Generation von polnischschreibenden litauischen Literaten durch Aleksander Sokołowski (*1935) vertreten, der auch der Vorsitzende der *Sekcja Literatów Polskich przy Związku Pisarzy Litwy* [Sektion der Polnischen Schriftsteller beim Litauischen Schriftstellerverband] ist.

Immer noch aktiv ist die Generation litauenpolnischer Dichter, die in den 1940–1960er Jahren geboren wurden. Diese »Generation 1940« hat Künstler wie Wojciech Piotrowicz (*1940), Maria Łotocka (*1944) oder Aleksander Śnieżko (*1945) hervorgebracht. Zu ihr gehörte auch Sławomir Worotyński (1942–1983), ein vielversprechender, aber vorzeitig verstorbener Dichter. Im literarischen Feld aktiv ist natürlich auch die »Generation 1950«, deren Vertreter Romuald Mieczkowski (*1950), Henryk Mażul (*1953) und Józef Szostakowski (*1953) sind. Bei den Dichtern der beiden genannten Generationen muss man wohl von einer gemeinsamen Generationserfahrung ausgehen, da sie ähnliche Erlebnisse hatte, nämlich einen Umzug vom Land in die Stadt. Sie verloren ihre ursprüngliche Heimat im Umland von Vilnius. Zu der Gruppe derer, die in den 1960er Jahren geborenen wurden, können die Dichter Alicja Rybałko (*1960), die heute in Deutschland lebt, Zbigniew Maciejewski (*1960), Alina Lassota (*1962), Leokadia Komaiszko (*1963) und Regina Pszczołowska (*1967) gerechnet werden. Die Lyrik von Alicja Rybałko wird besonders hochgeschätzt, und zwar für ihre kompositorische Transparenz, vollendete Form, ihren Antisentimentalismus und ihre tiefen Reflexionen. Wie bereits Podgórski (1994) feststellte, wird das Schaffen der »Generation 1960« von zwei Grundthemen beherrscht: Von Mickiewicz, der »eine camouflierte Standarte des Polentums war« (*był zakamuflowanym sztandarem polskości*), und von der »Strahlkraft von Vilnius und seines Umlandes« (*emancja Wilna i Wileńszczyzny*; Podgórski 1994: 223). Die in den 1970er Jahren geborenen Dichter – unter ihnen Lucyna Bukowska (*1973), Dariusz »Wierbajtis« Wierzbiewski (*1973) oder Maria Jakubowska (*1976) – nehmen nach ihren interessanten Debüts nicht mehr so sehr am literarischen Leben Litauens teil. Aus der »Generation 1980« verdienen es Alicja Mickielewicz, Romuald Ławrynowicz und Olga Generałowa erwähnt zu werden. Von ihnen ist derzeit aber nur Romuald Ławrynowicz aktiv, allerdings mehr im Bereich des Films. Die Lyrikergeneration der »1980er«, zurzeit die jüngste, besteht des weiteren aus Tomas Tamošiūnas, Marzena Mac-

---

1 [*Anm. des Übers.*: Adam Mickiewicz (1798–1855) ist der polnische Nationaldichter schlechthin. Er stammte aus Nowogródek, damals im Russischen Reich, heute in Weißrussland gelegen. Nowogródek hatte bis 1793 zum Großfürstentum Litauen gehört. Mickiewicz studierte 1815–1819 an der Universität Vilnius und arbeitete anschließend in Kaunas, bevor er 1824 nach Zentralrussland verbannt wurde.]

kojć, Dariusz Kaplewski und Daniel Krajczyński. Sie bezeichnen sich selber als die *Nowa Awangarda Wileńska* [Neue Avantgarde von Wilna].

Die Forscher Jacek Kajtoch und Krzysztof Woźniakowski haben das Schaffen der litauenpolnischen Dichter, die während der Sowjetzeit ihr Debüt gaben,[2] in drei Strömungen unterteilt, die sich durch ihre Themen und ihr künstlerisches Niveau unterscheiden. Bei der ersten Strömung handelt es sich um volkstümliche Literatur, die sich um die Natur, um Erinnerungen an eine arme Kindheit und um den Arbeitszyklus auf dem Feld dreht. Den zweiten Trend machen gesellschaftspolitische Themen bei traditionellem Vers- und Strophenbau aus. Am ausgereiftesten ist hingegen die dritte Strömung, die als moderne, synkretistische Kreativität charakterisiert werden kann. Sie wurde hauptsächlich von Autoren hervorgebracht, die zwar noch in der UdSSR ausgebildet wurden, aber dennoch verschiedenen literarischen Tendenzen gegenüber aufgeschlossen blieben (Kajtoch / Woźniakowski 1986: 8–11). In den Gedichten der »dritten Strömung« stellen die Landschaft der Region Vilnius und ihre Atmosphäre die wichtigsten Elemente dar und beides bildet die grundlegende emotionale Basis der Werke. Wie Tadeusz Bujnicki (2013: 301) meint, sei der Druck dieser beiden Elemente so stark, dass er ausgedehnte, oft stark konventionalisierte semantische Felder eines ›Kultes‹ um die Ikone Unserer Lieben Frau im Vilniusser Tor der Morgenröte [*Matka Boska Ostrobramska*], von der immer wieder die Rede sei, und um den Dichterpropheten Mickiewicz erzeuge. Darüber hinaus werde gerne die urbane Stadtlandschaft von Vilnius in starke Worte gefasst.

Besonders intensiv entwickelte sich die polnische Lyrik Litauens in den 1990er Jahren. Vor allem dank der großen verlegerischen Dynamik und dem großen Leserinteresse. Doch schon am Ende des Jahrzehnts seien, wie Bujnicki (2013) meint, erste Menetekel sichtbar geworden, weil eine gewisse Stagnation eingetreten sei, die künstlerische Produktion nachgelassen habe und einige Dichter in den Westen (Komaiszko, Rybałko) oder nach Polen (Mieczkowski) ausgewandert seien. Nach dem Millenium habe in Polen jedenfalls der Boom für Lyrik aus Vilnius und seinem Umland geendet (Bujnicki 2013: 302). Zudem wurden die Kriterien für die Beurteilung von Lyrik litauenpolnischer Autoren strenger.

Seit 2010 versucht nun die junge Dichtergeneration, Vilnius' polnisches Literaturmilieu wiederzubeleben und die bisherige Isolation der polnischschreibenden litauischen Autoren vom litauischen Literaturmilieu zu überwinden. Da die Polnischschreibenden ihre Texte bisher fast ausschließlich in der polnischsprachigen Presse veröffentlicht haben, sind in polnischen Verlagen nicht allzu viele Buchausgaben von ihnen erschienen. Bis vor kurzem übersetzten sie ihre Werke weder ins Litauische, noch nahmen sie am litauischen literarischen Leben teil. Erst in den letzten Jahren begann dank einiger aktiver Nachwuchsschriftsteller und dank deren äußerst aufgeschlossenen Einstellung ein Teil der litauenpolnischen Dichtergemeinschaft engere Kontakte zu litauischen Schriftstellern zu knüpfen (Krupka 2021: 478). Diese Kontakte äußern sich in gemeinsamen Buchpräsentationen, Treffen und Lyrikveranstaltungen. Solche Treffen polnischer mit litauischen Schriftstellern finden auch regelmäßig im Rahmen des bereits erwähnten Dichterfestivals »Maj nad Wilią« [Der Mai an der Neris] statt.[3]

---

2 [*Anm. des Übers.*: Litauen gehörte in der Sowjetzeit zur UdSSR, wo es den Status einer Sowjetrepublik hatte. Die litauenpolnischen Dichter jener Generationen sind somit in der UdSSR groß geworden.]

3 »Maj nad Wilią« ist ein internationales Lyrikfestival und findet seit 1994 statt. Initiator und Organisator der Veranstaltung ist Romuald Mieczkowski, Chefredakteur der Zeitschrift *Znad Wilii* [Von der Neris her] und selbst Dichter. Das Lyrikfestival für Autoren aus Litauen und vielen anderen Ländern der Welt dient vor allem dem Literatur- und Kunstmarketing, aber es ermöglicht den Künstlern auch, miteinander in Kontakt zu treten. Handfeste Ergebnisse des Festivals sind allerlei Neuerscheinungen, darunter auch Übersetzungen ins

Es besteht kein Zweifel, dass die Entwicklung der litauenpolnischen Literatur weitgehend mit der Situation der polnischen Minderheit zusammenhängt, die seit Jahren Kritik an ungelösten Probleme äußert. Zu den drängendsten zählten eine gewisse Schwäche des kulturellen Milieus, das von Amateurgruppen, hauptsächlich Folkloregruppen, dominiert wird, dann die sich verschlechternde demografische Situation der Litauenpolen und schließlich die schlechte wirtschaftliche Lage derjenigen Region, in der die Polen in Litauen hauptsächlich leben (Antonovič 2015). Hinzu kämen, dass ein professionelles Theater und der Zugang zu einem breiteren Angebot des polnischen Fernsehens fehle,[4] und vor allem auch, dass ein Großteil der Litauenpolen ein relativ niedriges Bildungsniveau besäßen.

Für die Zwecke dieses Artikels ist der Zustand des polnischen Kulturmilieus in Litauen von größter Bedeutung, zumal von ihm im Wesentlichen das Niveau der auf Polnisch verfassten Literatur abhängt. Der eher schlechte Zustand dieses Milieus resultiert aus einem Mangel an polnischen Intellektuellen im Litauen der Nachkriegszeit und aus dem nur langsamen Prozess der Erneuerung dieser Kreise. Erst heute können wir von einer sichtbaren Gruppe von Personen sprechen, die an Universitäten studiert haben und von der sowjetischen Ideologie unbeeinflusst blieben.

Die Litauenpolen, d. h. die größte nationale Minderheit Litauens, zeichnen sich derzeit durch ein relativ hohes Selbstbewusstsein aus. Nach dem Zweiten Weltkrieg war es jedoch zu enormen Veränderungen in der Bevölkerungsstruktur gekommen. Durch die Repatriierung nach Polen verließ fast die gesamte polnische Intelligenz die Region Vilnius, weshalb das kulturelle Leben der örtlichen Polen für mehrere Jahrzehnte erstarb, um erst im letzten Viertel des 20. Jahrhunderts wiederbelebt zu werden. Der Prozess der Wiederbelebung des polnischen Kulturlebens in Litauen begann mit der litauischen Unabhängigkeitsbewegung Ende der 1980er Jahre und intensiviert sich nach der Wiedererlangung der Unabhängigkeit des Landes in den Jahren 1990/91. Bald darauf erschienen Zeitschriften in polnischer Sprache, es nahm der Radiosender »Znad Wilii« [Von der Neris her] seine Arbeit auf, es entstand die Möglichkeit, polnisches Fernsehen zu empfangen, Treffen und Diskussionen frei zu organisieren oder Polonistik an der Universität Vilnius zu studieren.

2 Die Lyrik

Der ›Stammbaum‹ der litauenpolnischen intellektuellen Elite der oben genannten älteren Generationen ist meist provinziell, nämlich ländlich und kleinstädtisch.[1] Diese Tatsache hat die Art und Weise der Wiederbelebung des literarischen und kulturellen Lebens deutlich geprägt. Man sollte jedoch erwähnen, dass die in Litauen entstandene polnischsprachige Lyrik bereits in den 1980ern an Stärke gewann und auch zu einem Teil der gesamtpolnischen Literatur wurde. Wie Tadeusz Bujnicki (2014: 372) es gesagt hat, bilde die litauenpolnische Lyrik einen Teil der polnischen Literatur, bloß befinde sich dieser Teil in der Fremde [na obczyźnie], d. h. außerhalb Polens, wobei er weder den Charakter der polnischen Exilliteratur, noch den der polnischen Diaspora besitze. Was die litauenpolnische

---

Litauische, die in Zusammenarbeit mit dem Litauischen Schriftstellerverband entstanden.

4   Dieses Problem wurde teilweise gelöst, da es seit zwei Jahren TVP Wilno gibt, das sowohl von regionalen Problemen berichtet, als auch davon, was in Polen geschieht.

1   Diese erste neue ›Intelligencija‹ ist eine humanistische Intellektuellenschicht, die in den 1960–1980er Jahren entstand, und zwar hauptsächlich am Pädagogischen Institut Vilnius und dem dortigen Studiengang der Polonistik. An anderen Universitäten bzw. Fakultäten war ein Studium mit Unterrichtssprache Polnisch nicht möglich.

Literatur von der Exilliteratur unterscheide, sei ihre Verwurzelung im Raum und im nationalen Milieu der Region Vilnius, also ihre starke Beziehung zu einem Territorium, das etwas Eigenes darstelle, und die betreffenden Autoren seien in Litauen autochthon.

Am Ende der Sowjetzeit, als sich das polnische Literaturmilieu in Litauen herauszukristallisieren begann, war es noch verschiedenen ideologischen Beschränkungen unterworfen. Nach der Wiedererlangung der Unabhängigkeit Litauens stand das Milieu der Polnischsprachigen dann vor weiteren Herausforderungen, von denen die wichtigste darin bestand, die polnische Identität in einer Situation zu bewahren, in der sich der litauische Nationalismus verstärkte. Die Dichter haben in ihren Gedichten wiederholt ihre Sorge um das Schicksal der polnischen Sprache und Kultur in Litauen zum Ausdruck gebracht, wobei sie die Wiedergeburt[2] Litauens, den Status, den die litauische Sprache und Kultur wiedererlangten, und den Multikulturalismus nicht ablehnten. In diesem Zusammenhang bezogen sich die Künstler zumeist auf die Tradition ihrer Romantik und machten sie damit zu ihrer Schlüsseltradtion. Die Tradition der Zwischenkriegszeit hingegen, angeführt von der literarischen Gruppe »Żagary« [Holzscheit, Holzegge],[3] blieb bei den Dichtern im Abseits. Allerdings hätten die übereilte Aneignung der Tradition, die Unfähigkeit der Dichter, die komplizierteren Codes der zeitgenössischen Literatur zu lesen, und die Schwierigkeit, das Bild der Vergangenheit zu objektivieren, unweigerlich zu einer Mythologisierung geführt. In der litauenpolnischen Poesie der 1990er Jahre hätten Emotionen oft Vorrang vor intellektueller Reflexion gehabt und die poetische Visionen wären relativ schnell den romantischen und folkloristischen Konventionen gefolgt (Bujnicki 2014: 374). Im Ergebnis erhielten wir rustikale Landschaften und die legendäre Vergangenheit des Landes, die durch die Mauern von Vilnius, Trakai und anderen wichtigen Orten codiert werde, ohne den heutigen Tag und eine Reflexion über ihn zu berücksichtigen. Eine gewisse Entschuldigung für diese Lage der Lyrik sei die Tatsache, dass die überwiegende Mehrheit der litauenpolnischen Autoren in Vilnius und Umgebung geboren wurde, dort studiert hat und dass ihr weiteres Leben mit dieser Region verbunden blieb.

Neben den bisher genannten Themen wäre noch die Vorliebe der älteren Generationen zu erwähnen, Gedichte über Mickiewicz zu schreiben. Dabei handelt es sich weniger um einen Bezug auf das Œuvre des Dichtergenies, als auf seine Vilniusser Lebensphase und allgemeiner auf seine Zeit in Litauen. Zu den Lyrikern, die besonders viele Gedichte Mickiewicz und Vilnius gewidmet haben, gehören Michał Wołosewicz, Sławomir Worotyński, Wojciech Piotrowicz, Romuald Mieczkowski und Józef Szostakowski. Sie sind die Dichter, die auch den Kern des litauenpolnischen Literaturmilieus bilden. Ein weiteres wichtiges Thema in der dichterischen Reflexion älterer Autoren ist das bereits erwähnte Problem ihrer Identitätserhaltung, ihre Verbundenheit mit der polnischen Sprache und Kultur und

---

2 [Anm. d. Übers.: Im Original *odrodzenie* 'Wiedergeburt'. Der Begriff entspricht dem litauischen *atgimimas*, das zwischen 1990 und 2010 für eine bestimmte Weltanschauung stand. Dernach sei die Geschichte des modernen Litauen von drei nationalen ›Meilensteinen‹ bestimmt worden: Vom nationalen Erwachen in der zweiten Hälfte des 19. Jahrhunderts, von der tapfer erkämpften Unabhängigkeit 1918 und von der Wiedergeburt der Republik 1990. Die Verfasserin möchte also sagen, dass die litauenpolnischen Dichter die Restitution der Republik Litauen und die erläuterte politische Sichtweise nicht grundsätzlich in Frage gestellt haben.]

3 Die »Żagary« sind eine Gruppe von polnischen Lyrikern, die 1931 in Vilnius gegründet wurde und auch als »Avantgarde von Wilna« bezeichnet wird. Ihr gehörten unter anderem Czesław Miłosz, Teodor Bujnicki, Jerzy und Stefan Zagórski, Stefan Jędrychowski, Henryk Dembiński, Jerzy Putrament und Józef Maśliński an. Die Gruppe postulierte ein soziales Engagement der Literatur und verkündete die Parole, dass die Gesellschaft mit Hilfe der Poesie moralisch transformiert werden müsse. In den Werken der Gruppe waren die Gefühle einer Katastrophe und eines drohenden Untergangs, der Welt und Mensch gleichermaßen erfasst werde, allgegenwärtig.

die Notwendigkeit, diese zu pflegen und zu verteidigen. In diesen Zusammenhang fügt sich auch nahtlos das Thema der dichterischen Suche nach Spuren von Polentum in Vilnius und Umgebung ein.

Halina Bursztyńska charakterisiert die litauenpolnische Lyrik aus der Zeit nach 1980 wie folgt:

> Das ist Schmalspurdichtung, meist regionaler Natur. Es ist gut, dass es so etwas gibt, aber bei der Rezeption der Werke entsteht ein gewisses Unbehagen, weil der intellektuelle Gedanke nur schlecht in Worte gefasst wird. Es finden sich beispielsweise in den zeitgenössischen Gedichten zwar Motive aus der Architektur, aber sie verengen sich thematisch auf ›bekannte‹ Orte wie das Tor der Morgenröte, die St. Anna-Kirche oder die St. Peter und Paul-Kirche. Ist das eine Folge des engen intellektuellen Horizonts der Dichter oder die Folge eines Mangels an Techniken, oder muss man vielleicht in Betracht ziehen, dass es sich um Menschen handelt, die unter den sehr schwierigen Lebensbedingen der UdSSR gelebt haben und für die Dichtung bisher nur Flucht aus der Realität bedeutet hat? Ich meine auch, dass einige derjenigen lyrischen Texte, die die sogenannten existenzielle Themen behandeln, in ihren Versuchen, die Realität zu bewerten, sehr banal ausfallen. Man findet natürlich auch tolle Texte – aber riecht selbst deren problem-semantische Seite nicht nach Engstirnigkeit und thematischer Monotonie? (Bursztyńska 2005: 71)[4]

Wie Tadeusz Bujnicki (2014: 379) behauptet, sei die in Litauen entstandene Literatur verschiedenen Bedrohungen ausgesetzt gewesen, z. B. dass sie in eine für Nationalismus anfällige polnische Enklave eingesperrt gewesen sei, dass sie gefährlich in ideologische und politische Auseinandersetzungen verstrickt gewesen sei und also mit einiger Wahrscheinlichkeit eine traditionalistische Version des Polnischen, die zudem verteidigt werden müsse, verkündet habe; dass sie sich von der litauischen Kultur abgekapselt und ihr das Merkmal der Fremdheit verliehen habe, sowie sie auch ihr anachronistisches, gottesfürchtiges Polentum zur Schau gestellt habe. Krzysztof Woźniakowski (2000: 255) meint hingegen, dass die polnische Lyrik, die nach 1990 in Litauen entanden ist, raum- und zeitspezifische Reflexionen und Erfahrungen vermittele, ohne dabei nach besonderen handwerklichen Experimenten zu streben. Woźniakowski findet in der gemeinten Lyrik deshalb Bezüge zur Lyrik der Gruppe »Skamander«[5] und Absagen an Gałczyński, Grochowiak, Stachura oder Wojaczek.[6]

---

4 Orig.: »To jest poezja wąskiego toru, głównie o charakterze regionalnym. Dobrze, że takowa zaistniała, ale odnosi się pewien niedosyt w odbiorze dzieł, z uwagi na słabo wyartykułowaną stronę intelektualnego wypowiadania się. Dla przykładu: w wierszach współczesnych poetów pojawiają się motywy architektury, zresztą tematycznie zawężone do »ogranych« miejsc jak: Ostra Brama, kościoły świętej Anny, św. Piotra i Pawła. Czy to wynik wąskich horyzontów intelektualnych tych poetów, czy niedobór warsztatowy, a może należy brać pod uwagę, że to są ludzie, którzy żyli w bardzo trudnych realiach ZSRR i poezja stawała się jedynie ucieczką od życia? Wydaje się również, że niektóre teksty poetyckie, zawierające tzw. tematy egzystencjalne, rażą banałem w próbach wartościowania świata. Można znaleźć teksty świetne – ale czy problemowo-semantyczna strona tej poezji nie trąci zaściankowością i monotonią tematyczną?«

5 »Skamander« ist eine Gruppe von Lyrikern, die um 1916 in Warschau von Julian Tuwim, Antoni Słonimski, Jarosław Iwaszkiewicz, Kazimierz Wierzyński und Jan Lechoń zusammengebracht wurde und sich auf die monatliche Veröffentlichung ihrer Zeitschrift *Skamander* konzentrierte. Ihr Hauptunterscheidungsmerkmal von anderen Gruppen war ihre erklärte programmatische Enthaltsamkeit, die sie mit einem künstlerischen Freiheitspostulat begründeten. Außerdem vertraten »die Skamander« in ihrer Poesie eine Bewunderung des Lebens (einschließlich dessen biologischer Seite) und des Alltäglichen, erkoren den einfachen Mann zum Helden und bedienten sich auch entsprechender Themen, der Umgangssprache, der Dialekte und des Humors.

6 Konstanty Ildefons Gałczyński (1905–1953) war Übersetzer, Lyriker, Autor von Verssatiren und längerer Dichtung. In seiner Dichtung machte er sein lyrisches Ich zum Zigeunerdichter und flüchtete sich in diese dichterische Welt. Die zweite Richtung seiner Arbeit ist die Katastrophengroteske, in der er die soziale und politische Situation im Polen der Zwischenkriegszeit zum Thema erhebt. Stanisław Grochowiak (1934–1976) war Dichter, Dramatiker und Journalist und gilt aufgrund seines Interesses für das Physische, Hässliche und Brutale als Vertreter der Ästhetik des Hässlichen [*turpizm*]. Seine frühe Dichtung zeichnet sich zudem durch eine raffinierte Stilisierung und antiästhetische Themen aus. Grochowiak verwendet auch gerne Makabres und Groteskes und ließ sich von der Barockdichtung inspirieren. In seinem Spätwerk sind die klassizistischen

Die Überwindung von Stereotypen in der Imagination war in den Gedichten der polnischsprachigen Lyriker aus Vilnius schwierig: Die frühesten Veränderungen fanden in Sławomir Worotyńskis Œuvre statt und später bei Alicja Rybałko, deren Poesie die Grenzen des Regionalen überschreitet (Bujnicki 2014: 374).[7]

Doch trotz der verflossenen Jahre sei, so meint der Politologe Mariusz Antonowicz (2015), die polnische Kultur in Litauen bisher auf niedrigem Niveau verblieben. Sie habe einen provinziellen Charakter, weil sie von Folkloregruppen, literarischen Laientreffen, Erntedankfesten und religiösen Feiertagen dominiert werde. Die Gründe für diese Schwäche hat Antonowicz – ähnlich wie andere Forscher – im Ethnozentrismus der litauenpolnischen Kultur, in ihrer Fokussierung auf Selbsterkundung und in ihrem mangelnden Interesse an anderen ethnischen Gruppen ausgemacht. Dies schrecke all die Leser ab, die die Grenzen ihrer Nationalität überschreiten möchten (Antonowicz 2015). Die Folge sei eine Unattraktivität derjenigen Kultur, die dargestellt werde, und auch, dass die Leser dann nach anderen Kulturen griffen, um ihre kulturellen Bedürfnisse zu befriedigen, was im Falle der in Litauen lebenden Polen bedeute, dass sie nach der russischen Massenkultur griffen, die ihnen attraktiver als die polnische erscheine. Die junge Litauenpolen folgten zudem der litauischen Kultur. Die Lösung des Problems müsse darin bestehen, eine attraktive litauenpolnische Hochkultur zu schaffen, die eine Pflege des Polentums eben ermögliche.

Wie bereits erwähnt, begann der mühsame Prozess der Wiedergeburt der litauenpolnischen Kultur in der schwierigen Sowjetzeit, und von daher kennzeichnet sie ein gewisses Handicap. In letzter Zeit gibt es immer mehr Initiativen, durch die die Diskussion über die Tradition und den Zustand der polnischen Kultur in Litauen, die seit mehreren Jahren auf verschiedenen Wegen geführt wird, intensiviert wird. Diese Kulturinitiativen können auch als Vorschläge der litauenpolnischen Autoren interpretiert werden, ihr ›kulturelles Ghetto‹ zu verlassen und ihre Einstellung, eine ›belagerten Festung‹ zu sein, aufzugeben. Radikaler wäre es zu sagen, dass inzwischen einzelne Kreise, und insbesondere die Jugend, versuchen, sich von dem von der Mehrheit des litauenpolnischen Milieus akzeptierten Mythos des Grenzländertums [*mit kresowości*][8] und von der aus ihm resultierenden Notwendigkeit einer starken Traditionspflege zu distanzieren. Am sichtbarsten wird das am Aufkommen ›transkultureller‹ polnischer Teenie-Bands wie »Will'n'ska«, »Black Biceps« oder »Berser-

---

und metaphysischen Tendenzen offensichtlich. Edward Stachura (1937–1979) war Dichter, Prosaautor, Sänger und Übersetzer. In seinen dichterischen Werken, die beinahe lyrische Prosa sind, entsteht ein dramatischer Konflikt zwischen dem natürlichen Bedürfnis, das Leben, die Natur, den Menschen und elementare ethische Werte zu bejahen, und den Gefühlen der Entfremdung, der Existenzangst und des Ekels gegenüber der damaligen, die individuelle Freiheit einschränkenden Zivilisation. Rafał Wojaczek (1945–1971) war Dichter und Prosaautor. Die Hauptthemen seiner Dichtung sind der Tod, die Liebe und die Faszination für Weib- und Körperlichkeit. Meistens schreibt Wojaczek vom Schmerz, vom Gefühl, etwas Besonderes zu sein, und er rebelliert gegen die Heuchelei der Welt und der Gesellschaft. Er verwendet eine naturalistische und oft brutale Sprache.

7 Alicja Rybałko, geboren 1960, ist eine litauisch-polnische Dichterin und Übersetzerin litauischer und schwedischer Literatur ins Polnische. Sie lebt seit 1999 in Münster in Westfalen. Für ihre Arbeit erhielt sie von den Übersetzten den Beinamen »erste Dame der Wilnaer Poesie« (*pierwsza dama poezji wileńskiej*).
8 Die *Kresy* [Grenzlande, Marken] sind die ehemaligen Ostgebiete Polens, die nunmehr auf die Staatsgebiete der Ukraine, Weißrusslands und Litauens verteilt liegen. Heutzutage ist der Begriff Teil des historischen politischen Narrativs Polens und dadurch eine reiche Quelle historischer Mythen und Erinnerungen. Der Begriff *Kresy* wird manchmal von denjenigen Polen, die nach dem Zweiten Weltkrieg aus den entsprechenden Gebieten vertrieben wurden, als ein Synonym für »Heimat« verstanden. Die »Grenzland«-Idee ist hingegen weiterhin tief in der polnischen Kultur, einschließlich der Litauens, verankert. Die *Kresy* von vor dem Zweiten Weltkrieg werden oft in einem sentimentalen und erinnernden Kontext präsentiert, etwa als »Land der Kindheit« oder als verlorenes Paradies.

ker«, die Rock und Punk spielen und deren Liedtexte in Polnisch und anderen Sprachen verfasst sind. In Interviews betonen die Musiker die Multikulturalität von Vilnius und ihre polnische Herkunft. Und da sie für ein sehr differenziertes Publikum spielen, überwinden sie die traditionllen kulturellen Barrieren.

Katarzyna Korzeniewska (1999) behauptet, dass das, was die Polen, die in den verschiedenen Ländern östlich von Polen gelebt haben, am Ende des 20. Jahrhunderts verbunden habe, sei die sogenannte ›Pass-Identität‹ [tożsamość paszportowa] gewesen, d. h. die deklarative Eigenbezeichnung »Pole«. Das habe jedoch keine tieferen kulturellen Konsequenzen gehabt, sei nicht mit einer Notwendigkeit, Polnisch zu beherrschen, verbunden gewesen und habe in der Regel auch zu keinem tieferen Verständnis von polnischer Kultur geführt. Oder es habe dazu geführt, die polnische Kultur vor allem von der Folkloreseite her kennenzulernen. So verhalte es sich im Falle Litauens auch heute noch,[9] wo polnische Kultur auch fast ausschließlich auf einem volkstümlichen Niveau zur Schau gestellt werde. Darüber hinaus setze, wie Korzeniewska (1999) betont, diese Form der Bewahrung polnischer Kultur voraus, das Ghetto »nationale Minderheit« aufrechtzuerhalten, und könne deshalb kein sinnvolles Instrument sein, wenn man auf die litauenpolnischen Kultur positiv Einfluss nehmen wolle, sondern würde höchstens dazu führen, sie zu fossilisieren. Es ergebe überdies kein Potenzial, die lokalen Eliten zu beeinflussen und etwaige antipolnische Einstellungen in der die Minderheit umgebenden Gesellschaft zu neutralisieren.

Aus den genannten Gründen wurde ein Teil des litauenpolnischen Milieus der Lage müde; insbesondere verhielt es sich so in den Kreisen der jüngeren Polen. So machen sie eigene Vorschläge, wie sie ihren Platz im kulturellen und politischen Leben Litauens verstehen.[10] In diesem Zusammenhang war eine Gruppe junger Lyriker, die unter dem Namen *Nowa Awangarda Wileńska* [Neue Avantgarde von Wilna] agiert und deren Anfänge auf das Jahr 2011 zurückreichen, ein Novum auf der literarischen Landkarte von Vilnius. Das Neue bestand in ihrem gemeinsamen Auftreten und insbesondere in der Wahl des Namens, denn bis dahin war die dichterische Tätigkeit der Autoren der älteren Generationen nicht von dieser Art gewesen, obwohl letztere ebenfalls unter einem gemeinsamen Label firmierten und auch ihre Treffen, literarischen Veranstaltungen und Aufführungen gemeinsam organisierten. Das Stichwort für die jungen litauenpolnischen Dichter lautete jedoch »etwas Neues wagen«, was in ihrem Fall vor allem in dem Versuch bestand, das polnische literarische Leben Litauens zu reaktivieren.

Die jungen Dichter benutzen, um sich selbst zu beschreiben, einen etwas prätentiösen Namen, weil er insbesondere eine Reihe von Assoziationen literaturgeschichtlicher Natur hervorruft. Man muss dazusagen, dass es gar kein charakteristisches Merkmal der jungen Dichter ist, ein Avantgarde-Leben zu führen. Sie schlossen sich sogar dem *Krajowy Stowarzyszenie Literatów Polskich na Litwie* [Nationalverband polnischer Schriftsteller in Litauen] an, wobei sie unterstrichen, dass sie keinen bestimmten dichterischen Stil verfolgen würden, sondern in der Region Vilnius bloß das Interesse an Poesie beleben möchten. Es sei ihr klarer Wunsch, auf die (nicht näher bestimmte) Tradition der »Żagary« der Zwischen-

---

9   In Litauen gibt es derzeit eine große Anzahl an polnischen Folkloregruppen.
10 Eine der spannendsten Initiativen ist der *Polski Klub Dyskusyjny* [Polnische Diskussionsclub]. Seine Mitglieder schreiben, dass er eine Plattform für polnisch-litauenpolnische Diskussionen und den polnisch-litauischen Dialog sein solle. Ein Ort also, an dem sich alle Litauenpolen zu jedwedem Thema austauschen könnten, vorausgesetzt, sie betrieben keine politische Agitation oder Propaganda, verwendeten keine Hassreden und respektierten andere Menschen und ihre Ansichten, Meinungen und Überzeugungen. Die Tätigkeit des Diskussionsclubs stößt jedoch auf scharfe Kritik von Seiten der *Akcja Wyborcza Polaków na Litwie – Związek Chrześcijańskich Rodzin* [Wahlkampagne der Polen in Litauen – Union Christlicher Familien], die den Mitgliedern des Diskussionsclubs vorwirft, antipolnisch zu sein.

kriegszeit (s. Anm. 3 in diesem Kapitel) Bezug zu nehmen und zu versuchen, Einfluss auf das regionale polnische Milieu auszuüben.

Die Mitglieder der »Neuen Avantgarde von Wilna« praktizieren Lyrik und wiederholen gewissermaßen den kreativen Weg jener älteren Kollegen, die in den 1980ern ihr Debüt feierten. Jene begannen auf ähnliche Weise mit der Veröffentlichung ihrer Gedichte in Anthologien,[11] und erst mit der Zeit fingen sie an, eigene Gedichtbände zu veröffentlichen. Beispiele für neuere Buchausgaben von jungen Autoren sind u. a. die Publikationen *Na strunach duszy* [Auf den Fäden der Seele] von Kristina Užėnaitė (2018), *I pieśń gdzieś leci ode mnie echowa* [Und das Lied hallt irgendwo aus mir wider] von Mirosława Bartoszewicz (2018) und *Podróż długa jak życie* [Eine Reise so lang wie das Leben] von Dominika Olicka (2018).

Paweł Krupka ist seiner eigenen Meinung nach recht kritisch und er behauptet (Krupka 2019: 70), die polnischsprachige Lyrik aus der Region Vilnius sei im Allgemeinen konservativ und folge den Mustern der *Młoda Polska* [Junges Polen][12] und der *Skamandryci* [Skamandriten].[13] Sie trete eher in die Fußstapfen von Bujnicki und Zagórski als von Miłosz. Deshalb kämpften junge litauenpolnische Dichter noch heute mühevoll darum, sich von etablierten Klischees zu befreien, und ihre Arbeit stoße bei ihren litauischen Kollegen meist nicht auf Verständnis.

Vor diesem dichtungstraditionellen Hintergrund sticht das Werk einiger Dichter durch Originalität hervor, allen voran die Werke von Tomas Tamošiūnas, der einen litauisch-klingenden Vor- und Nachnamen hat, aber polnischer Herkunft ist. Er hat mehrere polnischsprachige Gedichtbände verfasst, darunter 2012 *Do krainy wyciszenia* [Ins Land der Stille] und 2018 *Piwo z Aniołem Stróżem* [Ein Bier mit dem Schutzengel]. Seine Gedichte zeichnen sich durch einen weiten Blick auf alltägliche Dinge aus. In seinen Werken gestaltet er oft ein synchrones Mosaik, das aus funktional gleichartigen Artefakten verschiedener Epochen und Kulturbereichen gebildet wird. Dies Verfahren macht seine Poesie attraktiv. Wie Paweł Krupka (2019: 70) meint, schreibe Tamošiūnas frei und ohne Respekt gegenüber Dingen, über die man mit Zurückhaltung sprechen und schreiben sollte. Die Psychologie, Erotik und Selbstreflexion seiner Gedichte brächten Tamošiūnas einer Ästhetik näher, die in der Lyrik seiner europäischen Altersgenossen weit verbreitet sei.

3 Die Prosa

Einerseits kann die totale Dominanz von Lyrik in der polnischen Literatur Litauens als Ausdruck einer Schwäche dieser Literatur, die praktisch der Prosa und deren breiteren epischen

---

11 Die Dichter der älteren Generation veröffentlichten 1985 in einem Kaunasser Verlag eine erste Anthologie mit polnischsprachigen Gedichten von fünfzehn Autoren, *Sponad Wilii cichych fal* [Über der Nėris' ruhigen Wellen] betitelt. 1986 erschien dann in Warschau die von Jacek Kajtoch und Krzysztof Woźniakowski herausgegebene *Współczesna polska poezja Wileńszczyzny* [Moderne polnische Dichtung aus Wilna und Umland], die die litauenpolnischen Dichter auch in Polen bekannt machte. Auch erste Sammelbände wie *Łamanie się opłatkiem wiersza poetów znad Wisły i Wilii* [Der Bruch der Gedichtoblate durch Dichter von Weichsel und Nėris] (Krakau 1988) oder *W stronę Wilna* [Richtung Vilnius] (Warschau 1989) sind erwähnenswert. 2019 erschien in Vilnius die Anthologie *Polska Pogoń Poetycka: Antologia polskiej poezji Litwy* [Der polnische poetische Vytis: Eine Anthologie litauenpolnischer Dichtungen], die Werke älterer und jüngerer Dichter enthält und sozusagen alle Grenzen zwischen ihnen aufhebt. Die Anthologie umfasst Texte von 37 Autoren, weshalb sie einen guten Überblick über das literarische Schaffens der litauischen Polen gibt.
12 [*Anm. d. Übers.:* Eine Strömung des polnischen Modernismus der Zwischenkriegszeit.]
13 [*Anm. d. Übers.:* Die Mitglieder der Gruppe »Skamander«; s. Anm. 5 in diesem Kapitel.]

Atemzugs beraubt ist, angesehen werden, aber andererseits kann dieser Umstand durch die eingeschränkten Publikationsmöglichkeiten verständlich erklärt werden. Die Autoren konnten bisher hauptsächlich nur kurze Gedichte veröffentlichen, während ihre eher umfangreichen Prosatexte keine eigenen Zeitungskolumnen bekamen. Von daher lassen sich die bisherigen Prosaausgaben an den Fingern einer Hand abzählen. Erwähnenswert sind ein Band mit ›kleiner‹ Prosa von Wojciech Piotrowicz, Romuald Mieczkowskis Memoiren und Aleksander Radczenkos *Cień słońca: Inne opowiadania* [Der Schatten der Sonne: Andere Geschichten], welches, soweit bekannt, der einzige polnischsprachige Vilnius-Roman ist, der in der zweiten Hälfte des 20. Jahrhunderts veröffentlicht wurde.

Wojciech Piotrowicz (*1940) gehört zur älteren Generation litauischer polnischsprachiger Künstler. Er stellt sich in die Tradition der regionalen Schriftsteller der Zwischenkriegszeit (Turkiewicz 2019: 164–165). Piotrowicz ist nicht nur Prosaschriftsteller, sondern auch Lyriker, Journalist, Kulturfunktionär und Sozialaktivist. Er repräsentiert das Milieu der litauenpolnischen Intelligenz der Nachkriegszeit, ist ein an der Universität Vilnius diplomierter Mathematiker und hat dort ebenfalls ein Lehramtsstudium für Physik und Mathematik abgeschlossen. In den 1980ern arbeitete er als Journalist bei der polnischsprachigen Tageszeitung *Czerwony Sztandar* [Rotes Banner].[1] Außerdem moderierte er polnischsprachige Programme im litauischen Rundfunk und Fernsehen (Fedorowicz / Geben 2021: 320–321).

Piotrowicz veröffentlicht Prosawerke seit 1998. 2015 erschien unter dem Titel *Moja czaso-przestrzeń: W głąb i z bliska* [Meine Raumzeit: In die Tiefe und hautnah] ein Zyklus von 84 Erzählungen in Buchform. Es ist eine Prosa, die dem Genre der künstlerischen Prosa mit Nähe zur Reportage angehört. Sie kann auch als autobiografische Prosa gelten, denn das Leitmotiv der Erzählungen sind Piotrowiczs Erinnerungen an seine in wirtschaftlicher und politischer Hinsicht schwierige Kindheit, die in die direkten Nachkriegsjahre und die Zeit des Sozialismus fiel. Die erzählte Zeit reicht von dort bis in die 1990er und somit bis zu den Ereignissen des politischen Umbruchs. Alles in allem erhalten wir eine nicht-fiktionalisierte Beschreibung der litauischen Realität, und zwar hauptsächlich die der 1940er und 1950er Jahre, in denen das Familienhaus die wesentlichen Rolle spielte.

Ein interessantes Literaturangebot ist das Buch *Cień słońca: Inne opowiadania* [Der Schatten der Sonne: Andere Geschichten] von Aleksander Radczenko, das 2015 in Vilnius neu aufgelegt wurde. Der Autor begann es 1997, und einige Jahre später wurden Teile des Werkes im Magazin *Chaos* vorabgedruckt. Die erste Auflage/Fassung von *Cień słońca* erschien dann 2004 in Vilnius bei »Niezależna Oficyna Wydawnicza TKM / W pasczu« [Unabhängiger Verlag der TKM ›Auf der Weide‹] (Widzniak 2012). Jedoch wurde die Ausgabe nicht angemessen vermarktet, sodass es 2015 zu einer zweiten, überarbeitete Ausgabe im Verlag des College of Eastern Europe in Wrocław kam. Der Kontext des Buches ist zweifelsohne die Biographie des Autors.[2] Das Buch erzählt von der Rebellion eines Punkers, der versucht, seinen Platz in der Welt zu finden. Der Autor selbst hob hervor (Radczenko 2015 a digital), dass er, als er »Schatten der Sonne« schrieb, gerade stark von Irvine Welsh

---

1 [*Anm. d. Übers.*: Eine in Vilnius, in der damaligen Litauischen Sozialistischen Sowjetrepublik verlegte Zeitschrift, die von 1953 bis 1990 erschien. Sie war ein Organ des Zentralkomitees der Kommunistischen Partei Litauens.]
2 Von 1994 bis 1996 war Radczenko Vorsitzender des *Klub Polskiej Młodzieży Alternatywnej na Litwie* [Polnischer Alternativer Jugendklub in Litauen] und er gründete die Gruppe unabhängiger Künstler »TKM«. Radczenko vertritt liberale Anschauungen. Von Beruf ist er Rechtsanwalt. Außerdem arbeitete er als Journalist für die Zeitungen *Słowo Wileńskie* und *Gazeta Wileńska*. Von 2000 bis 2002 war er Herausgeber des alternativen Magazins *Chaos*. Derzeit ist er hauptsächlich im juristischen Bereich tätig.

beeinflusst gewesen sei.³ Er habe versucht, ein Vilniusser *Trainspotting* zu schreiben, allerdings nicht über Drogenabhängige, sondern über alkoholkranke Journalisten:

> Und im Gegensatz zu dem, was die sagen, die den Roman bereits gelesen haben – es ist kein autobiografischer Roman. Es ist ein Roman über meine Generation. Über die Generation, die in den 1970ern geboren wurde, deren Kindheit in die Sowjetzeit fiel, die in der Zeit des Systemwandels Teenies waren und die während der Zeit des freien Marktes und der jungen Demokratie bereits zu Erwachsenen geworden waren. Über eine Generation, die gerade wegen dieser und keiner anderen Erfahrungen eine Generation von »Romantikern, verloren in einer Welt der Technokratie« ist. Ich finde, es ist jetzt höchste Zeit, ein Buch über diese Generation zu veröffentlichen. (Radczenko 2015a digital)⁴

Radczenkos Werk kann als die erste postmoderne Vilnius-Geschichte in polnischer Sprache charakterisiert werden. Vor allem sollte man hervorheben, dass es sich praktisch um den ersten Roman überhaupt handelt, den das litauenpolnische Literaturmilieu hervorgebracht hat. Das bisherige Fehlen dieser Gattung lässt sich aber einfach erklären: Es gibt im litauenpolnischen Milieu keine professionelle Prosaförderung. Der Roman wurde zweideutig aufgenommen. In seiner Einleitung zum Werk hob Jacek Kajtoch (2015: 5) hervor, dass es die Vielzahl der Handlungsfäden unmöglich mache, die Idee des Romans, der eindeutig ein Schlüsseltext sei, zu verstehen. »Eine übelriechende Brise aus der Vergangenheit. Im besten Sinne des Wortes«, schrieb ein anderer Rezensent (Rotkiewicz 2015).

»Der Schatten der Sonne« kann als Manifest einer Generation angesehen werden, die ihre Unabhängigkeit nicht erwarb, sondern sie konsumierte. Radczenko schreibt von der Zeit der Systemtransformation, während der diejenigen, die um 1975 geboren wurden, die entstandene axiologische Leere mit irgendetwas füllen mussten. Die Hauptfigur des Romans ist Aleks, ein kompromissloser Journalist einer Lokalzeitung, der angesichts seiner Bedrohung durch Mafia, Politiker und rivalisierende Medien vor der Notwendigkeit steht, eine Entscheidung zu treffen. Radczenko erzählt von einer Generation, die nicht weiß, was sie glauben soll. Sie sind zynische, verlorene Menschen, ihr religiöses Leben ist armselig und sie ergeben sich einem Konsumismus und Materialismus. Auch Aleks ist verloren und schafft es nicht, sich in einer Welt zurechtzufinden, derer er längst überdrüssig ist.

»Der Schatten der Sonne« erschien in einem für das litauenpolnische Milieu entscheidenden Moment, als sozusagen eine schrittweise Wachablösung einsetzte und ›Radczenko & Co.‹ immer mehr wichtige Positionen einnahmen, indem sie Personen ersetzten, die ihre persönliche Weltanschauung auf die Diskriminierung der in Litauen lebenden Polen gründeten und auf die Notwendigkeit, ein echtes Polentum um jeden Preis zu verteidigen. Das wichtigste Moment der Tätigkeiten der Neuen scheint es hingegen gewesen zu sein, das enge Verständnis von Polentum zu überschreiten und den Kontakt mit anderen, vor allem litauischen Künstlerkreisen zu suchen.

Bei seinem Versuch, sich von der recht verknöcherten Tradition der Vilnius-Romantik, die allen Autoren, die in Litauen auf Polnisch schreiben, eigen ist, zu befreien, tappt Radczenko jedoch in eine Falle. Wie Michał Rudnicki (2016) richtig festgestellt hat: »Aleks sucht die Liebe, welche ihm ›Seelenverwandtschaft‹ bedeutet; er ist ein Romantiker des

---

3 [*Anm. d. Übers.*: Irvine Welsh (*1958) aus Leith in Schottland wurde durch seinen Roman *Trainspotting* (1993) bekannt, der die von Drogen, Arbeitslosigkeit und Kriminalität geprägten Erlebnisse einer Gruppe junger Schotten aus Edinburgh zum Thema hat.]

4 Orig.: »No i wbrew temu co twierdzą ci, którzy już tę powieść przeczytali – nie jest to powieść autobiograficzna. To powieść o moim pokoleniu. Pokoleniu urodzonym w latach 70. Pokoleniu, którego dzieciństwo przypadło na okres sowiecki, młodość na czasy transformacji ustrojowej, a w wiek dojrzały już weszło w czasach wolnego rynku i demokracji. Pokoleniu, które właśnie z uwagi na takie a nie inne doświadczenia jest pokoleniem ›romantyków zagubionych w technokratyzmie‹. Wydaje mi się, że teraz jest najwyższy czas, żeby książkę o tym pokoleniu opublikować.«

19. Jahrhunderts, verloren in einer technokratischen Welt. Aber was kann man sonst von einem Autor aus Vilnius erwarten?«

2015 hatte der *Polski Klub Dyskusyjny* [Polnische Diskussionsklub; s. Anm. 10 in Kap. 2] einen Literaturwettbewerb um die beste Thrillergeschichte junger litauenpolnischer Autoren ausgelobt, in dessen Folge die Erzählsammlung *Thriller po wileńsku* [Thriller nach Vilnius-Art] veröffentlicht wurde. Trotz ihres bescheidenen Umfangs und Texten, von denen die meisten wohl eher als erste literarische Gehversuche gelten müssen, verdient die Veröffentlichung des Buches an sich Beachtung. Wie Radczenko (2015 b digital) zu Recht betont, sei »Thriller nach Vilnius-Art« der Versuch, den Grundstein für die Zukunft des Polentums in Litauen zu legen, weil dieses nur überdauern werde, wenn es nicht nur an Tradition und Folklore, sondern auch an die Gegenwart anknüpfe. Junge Autoren zu ermuntern, sich mit Genres wie Science-Fiction, Fantasy oder Thriller auseinanderzusetzen, soll nach Ansicht der Wettbewerbsorganisatoren dazu beitragen, das positive Image des Vilniusser Polentums zu festigen. Bis jetzt war dieser Literaturwettbewerb eine einmalige Aktion, aber er sollte unbedingt fortgesetzt werden. Es bedarf auf jeden Fall dieses Anreizes in Form eines Wettbewerbs oder einer anderen Veranstaltungsform.

Ein weiteres polnisches Prosa-Angebot eines gebürtigen Vilniusser sind Romuald Mieczkowskis Memoiren *Były sobie Fabianiszki* [Es war einmal ... Fabianiszki].[5] Das Buch handelt von Fabianiszki (einem Dorf), seinen Menschen (den Mieczkowskis) und dem Autor, der ein verdienter Multiplikator polnischer Kultur in Litauen ist und derzeit in Warschau lebt. Wie bereits ein Rezensent kommentierte (Snarski 2020), ist Mieczkowskis Buch auch eine echte Geschichtsstunde vom Leben in einem Litauen, das durch sowjetische Besatzung in Unfreiheit kam, von den Jahren seiner Transformation und von den darauffolgenden Jahren in einem bereits unabhängigen Land.

Andererseits behauptet Barbara Gruszka-Zych (2020), dass »Es war einmal ... Fabianiszki«, das ja nur die Lebensgeschichte einer einzigen Familie darstellt, eher eine symbolische Geschichte von den Polen sei, die in der Zwischenkriegszeit und nach dem Ende des Zweiten Weltkriegs in Vilnius gelebt haben. Es sei auch die Geschichte der Polen im Allgemeinen, einer Nation, die den zu ihrem Überleben unerlässlichen Patriotismus bereits mit der Muttermilch aufnähmen. Wie die Rezensentin es sieht, fange Mieczkowski das Wesen von Fabianiszkis dahinschwindendem Leben ebenso poetisch-nostalgisch wie humorvoll ein, und weil diese Momentaufnahme in Form von Literatur geschehe, werde sie ewigen Bestand haben.

Das Polentum in der Region Vilnius verlangt eine andere Art der Selbstpräsentation als bisher, zum Beispiel verlangt es einen Roman oder eine Erzählsammlung. Die im polnischen Kollektivbewusstsein immer noch stark präsente Region kämpft mit dem Problem ihrer Selbstdarstellung. Die ersten entsprechenden Versuche sind von unterschiedlicher Qualität. Sicherlich können die eher handwerklichen Mängel bald beseitigt werden.

4 Zusammenfassung

Paweł Krupka (2021: 482) beteuert, dass es alle Voraussetzungen dafür gebe, dass Litauens polnisches Literaturmilieu aktiv am literarischen Leben sowohl Litauens, als auch Polens teilnehmen und eine natürliche Brücke zwischen beiden Gesellschaften bilden könne. Es

---

5   [Anm. d. Übers.: Poln. *Fabianiszki*, lit. *Fabijoniškės* ist heute ein Stadtteil im Norden von Vilnius. Der Stadtteil diente 2019 als Drehort für die Fernsehserie »Chernobyl«, um die ukrainische Stadt Prypjat darzustellen.]

ließen sich jedoch nicht endgültig die Gründe dafür erhellen, warum es sich bisher anders verhalte. Vielleicht muss man die Antwort darauf im sozialen Bereich suchen, also im Konservatismus der Litauenpolen sowie darin, dass auf der künstlerischen ›Bühne‹ die Jugend zu langsam zum Durchbruch kommt.

Tadeusz Bujnicki (2002: 337) stellte in seiner Besprechung der Situation der litauenpolnischen Lyrik treffend fest, dass kritische Fragen nach der Eigenart der polnischen Literatur in Vilnius, nach ihrem Kontakt zu den literarischen Strömungen in Polen, nach ihrer Orientierung auf die litauische Literatur und nach der Funktion der Lyrik in Bezug auf andere Gattungen weiterhin angebracht seien. Eine Rückkehr in den recht anachronistischen Zustand der Exklave [*powrót do nieco anachronicznej »enklawy« poza granicami kraju*], d. h. in ein Reservat aus romantischen Emotionen, könne nämlich einen sehr ungünstigen Effekt zeitigen. Fast zwanzig Jahre nach dieser Feststellung müssen weitere kritische Fragen gestellt werden. Sie sollten in erster Linie die dichterischen Fähigkeiten der jungen Generation polnischsprachiger Kulturschaffender, die in Litauen leben, betreffen.

Aus dem Polnischen ins Deutsche übertragen von Stephan Kessler

5 Nachweise

5.1 Primärliteratur

Bartoszewicz, Mirosława (2018), *I pieśń gdzieś leci ode mnie echowa*, Vilnius: Jusida.
Bukowska, Lucyna Ł. (1994), *Okruchy liryczne*, Zielona Góra: Wydawnictwo Wyższej Szkoły Pedagogicznej im. Tadeusza Kotarbińskiego.
Komaiszko, Leokadia (1992), *W stronę światła*, Zielona Góra: Wydawnictwo Wyższej Szkoły Pedagogicznej im. Tadeusza Kotarbińskiego.
Kuncewicz, Krystyna J. (1997), *W tłumie ego*, Zielona Góra: Wydawnictwo Wyższej Szkoły Pedagogicznej im. Tadeusza Kotarbińskiego.
Łamanie się opłatkiem wiersza poetów znad Wisły i Wilii (1988), Anthologie, hrsg. v. Jacek Lubart-Krzysica, Kraków: Wydział Kultury UD Kraków-Podgórze.
Lassota, Alina (1992), *Wileńskie preludia*, Zielona Góra: Wydawnictwo Wyższej Szkoły Pedagogicznej im. Tadeusza Kotarbińskiego.
Mażul, Henryk (1991), *Doszukać się orła*, Wilno: Państwowe Centrum Wydawnicze.
Mieczkowski, Romuald (1992), *Powrócę*, Warszawa: Oficyna Literatów i Dziennikarzy »Pod wiatr«.
—, — (1994), *Podłoga w celi Konrada*, Warszawa: Oficyna Literatów i Dziennikarzy »Pod wiatr«.
—, — (1996), *Sen w ogrodach Moneta*, Zielona Góra: Wydawnictwo Wyższej Szkoły Pedagogicznej im. Tadeusza Kotarbińskiego.
—, — (2020), *Były sobie Fabianiszki*, Memoiren, Wilno: Wydawnictwo Znad Wilii.
Olicka, Dominika (2018), *Podróż długa jak życie*, Vilnius: Jusida.
Piotrowicz, Wojciech (1992), *Nec mergitur*, Warszawa: Oficyna Literatów i Dziennikarzy »Pod wiatr«.
—, — (1998), *Podzwonne sośnie*, Zielona Góra: Wydawnictwo Wyższej Szkoły Pedagogicznej im. Tadeusza Kotarbińskiego.
—, — (2015), *Moja czasoprzestrzeń: W głąb i z bliska*, Wilno: Muzeum Władysława Syrokomli.

Polska Pogoń Poetycka: Antologia polskiej poezji Litwy (2019), hrsg. v. Haliny Turkiewicz, Wilno: Krajowe Stowarzyszenie Literatów Polskich.

Pszczołowska, Regina (1996), *Muszelki miłości*, Zielona Góra: Wydawnictwo Wyższej Szkoły Pedagogicznej im. Tadeusza Kotarbińskiego.

Radczenko, Aleksander (2015), *Cień słońca: Inne opowiadania*. 2. Aufl., Wrocław: Kolegium Europy Wschodniej.

Rybałko, Alicja (1991), *Listy z Arki Noego*, Wilno: Państwowe Centrum Wydawnicze.

—, — (1992), *Będę musiała być prześliczna*, Warszawa: Oficyna Literatów i Dziennikarzy »Pod wiatr«.

Śnieżko, Aleksander (1993), *W kręgu Wilna*, Zielona Góra: Wydawnictwo Wyższej Szkoły Pedagogicznej im. Tadeusza Kotarbińskiego.

Sokołowski, Aleksander (1990), *Wiatraki historii*, Zielona Góra: Wydawnictwo Wyższej Szkoły Pedagogicznej im. Tadeusza Kotarbińskiego.

—, — (1992), *Kolce losu*, Wilno: Państwowe Centrum Wydawnicze.

—, — (1993a), *Kontrasty*, Zielona Góra: Wydawnictwo Wyższej Szkoły Pedagogicznej im. Tadeusza Kotarbińskiego.

—, — (1993b), *Podanie o zwrot ziemi*, Warszawa: Oficyna Literatów i Dziennikarzy »Pod wiatr«.

Sponad Wilii cichych fal (1985), Anthologie, hrsg. v. Stanisław Jakutis und Jadwiga Kudirko, Kaunas: Šviesa.

Szostakowski, Józef (1992), *Nie ucz się domu*, Warszawa: Oficyna Literatów i Dziennikarzy »Pod wiatr«.

Tamošiūnas, Tomas (2012), *Do krainy wyciszenia*, Wilno: Muzeum Władysława Syrokomli.

—, — (2018), *Piwo z Aniołem Stróżem*, Wilno: Wydawnictwo Znad Wilii.

Thriller po wileńsku: Antologia opowiadań z Wilna (2015), Vilnius: Ciklonas.

Užėnaitė, Kristina (2018), *Na strunach duszy*, Vilnius: Jusida.

Wierbajtis [i.e. Wierzbiewski], Dariusz (1995), *Wiosenne wzloty*, Zielona Góra: Wydawnictwo Wyższej Szkoły Pedagogicznej im. Tadeusza Kotarbińskiego.

W stronę Wilna: Anthologie (1989), ausgew. und hrsg. v. Tomasz Jodełka-Burzecki. Warszawa: ZLP.

5.2 Sekundärliteratur

5.2.1 Gedruckte Titel

Antonovič, Marijuš (2015), »Quo vadis Wileńszczyzna?«, *Naujasis židinys-Aidai* 5, S. 15–23.

Bujnicki, Tadeusz (2002), »Polskie życie literackie we współczesnym Wilnie (pierwsza dekada w niepodległej Litwie)« [Polnisches literarisches Leben im Vilnius der Gegenwart (das erste Jahrzehnt des unabhängigen Litauen)], in Tadeusz Bujnicki, *Szkice wileńskie*, Kraków: Collegium Columbinum, S. 319–338.

—, — (2013), »Henryk Szylkin i poeci wileńscy lat 90« [Henryk Szylkin und die Vilniusser Dichter der 1990er], in Małgorzata Mikołajczak (Hg.), *Miejsce i tożsamość: Literatura lubuska w perspektywie poetyki przestrzeni i antropologii*, Zielona Góra: Oficyna Wydawnicza UZ, S. 291–303.

—, — (2014), *Na pograniczach, kresach i poza granicami*, Białystok: Książnica Podlaska w Białymstoku.

Bursztyńska, Halina (2005), »Refleksje o współczesnej poezji polskiej na Litwie« [Reflexionen über die polnische Gegenwartslyrik in Litauen], *Konspekt* 1 (21), S. 69–73.

Kajtoch, Jacek (2015), »Wstęp« [Vorwort], in Aleksander Radczenko, *Cień słońca: Inne opowiadania*, Wrocław: Kolegium Europy Wschodniej, S. 5–11.

—, —/ Krzysztof **Woźniakowski** (1986), Hrsg., *Współczesna polska poezja Wileńszczyzny*. Warszawa: Polonia.

Krupka, Paweł (2019), »Tomas Tamošiūnas pije ›Piwo z Aniołem Stróżem‹« [Tomas Tamošiūnas trinkt ein »Bier mit dem Schutzengel«], *Znad Wilii* 2 (78), S. 70.

—, — (2021), »Rola polskich pisarzy z Litwy w rozwoju polsko-litewskich relacji literackich w XXI wieku« [Die Rolle der litauenpolnischen Schriftsteller bei der Entwicklung der polnisch-litauischen Literaturbeziehungen des 21. Jahrhunderts], in Irena Fedorowicz / Mirosław Dawlewicz / Kinga Geben (Hg.), *Pod znakiem Orła i Pogoni: Polsko-litewskie związki naukowe i kulturowe w dziejach Uniwersytetu Wileńskiego: Zbiór studiów*, Vilnius: Vilniaus universiteto leidykla, S. 476–483.

Kurzawa, Eugeniusz (1995), *Słownik polskich pisarzy współczesnych Wileńszczyzny* [Lexikon der zeitgenössischen polnischen Schriftsteller der Region Vilnius], Zielona Góra: Lubuska Oficyna Wydawnicza.

Podgórski, Wojciech Jerzy (1994), »›Czy wróci tu kiedyś poeta?‹ Poezja polskiego Wilna – dzisiaj« [»Wirst du jemals hierher zurückkommen, Dichter?« Die Lyrik des polnischen Vilnius heute], in Wojciech Jerzy Podgórski, *Litwa: Polska XIX i XX wieku: Inspiracje literackie, kulturalne, oświatowe*, Warszawa: Interlibro, S. 215–261.

PPzW (2001), *Polskie pióra znad Wilii: Bibliografia polskich współczesnych pisarzy Wileńszczyzny 1985–2000* [Polnische Schreibfedern entlang der Neris: Bibliographie zeitgenössischer polnischer Schriftsteller aus der Region Vilnius, 1985–2000], hrsg. v. Henryk Szylkin und Dorota Szagun, Zielona Góra: Pro Libris.

Turkiewicz, Halina (1995), »Współczesna polska poezja Wileńszczyzny« [Zeitgenössische polnische Lyrik aus der Region Vilnius], in Tomasz Wroczyński (Hg.), *Literatura polska XX wieku*, Kaunas: Šviesa, S. 323–350.

—, — (1996), »Wilno w twórczości współczesnych polskich poetów Litwy« [Vilnius in den Werken zeitgenössischer litauenpolnischer Dichter], in Elżbieta Feliksiak (Hg.), *Wilno i kresy północno-wschodnie*, t. IV, Białystok: Biblioteka Pamięci i Myśli, S. 287–306.

—, — (2005), »Był zbyt wrażliwy dla miłości?« [War er zu sensibel um zu lieben?], in Sławomir Worotyński, *Złamana gałązka bzu*, Wilno: Poldicta, S. 25–34.

—, — (2019), »Inspiracje Mickiewiczowskie w najnowszej polskojęzycznej poezji Litwy« [Inspiriert von Mickiewicz: Die neueste polnischsprachige Lyrik Litauens], *Bibliotekarz Podlaski: Ogólnopolskie naukowe pismo bibliotekoznawcze i bibliologiczne* 2, S. 161–176.

Woźniakowski, Krzysztof (1985), *Polska literatura Wileńszczyzny 1944–1984* [Die polnische Literatur der Region Vilnius 1944–1984], Wrocław: Zakład Narodowy im. Ossolińskich.

—, — (2000), »Główne tendencje rozwojowe polskiej literatury Wileńszczyzny w latach 1985–1998« [Die hauptsächlichen Entwicklungstendenzen in der polnischen Literatur der Region Vilnius 1985–1998], in Halina Bursztyńska (Hg.), *Od strony kresów: Studia i szkice, cz. 2*, Kraków: Wydawnictwo Naukowe Akademii Pedagogicznej, S. 247–258.

5.2.2 Digitale Titel

 Fedorowicz, Irena / Kinga **Geben** (2021), »Językowy obraz domu w prozie wspomnieniowej Wojciecha Piotrowicza« [Das sprachliche Bild des Hauses in den Memoiren von Wojciech Piotrowicz], in *Vertybės lietuvių ir lenkų kalbų pasaulėvaizdyje*, S. 318–333, digitale Edition. (Vilnius University Open Series 2.)

 Gruszka-Zych, Barbara (2020), »Fabianiszki – moja miłość« [Fabianiszki ist meine Liebe], *Gość.pl* 34, digitales Periodikum.

 Korzeniewska, Katarzyna (1999), »Obecność kultury polskiej na Wschodzie« [Die Präsenz der polnischen Kultur im Osten], auf den Internetseiten des Krakauer Vereins »Ośrodek Myśli Politycznej«, Webseite.

 Radczenko, Aleksander (2015a), »Prezentacja pierwszej postmodernistycznej powieści wileńskiej« [Die Präsentation des ersten postmodernen Wilna-Romans], Blogbeitrag.

 —, — (2015b), »Poetycki thriller wileński« [Ein poetischer Vilnius-Thriller], Blogbeitrag.

 Rotkiewicz, Ryszard (2015), »Cuchnący powiew z przeszłości, czyli jak odebrałem ›Cień słońca‹ Aleksandra Radczenki« [Eine übelriechende Brise aus der Vergangenheit, oder: Wie ich »Cień słońca« von Aleksander Radczenko erhielt], *pl.delfi.lt*, 04.06.2015, digitales Periodikum.

 Rudnicki, Michał (2016), »Cień słońca: Recenzja« [»Cień słońca«, Rezension], *zw.lt*, digitales Periodikum.

 **Snarski**, Tomasz (2020), »Były sobie Fabianiszki?« [War es einmal Fabianiszki?], in *Przegląd Bałtycki*, 03.05.2020, digitale Edition.

 Wiszniak, Gabriela (2012), »Historia wileńskiego ›Chaosu‹, 4: Twórczość literacka na łamach pisma« [Die Geschichte des Wilnaer »Chaos«, Folge 4: Schöne Literatur in den Kolumnen der Zeitschrift], *3obieg.pl*, 17.05.2012, digitales Periodikum.

The Culture of Happy Endings, the Basic Structure of Narration, and Maks Fraj's *Skazki starogo Vil'nûsa*

A sketch of a semiotic framework of narration
by Stephan Kessler (Greifswald)

Outline

The happy ending characterises modern fiction. If the happy ending is not simply viewed as the author's narrative craftwork (section 1), but is viewed as a purposeful function, then, for the happy ending to occur, the plot must be brought to a logical conclusion (sections 2 and 3). This draws attention to what a logical ending of a piece of fiction is and when it can occur. The finding of a basic structure of narration provides the answer (section 4). The basic narrative structure represents a logical framework along which the fiction's plotline runs, if one may call it 'narrative' (section 5). That framework consists of five stages to which the protagonists are subjected — the status quo (stage A), the peripety (stage P), the new values (stage B), the resumption (stage R), and the status quo plus (stage C). In an abbreviated form, it can also be just three stages (A–P–B). We then have a closer look at Maks Fraj's seven-volume work Сказки старого Вильнюса [Fairy tales of old Vilnius], the 22 stories in volume five, and herein story №6, 'Simonas Daukantas Square' (section 6). In conclusion, there is an international cultural practice realised in the stories of volume five so that the 22 Fairy tales can be received regardless of what the reader knows about the cultural details represented or referenced.

Structure

1	How to finish a narrative technically?	29
2	Technical and logical endings connected with the communicative levels in fiction	31
3	How to finish a narrative logically? A definition of the happy ending	33
4	The basic structure of narration, the peripety, and the catastrophe	34
5	The principle of causality and two more examples	38
6	Maks Fraj's *Skazki starogo Vil'nûsa* [Fairy tales of old Vilnius]	40
7	Conclusion	44
8	References	45
8.1	The stories (streets) of volume five of Maks Fraj's *Skazki starogo Vil'nûsa*	45
8.2	Fiction and films cited as examples	46
8.3	Educational video	47
8.4	Bibliography	47

8.4.1 Printed titles ... 47 — 8.4.2 Digital titles ... 48

1 How to finish a narrative technically?

Hardly anyone who peruses the current artistic narratives—be it fiction, film series or feature films—will miss the fact that there is a culture of happy endings. Rather than the art itself of crowning a fictional work with a happy conclusion, which one would easily explain from the needs of readers and viewers, whom neither an author nor a director wants to disregard if they rely financially on their craftsmanship, one must be amazed at the widespread use of the happy ending. This finding must certainly be the endpoint of a long development and dissemination of specific aesthetic codes and communicative schemata.

However, scrutinising this is not the aim of this contribution. Instead, the focus of this contribution is about what a happy ending is and why it is part of a particular culture. In order to demonstrate this, a model of narration that gives meaning to happy endings in fiction and film is first introduced. The point is to create a larger narratological framework in which the happy ending, narrative closure, the peripety, or the catastrophe then finds their place. It is the idea that these narrative features can never be observed or understood in isolation from a basic structure of narration, and it is this enriched framework that is a particular culture. The basic structure will be presented in the first five sections before the contribution delves into the realm of the author Maks Fraj (Макс Фрай) in the sixth chapter. In the beginning, there is the fundamental decision between technical and logical endings.

Since the author eventually has to end his/her story, every narrative needs a real ending. As banal as this is, it divides the use of narrative conclusion into two categories: on the one hand, there are the stories' technical cessations, and on the other hand, the logical endings required by the plots. In specialist literature, this distinction is sometimes similarly named, for instance, by 'conclusion/resolution of the story' and 'closure of the narrative discourse' (cf. Neupert 1995: 16–21, 32–33). However, these terms still do not discriminate enough between the purely technical, formal manner with which the text can find an accepted end and the completely different question of whether the story's ending is, for instance, happy, satisfactory, and credible, or tragic, unsatisfactory, and incredible.

The category labelled as 'logical endings' therefore contrasts with the category of technical endings (an common distinction, see op. cit.: 12–14, for an overview). The latter is about artistically handling the plotlines and how the entire story is then finished at the end of the book in the last paragraph. It is a question of aesthetics and a question of style whether an author prefers to cease telling the story in this way or that way. Without being necessary to name all the possibilities of technically finishing a story (as Neupert does), a list of four common cessations inspired by MacDowell (2014) may give some evidence.

The **first** technical conclusion is simply a final joke, a punch line, or some other exhilarating moment (MacDowell 2014: 120). This technique was widely used during the early modern period—an absurd ending of a story or a poem was trendy, for example, in the baroque era. The terminology used for this type of farfetched ending is a conceit. The **second** type of conclusion, also prevalent in certain narratives, is one that somehow echoes the story's opening. It gives the impression that the storyline is somehow repeating itself, that it is in a narrative cycle, that the whole story is 'biting its tail'. In more general terms, the parallelism of the opening and the ending creates a mirroring, bracketing effect.

Another variant of the technical possibilities for creating an ending of a story is often associated with romanticism and is especially associated with modernism. It is also a style characteristic of the short story. The point is that the story does not, in fact, seem to end in any way. Of course, the narration has to break off at some point, but this does not correspond to a narrative conclusion. Instead, central plotlines are left dangling so that we struggle with the story's 'loose ends' (MacDowell, 2014: 151–152, discusses several synonyms for such 'aperture'). Here, too, it is generally formulated that the narrative has an implied continuation (op. cit.: 35, 40), for the author may not have outrightly resolved the plotlines, but s/he has told the story's ending in a way that the reader can infer the remainder.

Last, closure happens when all plotlines reach a resolution—all lovers become couples, quarrels are smoothed, the heroes win, the timid fawns get their rights, the enemies are destroyed, the bad ones are punished, and so on, if the author intends to show that. Beyond that, any 'question saliently posed by the narrative' is answered (op. cit.: 70). If there is a closure, the narrator (the voice) does not have to continue the story because nothing hereafter is worth reporting. This fourth kind of narrative conclusion is perhaps the typical norm. The fact is that the closure is a widespread, worldwide technical ending and in all genres at hand. It occurs in classicism, realism, and other epochal aesthetic codes and is present in various literary traditions. It is difficult to say whether a closure occurs so often because of an anthropologically constant expectation of the reader, a gestalt-psychological necessity regarding the notion of an ideal, complete narrative, or the successful dissemination of a once specific form of ending a story.

Technical endings are accomplished through particular aesthetic signifiers of finality. This is a concept of MacDowell (2014: 65–66) defining signifiers of finality as conventional closure devices that constitute the rhetoric of the ending: for any reader or viewer, the appearance of such a signifier was 'likely to encourage an intertextually-learned sense that this ending feels like an ending—an appropriate cessation—and thus feels "closed"'. For instance, a 'final' couple (symbolised by a kiss, a joint journey, a proposal, a wedding, or the like) is, according to MacDowell, an ultimate signifier of concluding a story technically. This is a particular artistic, aesthetic convention, of course, but has a long tradition: a final couple has already been used in the ancient Greek novel *Daphnis and Chloe* written by Longus (Λόγγος) in the Roman Empire in the second century AD (see index of cited examples below). Eventually, Chloe, who is an orphan, marries Daphnis, finds her parents, and becomes a seasoned lover of her husband—what more could a story of a man and a woman achieve? More recent examples of final couples and signifiers of finality, respectively, are the double weddings in Jane Austen's *Sense and Sensibility* (1811) and her *Pride and Prejudice* (1813). The author's presentation focuses less on the marriage proposal, and certainly not on the consummation of the marriage, but sets forth the explanation of the lovers' hearts and the turns they have taken. For Austen, the proper steps that lead to marriage are not that important, even if the narrator needs those steps to signify the end of the story; what is more important to depict is the final social harmony that results from the right pairing. Also set in the Regency era is the streaming series *Bridgerton* (2020), based on Julia Quinn's alias Julie Pottinger's contemporary novels with the same title. However, the times of sentimentalism and body taboos have gone so far that *Bridgerton*'s imminent ending signifies the already married couple fulfilling their desire to have children and thus finishing a long fermenting argument.

A joint journey signifies, for instance, the endings of the films *Sleepless in Seattle* (1993) and *Leap Year* (2010). However, the modes of transport are different. In *Sleepless in Seattle*, the lovers, who have frequently missed the opportunity to meet, finally encounter each other on the observation deck of the Empire State Building. They silently, but consensually, enter the elevator to descend together. This is a sort of implied continuation (cf. MacDowell 2014: 59–62). A similar tacit agreement finishes *Leap Year*. One of the lovers proposes to the other on the nearby cliffside, and then they drive away, leaving their destination open to fate. The scene ends with the car disappearing along the horizon.

As much as these are examples of different signifiers of finality, they do not prove the theoretical independence of the technical endings from the logical endings because the conclusions of the examples are only happy. Therefore, one could argue that a final couple does not indicate the story's imminent ending but rather the happiness of the conclusion. However, there are counterexamples where a final couple is the signifier of finality, but the end of the story is unhappy. Consequently, technical endings are a category of their own. In the historical television series *The Princess Weiyoung* (2016), based on Qin Jian's (秦简) novel *The Poisonous Daughter* (2013), the main male character, Prince Tuoba Jun, marries twice. First, he enters into an aristocratic arranged marriage and only in the second attempt can he marry the heroine of the title, Wei Yang. However, both marriages are unhappy: in the first one, the hero does not love his scheming spouse; and in the second, he loves Yang but has been poisoned and will soon die. While the representation of the arranged wedding is shown in detail, becomes a signifier of finality, logically divides the series into two parts, and is also used for the episode's cliffhanger, the second wedding is only implied. Instead, Jun's and Yang's plotline focuses on the vanquishment of all family enemies, the suffering of the poisoned husband, and the implied continuation of the dynasty as the couple has a son after their coronation. Thus, the last scene melodramatically shows the lonely dowager with her still very young child during a snowfall which is depicted in cool colours. However, after 54 episodes, several signifiers allude to the imminent end of the series, starting with one more unhappy marriage. Once the current king dies, another prince, Yu, ensures that he is proclaimed the successor and forces Yang to marry him because he has fallen for her beauty and intelligence. Jun breaks up the wedding, and an all decisive battle (a signifier) for the throne begins. Yu the bad dies in an undisturbed duel (a signifier) with Jun the good, for which they are given plenty of film time. Other evildoers of Yu's party commit suicide (signifiers) because of unfulfilled love or success; in contrast, among Jun's followers, the lovers find each other to mate (signifiers).

The end of the feature film *La La Land* (2016) is just as unfortunate but not nearly as bloody. Although they develop the beginning of a relationship, the lovers cannot proceed happily due to different career goals. The film's ending is thus a final couple scene where the lovers meet by chance and imagine what might have been had their relationship thrived alongside their careers. Due to this scene signifying finality, romantic viewers may expect that the lovers will come together again and attempt a new beginning. However, that does not happen. The inamorata is then married to another man so that the ending is unhappy from the viewpoint of the love story the film has told.

2 Technical and logical endings connected with the communicative levels in fiction

Since ancient times, happy and unhappy endings have been used to distinguish comedy from tragedy. A comedy is a play with a plot that concludes positively in some way. Conversely, a tragedy is something that leads to disaster. This ancient theory is interesting because the distinction the theory makes shows the staple difference between logical and technical endings: logical endings deal with fate <u>within</u> fiction and how we may understand it. Herein, the plot conclusion's happiness or unhappiness is usually decided either from the narrator's or the characters' viewpoint. However, I am abstaining from more examples here as the whole matter is a little more involved.

In narratology, a distinction is made between several communicative levels. It is standard to distinguish the story world (intradiegetic level, characters' level, the 'showing') and the discourse (the voice, narrator's level, the 'telling'). I follow the model of Kahrmann et al. (1991), the innovators who discriminate between **five levels** that affect the author's communication with the readership. Levels 4 and 5 are outside of fiction and are part of social life. Levels 1 to 3 concern the narrative, i.e. relating to the fiction and the narration itself. Level 2 matches the narrator's communication (the voice that tells us about everything), and level 1 is the world that the narrator presents to us. So Kahrmann et al. bring into use level 3, which is the narrative schema that we perceive as the plot. The scholars also name level 3 'the abstract author', for the third communicative level is the fact that the author has plotted his/her work, and hence lacks any concreteness while the narrated characters and frequently the narrator are concrete, depicted, formulated, present (at least, implicitly).

The following theoretical step concerns how the five narrative levels are distributed throughout our previously established distinction between technical and logical endings. On the technical endings' site, we find levels 4 and 5. The author's style and preferences may favour some technical endings, of course. However, in a historical dimension, technical endings raise questions about the style and the aesthetics of the era (cf. MacDowell 2014: 69). The latter does not just question the allowed forms or shapes of the artwork that must come to an appropriate end then, but fundamentally is also what was considered good storytelling. The genre can also impose restrictions on the narrative's technical conclusion. Consider a detective novel with an implied continuation before the detective caught the perpetrator. In that case, we would perceive a cliffhanger and hence expect the story to be continued in another book. The instance shows that a technical ending is not possible at a random point in the plot but that a detective story requires an investigator to catch the culprit first.

That said, the author has to decide on a concrete logical conclusion of the story s/he has in mind. In doing so, the author considers the effect his/her selection will have on the reader. 'Effect' is not just about aesthetics but also the influence that a particular ending will have on the reader's understanding of the fiction or film (cf. MacDowell 2014: 133–135). Because it is clear: if the author devises the story so that the protagonist dies at the end, then everyone will understand that the opinions and worldview that the protagonist expressed or embodied are not the right ones, but rather the wrong ones. And therefore they are doomed unless there are reasons why the protagonist should die despite the correct values he or she advocates (for an example see next paragraph). Thus, the logical, (un)happy endings fall under the narrative levels 1 to 3 because they are essential information for the reader's understanding of the fiction or film.

On **level one**, the characters are very fortunate that they are the subjects of an expected conclusion. Nevertheless, they also have the misfortune of not choosing how they end up — happy, unhappy, or it does not matter how. It is not true that we would only deem a story ending as happy or unhappy when the characters become happy or unhappy, respectively. For instance, Albus Dumbledore must die at the end of book six of Joanne Rowling's *Harry-Potter*-saga because only in this way the wizard prevents evil traitors from prevailing. Of course, Professor Dumbledore's death is horrible for him and tragic in the eyes of the reader. However, on the other hand, only then is Harry Potter able to become a complex mature individual who shows a willingness to valiantly fight for the good. This is an ending as ideally happy as intended by the narrative framework, the details of which I shall go into in a moment.

On **level two**, the narrator (voice) must plausibly tell the story's logical end and achieve the reader's (listener's) happy or unhappy feelings, no matter what the characters say about the conclusion. So the narrator has to first satisfy the reader regarding the (un)happiness of finishing his/her narrative. In doing so, the narrator must consider that the values of the intended audience are not the same as the values of the fictional world being told. Therefore, the narrator observes a 'higher' logic (i.e. the narrative framework) than the characters' impressions of their fate. By the way, there is no happy or unhappy ending for the voice itself, although such an ending is plausible with a first-person narrator.

On **level three**, the author's decisions result in a blueprint for the future story—s/he plots the narrative. Interestingly, there is no logical ending that is irrelevant to the readers' interpretation. If the real author had to make a fundamental decision first as to which technical and logical ending suited his/her intention best, this has now led to a more precise plan of which characters, to what extent, through which actions, should become happy or unhappy at which point in the story and, what is crucial, how the intended readership would assess that story's conclusion.

3 How to finish a narrative logically? A definition of the happy ending

So far, I have compared technical endings and logical endings. It became clear that only the logical endings make sense to speak of happiness or unhappiness of a narrative's conclusion. Then, I presented the communicative levels that narratology differentiates within any narrative. Thus, it was possible to determine more precisely for which text-immanent levels the question of happily ending a story plays a role and to what extent.

The discovery is that there are two types of happiness. The first is that of the narrated characters. However, from a narratological perspective, the characters' happiness is of no interest, as it is functionalised in a story's narrative plan, i.e. actually, the plot. Furthermore, the characters are fictional—why should we care about their fate? Only insofar as one experiences the story, the reader would like the heroines and heroes with whom he/she identifies to find a happy status for their fictional life. Yet, from this specific psychological process of reception, the narratological question about a story ending's happiness or unhappiness must be distinguished. What the reader likes in any way is the appropriate conclusion of the narrative that, in some instances, as MacDowell (2014: 100–104) points out, can only be devised at the cost of a story's plain unrealism. However, we are willing to accept such trifles once the narrative closure satisfies us. The question arises: why can a plot's shape, which requires a specific ending, triumph over the story's plausibility?

While we could quite easily put together a small list of ideas regarding the characters that may be culture-specific or genre-specific, but that many people would call happy—I am thinking, for instance, of a wedding in a romantic comedy or the revelation of the culprit's identity in a detective novel—it is not so easy to determine what should be considered happy or unhappy on the plot level. On behalf of various other researchers who have expressed similar ideas, I refer here only to Barbara Creed. She brings together several strands of the scholarly view of our subject when she describes the happy ending as the 'classic realist' story's conclusion 'in which all loose ends are usually neatly tied up, and the values of the status quo confirmed—the couple, family, society and the law' (Creed 1995: 155). The quotation includes two statements that we will trace now by questioning what the statements mean for plotting any narrative. I begin with Creed's first statement: a happy ending is a conclusion 'in which all loose ends are usually neatly tied up.' (Please note, Creed does not speak of technical matters here, but does speak of plot structure.)

It seems to be the basis of a universal aesthetic that art should be 'completed', that the artwork is an inherent perfection that arises from its formal and creative wholeness. This completeness is thus an enactment, but it also affects the schema of a particular narrative. The notion of completeness may have been confirmed or undermined in particular arts, genres, or epochs. However, it still seems to be an anthropological-historical constant of sorts that leads us to 'properly' conclude the plotlines being told. When are the plotlines correctly concluded from the viewpoint of narrative logic? The measure of correctness lies within any possible logical universe of the fictional world, which must generally be understood as the plot's precepts. Therefore, 'happy' means closing the story according to the plot's precepts.

However, 'unhappy' does not mean the opposite. Instead, it means that the protagonists cannot comply with the plot's precepts; they cannot fulfil or uphold what the story requires of them—they fail because of the circumstances or lack of abilities. Still, it is not the convention of concluding the plot that goes wrong then. Therefore, the actual **definition** of a **happy ending** must be:

The narrator finishes the story (level 2) according to the plot's precepts (level 3) by narrating characters who can fulfil or uphold what is required of them (level 1).

That is not all. From a narratological viewpoint, specific values and a specific plot pattern also come into play.

4 The basic structure of narration, the peripety, and the catastrophe

I refer to Creed's second statement now: a happy ending was a conclusion in which 'the values of the status quo [are] confirmed—the couple, family, society and the law.' This aspect has especially not been obscured from film and literary studies. Moreover, any recipient who does not share the values affirmed by the story's conclusion immediately encounters that the ending should not behave as the story's cessation has asserted.

Lotman (1977: 231–239, 1990: 151–170), Campbell (2008 [1949]) and Greimas (1971, pp. 157–205) have expressed themselves somewhat more substantially. Lotman thinks that every fictional narrative leads its protagonists through two states of social meaning, personal values, or world understanding. Lotman named it two different semiospheres, i.e. two sets of societal frames of meanings represented by all prevalent signs in the respective frame (Lotman 1984; cf. Lotman, 1990: part 2, and 2010; see also the outline of Fleischer, 1989: 146–157).[1] The narrative's fulcrum becomes the transition between the two states (the so-called peripety, or turning point). Campbell has discovered throughout historical material from around the world (in myths, epics, fairy tales, and other narratives) that the

---

1 In fiction, spaces or spatial relations often represent the two states or semiospheres. That is why scientific terminology often uses spatial terms for them, too. Therefore, we might not forget that the spaces or spatial relations narrated by the voice are objective spaces of the protagonists' action, but that they are to be understood as metaphors on the level of the plot (see Lotman 1990: 171–202).

Figure 1: The basic structure of narration

Stage A	Peripety	Stage B	Resumption	Stage C
Status quo — the fictional world and values (semiosphere I)	An event happens — a boundary is crossed literally or figuratively	New values obtained — another world, other values (semiosphere II)	An event happens — characters return across the boundary	Status quo plus — former world, values confirmed (semiosphere I+)
A run of happy endings		The protagonists are allowed to live in their new world and with its values		The protagonists maintain the modified values of the traditional world
A run of unhappy endings		The protagonists fail in the new world and cannot comply with the values		The protagonists can not find their way in the (modified) status quo
	The author designs events, but only one of them becomes the narrative's turning point at the peripety stage. On the other hand, the peripety gives an event a special status, namely being a turning point within a three- or five-stage narrative.			
		A technical ending is possible (e.g. an implied continuation)	*The catastrophe: in order to fulfil what is required by the precepts of the fictional world, the characters may suffer a bad or even terrible fate.*	A technical ending must take place (e.g. a closure)

© Stephan Kessler, 2021

This figure is also available as more elaborate infographic (download here, or from 'academia.edu').

idea of the new status the protagonists reach is that they return changed to the old status — enriched, more capable, recognised, socially ascended. Greimas' theoretical considerations support Campbell's observations. Greimas can reduce the manyness of narrated actions of any fictional world to a few narrative functions that structure the narration and have an 'ordeal' or 'trial' (*épreuve*) of the main characters as their pivotal point.

When we put all of this together, we come to a basic structure of narration, and we also recognise the positions a happy or unhappy ending can take in it. The point is that every narrative has a basic structure on the plot level that consists of a minimum of three and a maximum of five stages that the protagonists traverse (see Figure 1). However, the author can, of course, work with flashbacks, foreshadowing, or 'foregone conclusions' (MacDowell 2014: 71) so that the framework can have a complex implementation on the story level. Still, if you leave that aside, every fictional narrative logically begins with a status quo (**stage A**) which is soon overturned by a turning point event. It may not be our world that the narrator depicts in stage A, but the world that the characters know and whose values and precepts confront them. Then something symbolic happens to the narrated characters, leading them to or across a border or boundary (cf. Lotman 1990: 131–142). There on the border or beyond, the world is a different one. The way across the boundary is the stage of **peripety**, and it throws the protagonists beyond the limits of their previous everyday lives, beyond their recognised values, or in a very visual way which can be depicted very clearly in a novel or film, beyond the physical-geographical world the protagonists know into a new world (like in Jules Verne's French science fiction *20,000 Leagues Under the Seas*, 1869–1870, Antal Szerb's Hungary mystery story *The Pendragon Legend*, 1934, or Douglas Adams' novel *The Hitchhiker's Guide to the Galaxy*, 1980). The new world, be it natural or symbolical—that is **stage B**. At this point, the narrator can stop storytelling. The happy ending is then that the protagonists remain in the status reached and can (or dare to) live their new values and worldviews. So, a technical ending is possible and would be accepted by the reader as a final one.

No doubt, a three-stage plot is the narrative schema of a host of utopian science fiction. For example, in Ernest Callenbach's *Ecotopia* (1975), a reporter visits this isolated state based on alternative ways of life but is sceptical. Instead, he would like to enlighten the 'normal' world about what he thinks is madness. Nevertheless, he begins to like the eco-semiosphere more and more, and in the end, he does not want to go back home. What a reporter is in Callenbach's work is a young rebel in Arthur Clarke's *The Lion of Comarre* (1949) who does not want to be satisfied with the status quo: scientists already know everything, and technicians have already built every imaginable aid for the people. They think. Despite this, the hero knows the legend of Comarre, a city with even more yet-to-be-discovered possibilities based on a new area of science. However, a powerful world government has suppressed any information about this city. The hero, of course, finds a way there and can free the new knowledge for humanity. So, stage B is the world that knows Comarre's abundant treasures.

In a future England, a clerical regime rules a society that lives in medieval conditions because of a past about which there is only speculative information. This is the status quo of *The Second Sleep* (2019), written by Robert Harris. The peripety occurs because, due to special circumstances, a priest is sent to a strange village where he soon becomes active in historical-archaeological matters and reconstructs the history of a societal catastrophe resulting from the complete loss of electricity. As is the case in Clarke's story, so with Harris's novel, too, the uncovering of the long-suppressed truth of how good civilisation has once been and which atrocities men have committed since then is the stage-B semiosphere. For the protagonists, however, the new knowledge means their tragic end.

Despite these and other instances, the narrative framework does not necessarily end in stage B. Consider the status B values as the wrong ones. Then the author could bring the story to an unfortunate end (like with *The Second Sleep*) and thereby indicate to the reader that the values of status B should not be the right ones as with Harris's novel. From the vantage point of the clerical regime, the protagonist's stage-B knowledge is hence inadmissible. However, in doing so, the author could not, in a positive way, show which values are the right ones from his/her standpoint. That may implicitly lead the reader to infer that the author seriously considers the values of stage A the right ones—an inference that may be accurate or, as with Harris's novel, may not. Not to mention the possibility that the protagonist may also be an obvious culprit. Then status B would be characterised by the victory of the perpetrator's misdeeds. However, of course, this must not remain permanent! Such a status B calls for the decline of evil and the triumph of good—it calls for a continuation of the story.

The narrative framework is continued so that the protagonists must leave the semiosphere of status B that they have just achieved. In stage B, the protagonists can grapple with the B-values. They may or may not comply with these values. No matter, something can happen again that brings the protagonists back to their former world. They literally or figuratively recross the boundary that they have already crossed once during the peripety. In this respect, it is about a **resumption** of status A. After the resumption, the protagonists are confronted with the 'old' world's (semiosphere's) values. However, the recently achieved **status C** is not entirely identical to the former stage A (Todorov 2018: 200–202). A lot has happened in the meantime. The protagonists have become more experienced or recognised by others, for instance, because they dared to cross the boundary or did something heroic in the world of stage B. Alternatively, the former world (semiosphere) has changed, for example, because the protagonists' social environment was ready to change its behaviour due to the protagonists' symbolic or actual absence. So stage C is a status quo plus of sorts because the values of stage C correspond to those of stage A, albeit modified. That said, the crucial point is that the protagonists will now accept the traditional A/C-stages' values. Their insight or progress brings the story to a happy ending.

The exciting concept about the basic structure of narration is that it also applies equally to unhappy endings. The unfortunate aspect in a three-stage narrative is that the protagonists either do not wish, do not try, or cannot live under stage B's values (under its semiosphere). In their point of view, the peripety that brings them into stage B is a horrific trip. So they fail there—and <u>must</u> fail if stage B indeed turns out to be a world of terror and crimes against humanity. Only then will the reader notice that the values achieved in status B are the wrong ones. For example, in the 1985 film *Brazil*, a free film adaptation of George Orwell's *1984*, the protagonist is such an ill-fated person that we need to critically assess the strange world of modern dictatorship.

It is similar to the unhappy five-stage pattern. For whatever reason, the protagonists have to return from the semiosphere B by crossing a new boundary or by recrossing the previous one. Then, consider an unhappy ending; they cannot come to terms with the world of stage C. Why should that happen, especially when stage C is only a modified status quo? First, if the protagonists' time spent in the world of stage B created the prerequisites for them to be allowed to return to stage C at all (for example, because they have to fulfil an obligation there), then it may be that they fail at stage C because they did not do what was demanded of them at stage B. Second, the final stay at stage C could even be a punishment for the protagonists. If the hero or heroine is a morally positive character but the surrounding values are evil, the protagonists' punishment would, of course, be a very downtrodden ending (as in *Brazil*). However, if the hero or heroine is a culprit like the perpetrator in a murder mystery, a final punishment would be unfortunate for the character but justified in the readers' eyes. Since crime is seen as the disruption of an existing order, the detective's only task is to restore order or, at least, enable its resumption by finding and punishing the criminal (cf. Marsch 1983: 89–98; Linder/Ort 2012 [1999]: 33–35). Then, the happy ending is the culprit who is apprehended and has regrets—his/her remorse signifies acceptance of the stage-C values. The unhappy ending, however, is the perpetrator-hero or heroine who regretlessly opposes the order to be restored.

By the way, I can now ascertain the **peripety** and the **catastrophe** more precisely. The idea of peripety is closely connected with particular narrated events (or one such event). The author devises many events in which the protagonists are involved (or, at least, with which they have to struggle within their consciousness), but only one of these events becomes the narrative's turning point at the peripety stage. On the other hand, the peripety gives an event a special status, namely being a turning point within a three- or five-stage narrative. As a result, the peripety can never be observed or understood in isolation from the basic structure of narration (cf. Kermode 2000 [1967]: 17–18, 44–45).

As for the catastrophe, I only want to remind you of the example from *Harry Potter* given at the beginning. The catastrophe presents itself as a tension between what a happy ending means regarding a particular plot and its precepts, and the characters who cannot achieve this happy ending although they fulfil or uphold what is required of them. Dumbledore's death is a tragic moment in terms of this theory. Dumbledore represents the values of democracy and tolerance and hence fights for the good of the wizard's community.

However, he cannot experience the victory over the embodiment of evil, Voldemort, because he sacrificed himself.

5 The principle of causality and two more examples

I was surprised myself, so to speak, that the aforementioned narrative framework can be based on very diverse narratives in terms of time, media, and language. Therefore, the idea arose that using the basic structure in a narrative is an item that aligns itself with a particular culture. Whether that culture is as global as indicated at the beginning of my contribution and whether one could map its items as the archaeologists do with the discovered artefacts of the Corded Ware culture has to be clarified elsewhere. As in archaeological research, it is also true for mapping the suggested basic structure that this framework may only be a <u>variety of</u> artistic <u>possibilities</u> in the realm of fiction and film, even if it may appear to us in many contexts as the epitome of narration itself.

Scholars investigating the meaning of narration often emphasise the principle of causality. The relationship between cause and effect must exist between represented textual parts so that a piece of fiction becomes a narrative instead of solely an enumeration of (fictional) facts. Forster first noted the principle in 1927 (1990: 87), and it is often quoted today in the more elaborated version of Danto (1985: 233–241).[1] The principle of causality is a condition of the presented framework because 'stories, or narratives, are forms of explanation', as Danto (1985: 233) says. In other words, the basic structure of narration does not emerge if the principle of causality, or the explanatory force, is undermined. Such force implies that the event determined by the narrator links two states in time (Danto 1985: 236). So, the microstructure of narration at least partly mirrors the narrative framework. However, one can also write fiction or make a movie without observing the principle of causality, and as a corollary, the narrative framework. Such fiction or movies should then not be named a narrative but, as White (1969: 222–223) writes, a chronicle.[2] For example, Olga Tokarczuk's Polish novel *Primeval and Other Times* (1999–2000) or Lilian Nattel's beautiful work *The River Midnight* (1999) are such an annalistic fiction, among other similarities between both works (e.g. depicting historical life in a fictional Polish village as a hermetic world). Another example of a modern chronicle would be James Joyce's *Ulysses* (1922), which documents one day in the life of the character Bloom.

Without making the proposed framework then absolute, this section aims to show two international examples of how it allows the authors to cleverly structure their plots. The first example is *Oh my Venus* (2015), a South Korean television series that received exceptional ratings and was also distributed worldwide. The whole story is romantic in the truest sense of literary history, as in the series, a socially and financially simple heroine and a 'modern aristocrat' fall in love. In stage A, Young-ho ('he') and Joo-eun ('she') live separate lives in different social circles. Young-ho is upper class but had been very sick in his youth and was therefore estranged from his family. Joo-eun was a beauty in her youth, and attempted a career as a lawyer which led her to become overweight. The peripety is that the protagonists meet 'unrecognised' because Young-ho leads a double life as a fitness trainer.

---

[1] However, Danto's formula which he uses to give Foster's findings a practical shape already occurs in White's (1969: 225–227) argumentation.

[2] Kermode (2000 [1967]: 44–48, 50–52) too distinguished these two types of plots. Yet he does not speak of annalistic and narrative plots but sophisticatedly of *chrónos* (χρόνος) and *kairós* (καιρός) [the times and the seasons].

He can therefore train Joo-eun, and she slims. Conversely, Young-ho, supported by Joo-eun, learns to live with the mental and emotional anguish of his illness.

The story soon reaches a happy ending at stage B — the two become a couple (presented as a signifier of finality), but with their own rules ignoring expectations and traditions (for instance, they embrace modern values, have an equal relationship, and use their own exclusive code). The last, 'romantic' point is only deemed superficially happy as we shall see in a moment. Being truly happy (i.e. fulfilling what is required of them according to the plot's precepts) is when Joo-eun has more success at work and Young-ho is ready to take on a company inheritance. However, 'final couple' here implies that Joo-eun and Young-ho behave secretly, i.e. breaking the tradition of the conservative family and society, the couple's relationship remains a problem in status B.

Then, Young-ho has a bad car accident. This ultimately brings all family members together, and they can work through old quarrels. (This is an exemplary resumption.) Furthermore, Young-ho's rehab abroad tests the couple's relationship. Ultimately, his parents recognise Joo-eun's seriousness. Conservative as Young-ho's parents are, they had rejected Joo-eun at first. The couple's integration into his social circle (her family do not count because of their low social status) without adhering to outdated traditions creates the second happy ending at stage C. However, Joo-eun must acknowledge compromising her previous stage-B values, 'Let's make sure nobody gets hurt' (episode 16, minute −53.03). Similarly, Young-ho remembers, 'I vowed never to live as my father did' (episode 16, minute −25.05). Nevertheless, he then perfectly fulfils the duties of his father's CEO job in the company.

Technical and logical endings are possible on the same two stages B and C. However, they are optional for a five-stage pattern on stage B. As we can see in *Oh my Venus*, this creates the possibility of meaningfully structuring the narrative. Nevertheless, the framework alone can arrange the story, as in Adolphsen's disturbing, structurally complex piece of fiction, *The Brummstein* [The humming stone], first published in 2003 in Danish.³ Stage A: The status quo is the world as we know it, and the story opens with the emergence of the Alps. This is told with precise 'geological' realism. Mr Siedler, an obscurant and dreamer from Augsburg, eventually enters this world. He is looking for power which he seeks in the form of a still unknown, unique physical force which is most likely controlled by the underworld. Peripety (P): Siedler descends into the Swiss Hölloch Cave in 1907 to enter what he believes is the underworld. However, at the deepest point of Hölloch, Siedler finds the end of a rock vein that hums. Stage B: The stone allows Siedler to have a numinous experience. Resumption (R): Siedler returns to Augsburg. Stage C: Siedler cannot do anything with his experience; he cannot understand it. He leaves a rock sample with a report that is not true to his experience (Adolphsen 2011: 27). Siedler dies in a banal accident.

Interestingly, the story does not end with Mr Siedler's death. Although it is a strong signifier of finality, there is a second run through the basic structure. Every run comprises the entire basic structure and finishes technically with a closure. Therefore, *The Brummstein* is not a novel, but is in fact, a novella. Stage A_2: It is reported with precise accuracy how the rock sample gets to Ms Breslauer in Düsseldorf around 1994. This story allows the narrator to discuss various aspects of the GDR's and FRG's history. Stage P_2: Breslauer works for a museum and is supposed to catalogue bequests. The rock sample must be analysed; a geologist cannot explain its hum. He encourages Breslauer to check the origin of the

---

3   The complexity of Adolphsen's work can only be touched on here. Whoever is further interested in the *Humming stone's* narrative schema may take a look at my respective lecture on Happy Endings #3 (Kessler 2021) although these findings and explanations are provisional.

sample. Breslauer goes to Hölloch and repeats Siedler's expedition—at her own risk as this part of Hölloch is now banned. Stage B_2: Breslauer has the same mystical numinous experience as Siedler had. She makes an audio recording. Stage R_2: Breslauer returns to Düsseldorf. She, too, cannot do anything with her experience (stage C_2) nor has the opportunity to do so later because, on her way back to Düsseldorf, she causes a car accident and dies. The audio recording and the rock samples are lost.

The additional observation that Adolphsen's novella has an epilogue is crucial regarding our basic structure of narration because the epilogue does not contain or continue stage C_2 or, respectively, the second run that is already 'closed' technically as well as logically, but instead expands the story. In the epilogue (Adolphsen 2011: 78), the narrator, as successor to Breslauer's job, wants to reconstruct the true history of the rock sample that is still catalogued. He has become as curious about the humming stone and the truth hidden behind it as Breslauer once had been, and he is determined to make his way into Hölloch. In other words, the story will repeat itself again! So, the epilogue opens the third run through the narrative framework, and as one might assume, with the same actions and consequences as far as the narrator is concerned. However, that run is not being told. Thus, the epilogue is, in fact, an open end to the novella, only implying another ill-fated cycle.

In every run through the basic structure of narration, the main emphasis lies in representing stage A. By far, stage A_2 is the most expansive part—it encompasses 52 % of the novella (41 of 78 pages). Here, the narrator represents the 20th-century history of Germany from an unusual angle, telling the fate of persons who have been forgotten in the recent collective memory. This perspective explains, for instance, why the narrator is more or less only hinting at the fate of the Jews after 1938 (Adolphsen 2011: 36) because their fate is very well remembered collectively. The narrator need only say little to evoke a long chain of associations in the reader related to the history of the Jews during the Second World War. Instead, the narrator emphasises, for example, how they experienced and survived the war and the immediate post-war period, who were neither followers, soldiers, partisans, business people, nor were involved in the Third Reich in any other way (Adolphsen 2011: 36–55). The selected aspects of German history at stage A_2 are strangely contrasted by stage A_1, which speaks of several million years of geological development of the Alps. Against the background of these incredibly long and potent processes, what happened in Germany in the 20th century seems slight and miniscule. Moreover, the protagonists cannot understand the processes' power which the humming stone symbolises nor is their incomprehension of any impact. Consequently, their fate is only briefly depicted, although just the stages P–C comprise actions and events that generate the entire narrative.

We can now clearly understand the importance of the narrative framework based on the last two sample texts. It is the essential structure for generating narrative fiction, and it enables us to divide a story into reasonable sections and to weight them by their narrative function.

6 Maks Fraj's *Skazki starogo Vil'nûsa* [Fairy tales of old Vilnius]

Fraj's work is a collection of short stories that now fills seven volumes published regularly from 2012 onward (first stories appeared from 2000). The titles of the stories are names of streets in Vilnius. The word 'old' in the opus' overall title refers to the old town of Vilnius. So it makes sense to map the street names once used by Fraj. For purely practical reasons, the following analysis refers only to the fifth volume of Fraj's opus (Fraj 2019 b), comprising

Figure 2: Map of the city centre of Vilnius displaying the streets after whom the stories are named in volume five of Maks Fraj's collection *Сказки старого Вильнюса*

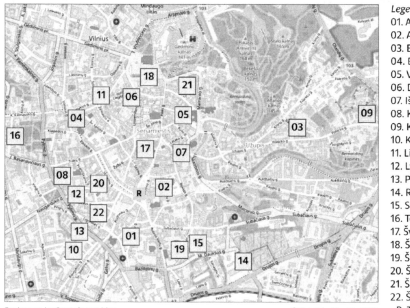

Legend:
01. Arklių Street
02. Augustijonų Street
03. Baltasis Lane
04. Benediktinų Street
05. Volano Street
06. Daukanto Square
07. Išganytojo Street
08. Kėdainių Street
09. Kreivasis Lane
10. Kruopų Street
11. Liejyklos Street
12. Lydos Street
13. Pllačioji Street
14. Rasų Street
15. Strazdelio Street
16. Teatro Street
17. Švarco Street
18. Šventaragio Street
19. Šv. Dvasios Street
20. Šv. Mikalojaus Street
21. Šiltadaržio Lane
22. Šiaulių Street
R. Town Hall (Rotušė)

Basic map by Open Street Map   © Stephan Kessler, 2021

22 stories whose respective streets are grouped, more or less, concentrically around the town hall (see Figure 2). Only streets №s 3 and 9 are separate; they are in a district called Užupis. This district is actually no less historical than the old town but is recognised collectively as the Jewish suburb.

Each story tries to establish a connection to the location of its street. For example, in the first story (see № 1 in the stories' index below), the fictional protagonists gather at a puppet theatre that is really located on the street in question, on Horse Street (Fraj 2019 b: 12). As for other stories, the affiliations to the streets and their names are rather associative. For instance, the Simonas Daukantas Square of story № 6 is opposite Lithuania's presidential palace next to the University of Vilnius, which comprises several inner courtyards. The story is an allegory of our brain's inner mechanism that creates reality by differentiating conscious items from everything else (unconscious, unreal, the rest of the world). In this respect, a world-creating line is set there, which is called *линия мира* [line of the world] in story № 6 (Fraj 2019 b: 109 et passim), and beyond that line, there is no perception of the world (not even of oneself), but darkness (represented as 'the night'). The 'daylight' mechanism that sets the line is personified in the text as a character. This allows the narrator to interweave two text blocks: the perceptions or experiences of the character Anna-Alëna and the thoughts of the character who sets the line of the world and judges things a little differently. The story itself is simple. Anna gets lost in the darkened yards while she is daydreaming. So there is a gap in her awareness. However, after the line-setting character has fixed Anna's consciousness, she realises what she has to be reminiscent of and where she stands. It is Simonas Daukantas Square, but as one has to consider, the place where she got lost was the university courtyards. As a result, the metaphorical 'dark yards' of consciousness are subsequently legitimised as the University's real courtyards. This representation of Anna's brain activity is connected to Simonas Daukantas (1793–1864) apparently as well as subtly. Today, Daukantas is considered the forefather and ideologue of the emerging Lithuanian national movement of the 19th century. Therefore, he is as much a person fixing a world-creating line as the personification of story №6.

The author Fraj is, in fact, a married couple. Svetlana Martynčik (Светлана Юрьевна Мартынчик) was born in 1965 in Odessa. Until she was nine years old, she lived in Germany with her father, a working military musician. Martynchik has been a presenter of the radio program *Свободный вход* [Free entry] from *Радио России* [The radio of Russia] in Moscow where she lived from 1993 on. Nevertheless, since 2004, she has been a citizen of Ukraine with residence in Lithuania. Igor' Stëpin, (Игорь Викторович Стёпин) born in 1967 also in Odessa, was an artist. Stëpin inspired Martynčik with the idea of a plasticine world project. So they created toy people, buildings, culture, history, myths, and even a calendar. Later, the project became an international travelling exhibition under the name 'Homan's Planet'. Stëpin is also known as one of the founders of the cult Odessa punk group *Клуб Унылых Лиц* [Club of Sad Faces]. He died in 2018. The true identity of the author Fraj remained a mystery for a long time. Martynčik and Stëpin only disclosed their Fraj identity when a legal dispute arose over ghostwriters and plagiarism (Gustė 2014).

The author duo writes about their Maks Fraj project:

> It should be admitted that no one knows the exact number of streets in the old town of Vilnius. There is no more hope even for the geniuses of the place. They said, 'One hundred and eight,' then corrected themselves. 'Oh, no, excuse us! One hundred and thirty-one!' However, once we had made a trip to the new unknown quarters and wrote down the stories included in the sixth volume of our Fairy tales, the streets were re-counted, and as a result, there were one hundred forty-six of them. This means that instead of the planned five volumes, we will have as many as seven. On one hand, this is good news. On the other hand, this means anarchy and chaos, and we shall complain about it. (Fraj 2017: 4)[1]

On this occasion, the authors outline the content of their fairy tales as follows:

> Furthermore, life in our city flows calmly and measuredly. The police make regular raids to catch especially evil demons; city spirits bake cookies; and ordinary Vilnius inhabitants drink cherry beer,[2] sincerely talk to the bottomlessness, look at dreams, and surmount death. Everything is as always. (Fraj 2017: 4)[3]

The statement that everything was as always is just as much an understatement as it expresses the authors' intention. A golden thread runs through, for instance, all 22 stories of the fifth volume — the notion of a supernatural, fantastic world in which the inhabitants can suddenly reveal themselves to us. How the characters act on these beings and how discovering the 'additional' sphere affects their lives is also a permanent subject. Insofar, if you take a metaphysical parallel universe for a fact, then in Fraj's fiction, everything happens as always, of course.

However, if supernatural, fantastic beings are not part of your average everyday life, you might be surprised by Fraj's stories. And you may be further surprised because the supernatural beings are part of a cosmic order in which the earthly individual and his/her

---

1 Orig.: 'Следует признать, что точного числа улиц в Старом Городе Вильнюса не знает никто. Даже на гениев места больше никакой надежды – то говорили, сто восемь, потом исправились: ой, нет, извините, сто тридцать одна! А пока мы совершали обход новых незнакомых кварталов и записывали истории, вошедшие в шестой том сказок, улицы пересчитали заново, и их оказалось сто сорок шесть. Значит, вместо задуманных пяти томов у нас будет целых семь. Что, с одной стороны, хорошая новость. А с другой – анархия и бардак, мы будем жаловаться.'
2 Cherry beer is a regional specialty.
3 Orig.: 'В остальном же у нас в городе жизнь течет спокойно и размеренно: полицейские совершают регулярные рейды по отлову особо злобных демонов, городские духи пекут печенье, а простые виленские обыватели пьют вишневое пиво, задушевно беседуют с бездной, видят сны и побеждают смерть – все как всегда.'

unsuspecting soul have to prove themselves. Unlike in fantasy literature, where the supernatural is usually an extension of the protagonists' normality and thus their possibilities, Fraj's universe is a gnostic one (very clearly in story № 8). In that cosmos, the human does not have fate in his/her own hands, but s/he can only think about how s/he wants to react to the overpowering forces (cf. Hartmann 1980: 24–28). Unlike Gnosis, in Fraj's tales, these powers are by and large benevolent to man (as in № 3, for instance). So, Fraj's tales may belong to a popular sub-genre of horror fiction, that Bārbala Simsone (2015: pp. 127–133) calls Urban fantasy literature, which is characterised, as she (p. 127) puts it, by the fact that 'the elements of horror literature are virtually eliminated' (*šausmu žanra elementi it kā izšķīst*). However, it may be misleading that something is a subgenre of horror fiction that does not have horror fiction characteristics. A second, cultural-semiotic Fraj reception rightly focuses on the *Fairy tales* resulting in a Vilnius novel. As Romanenkova (2020) sees it, the book series was a testament to the appropriation of a foreign (Lithuanian) semiosphere through recognising one's own (Russian) signs, and the means for this were the fictional memory of a fairytale-like (fantastic) town world. This reception can draw parallels to the biography of the author duo, who moved from Moscow to Vilnius, where, as one can assume, they had to settle into a new semiosphere. On the other hand, the *Fairy tales* do not deal with what is familiar and foreign, but rather that the past can be rewritten.[4] So the discussion about this work of fiction remains exciting.

In story № 6, already interpreted above, paying attention to the narrative framework is all the more important as both characters, Anna-Alëna and the personification of the line-setting brain, are narrators in their respective text paragraphs. While the ego-line character narrates in the first person, Anna's absenteeism appears in the third person and in italics. This emphasises the line-setting character, whereas Anna's thinking only seems like an echo or comment of his work. Moreover, Anna's thinking does echo something insofar as the story ends with an acquaintance tracking her down after calling out to her. The story begins with Anna recognising that she has lost her way, 'Anna-Alëna, Anna-Alëna, where did you end up?' (*Анна-Алена, Анна-Алена, куда тебя понесло?*, Fraj 2019 b: 98). However, this opening could as well be Anna's acquaintance's first calling out to her. Therefore, it is wise that the authors adhere to the international, basic structure of narration so that the readers have a receptive framework at hand. We thus see the story's first sentence already starts with the peripety, but its condition implies that Anna had orientated herself beforehand (untold stage A). After the first sentence, the story's focus pans over to the line-setting character who has slept and did not do his consciousness-creating duties (as he admits), and that is how Anna got lost in her thoughts (overwhelmed by 'the night', as the line-setting character argues). His nap, his explanation and his self-reproach are the peripety.

Anna's new state is apparently going around the University's courtyards, but she takes a strange path and does not find her way out. Stage B is thus Anna being confused. The attraction of story № 6 is that stage B is not a desirable condition for Anna, even if she does

---

4   For example, the first-person narrator says (Fraj 2019 a: 152) that '"Living in order" now, in any case, is not an option. Because the dull townships at the fair have pissed you off tonight. And if we want not just to improve your mood, but to find that your mood has remained beautiful all day, we must change what has already happened to them. Must rewrite the past, or at least what we remember about it' («*Жить по порядку*» *сейчас, в любом случае, не вариант. Потому что унылые горожане на ярмарке взбесили тебя сегодня. И если мы хотим не просто поднять тебе настроение, а обнаружить, что оно оставалось прекрасным весь день, надо менять то, что с ними уже случилось. Переписывать прошлое или хотя бы то, что мы помним о нем*). Romanenkova (2020: 131) also quotes this passage (but from Fraj 2014: 167).

not feel uncomfortable. However, the line-setting character soon begins his work (on page 108 of Fraj 2019 b). Anna notices an incoming mobile phone call from her acquaintance, which initiates the narrative resumption. The line-setting character entangled with Anna's consciousness tries to reconstruct how Anna could get lost. Such a reconstruction is, of course, no longer possible according to logical criteria since Anna's confusion happened in the realm of the irrational. So Anna's explanations seem like excuses to the reader.

Stage C is reached when Anna meets on her date in front of the presidential palace. The change in the narrated space clarifies that Anna has finally escaped both the 'yards of the night' and the University's courtyards. In the end, Anna's acquaintance greets her with 'a warm welcome home' (*добро пажаловать домой*, Fraj 2019 b: 111) so that we are informed that Anna could probably get lost because she had not been in Vilnius for a long time. However, the line-setting character anticipates such a rational explanation arguing that Anna's acquaintance, of course, had nothing to do with her temporally getting confused (*он, конечно же, ни при чем*, op. cit.: 111).

7 Conclusion

The starting point for our deliberations was the happy ending that characterises modern fiction. If the happy ending is not simply viewed as a technical procedure, but that for the happy ending to occur, the fictional work must be brought to a logical end, the question is what a logical end to a fictional text is and when it can occur. The basic structure of narration answers this. It represents a (narrato)logical schema along which the fiction's plot runs, if one may call it a narrative. This narrative framework consists of five stages to which the protagonists are subjected—the status quo (stage A), the peripety (stage P), the new values (stage B), the resumption (stage R), and the status quo plus (stage C). In a shortened form, it can also be just three stages (A–P–B).

We took a closer look at Fraj's seven-volume work *Fairy tales of old Vilnius*, the 22 stories in volume 5, and story № 6, 'Simonas Daukantas Square'. Here, one could say a lot about the fantastic worlds and their beings that we encounter in the stories, about the worldview of the authors, whether it is gnostic or not, about the mixing of styles, about the contribution that Fraj makes to Russian-language literature, although both authors do not live in Russia. Or, on the other hand, one could ponder the peculiarity that all the stories are situated in Vilnius, where the Fraj-authors may have found their new home or where their local history, in which the experiences of different cultures are merged, fascinates them. Also, it would certainly be very worthwhile to take a closer look at which of the 22 stories are to be understood as a parable, as was story № 6. And while all of this <u>could</u> not only be said, but <u>should</u> be said once, this contribution focuses on another aspect. Hence, the question arises as to how the reader is actually able to receive a piece of fiction that ultimately draws its source from the mixture of everything (locations, cultures, histories, realities) but at the same time presupposes that the mixture's details can be recognised by the readers and put into context (for instance, the proximity of the University of Vilnius and Simonas Daukantas Square which is named after a historical figure important to contemporary Lithuanian self-imagination). The question weighs even more as the authors offer their results to a Russian-speaking yet international audience. The answer is again in favour of the narrative framework presented here. This widespread, internationally and transculturally shared, communicative and aesthetic code enables the Fraj-authors to reach an international audience who can ultimately comprehend their narratives. Of course, Fraj's stories' concrete reception still depends on which details of the 'fictional mix' one recognises or, to stay with the example of № 6, that one knows Vilnius University has several inner courtyards. However, a meaningful, structured reception is always possible because Fraj's tales' plot schemata follow the international framework.

Such considerations have long been the norm in the film sciences. For example, Kuhn (2018: 45–46) not only describes a 'classic narrative structure,' which resembles the narrative framework presented here, but she also explicitly puts forth these findings into literary studies when she suggests (Kuhn 2018: 46) that film and fiction were similar in terms of the basic plot structure. Why is it then that literary studies continue to view the objects of investigation from a national and author-centred point of view? Why not finally recognise, as film studies have long done for the cinema, that every international reception of a work of fiction is based on a communicative and thus cultural commonality? Perhaps not all people in this world share a cultural practice that I have tried to describe through the basic structure of narration. However, it would finally be time for literary scholars to become more explicit about the validity of this cultural practice, its scope, and its dissemination.

8 References

8.1 The stories (streets) of volume five of Maks Fraj's *Skazki starogo Vil'nûsa*

01. 'Улица Арклю (Arklių g.): Встреча выпускников' [Arklių Street (Horse Street): The graduate meeting], Fraj 2019b: 7–30.
02. 'Улица Аугустиону (Augustijonų g.): Билет и чемодан' [Augustijonų Street (Augustinian Street): Ticket and suitcase], pp. 31–46.
03. 'Переулок Балтасис (Baltasis skg.): Дело в шляпе' [Baltasis Lane (White Lane): Done deal!], pp. 47–62.
04. 'Улица Бенедиктину (Benediktinų g.): Кайпиринья сердца' [Benediktinų Street (Benedictines Street): A caipirinha from the heart], pp. 63–92.
05. 'Улица Волано (A. Volano g.): Культурная миссия' [Volano Street (Andreas Volanus Street): On a cultural mission], pp. 93–97.
06. 'Площадь Дауканто (S. Daukanto a.): Я или ночь' [Daukanto Square (Simonas Daukantas Square): Me or the night], pp. 98–111.
07. 'Улица Ишганитойо (Išganytojo g.): Дурацкие зеркала' [Išganytojo Street (Christus Salvator Street): Stupid mirrors], pp. 112–141.
08. 'Улица Кедайню (Kėdainių g.): Требуется чудовище' [Kėdainių Street (Kėdainiai Street): We are hiring: a monster], pp. 142–171.
09. 'Переулок Крейвасис (Kreivasis skg.): Темнее, чем просто тьма' [Kreivasis Lane (Crooked Lane): Darker than just darkness], pp. 172–187.
10. 'Улица Круопу (Kruopų g.): Заверните, беру' [Kruopų Street (Groat Street): Wrap it up, I'll take it], pp. 188–211.
11. 'Улица Лейиклос (Liejyklos g.): Площадь Восьмидесяти Тоскующих Мостов' [Liejyklos Street (Foundry Street): Eighty Yearning Bridges Square], pp. 212–237.
12. 'Улица Лидос (Lydos g.): Белые стволы, алые стены' [Lydos Street (Lida Street): White trunks, scarlet walls], pp. 238–257.
13. 'Улица Плачойи (Plačioji g.): 1+1' [Plačioji Street (Wide Street): 1+1], pp. 258–269.
14. 'Улица Расу (Rasų g.): А вы как хотите' [Rasų Street (Rasos Cemetery Street): And for you, as you want], pp. 270–304.

15. 'Улица Стразделе (A. Strazdelio g.): Мне нравится это девочка' [Strazdelio Street (Antanas Strazdas Street): I like this girl], pp. 305–326.
16. 'Улица Театро (Teatro g.): Вредные привычки' [Teatro Street (Theater Street): Bad habits], pp. 327–362.
17. 'Улица Шварцо (Švarco g.): Чье чудовище прекрасней' [Švarco Street (Schwartz Street): Whose monster is more beautiful], pp. 363–374.
18. 'Улица Швентараге (Šventaragio g.): Строительный материал' [Šventaragio Street (Šventaragis Street): Construction material], pp. 375–400.
19. 'Улица Швенто Двасес (Šv. Dvasios g.): Открытый финал' [Šventosios Dvasios Street (Holy Spirit Street): An end with an open outcome], pp. 401–421.
20. 'Улица Швенто Микалояус (Šv. Mikalojaus g.): Позвоните Барбаре' [Šventojo Mikalojaus Street (Saint Nicholas Street): Call Barbara!], pp. 422–439.
21. 'Переулок Шилтадарже (Šiltadaržio skg.): Это делается так' [Šiltadaržio Lane (Greenhouse Lane): This is to be done in that way], pp. 440–452.
22. 'Улица Шяулю (Šiaulių g.): Третья сторона' [Šiaulių Street (Šiauliai Street): A third party], pp. 453–479.

8.2 Fiction and films cited as examples

Adams, Douglas (2008), *The Hitchhiker's Guide to the Galaxy*, ed. by Reinhard Gratzke, Stuttgart: Reclam.
Adolphsen, Peter (2011), *The Brummstein*, translated by Charlotte Barslund, Las Vegas: Amazon Crossing.
Austen, Jane (2008), *The Complete Works*, with an introduction to each volume by Katie Halsey, Newcastle-upon-Tyne: Cambridge Scholars Publishing Classic Texts.
Brazil (1985), U.K. & U.S. science fiction film directed by Terry Gilliam and written by Terry Gilliam, Charles McKeown, and Tom Stoppard.
Bridgerton (2020), U.S. streaming television series created by Chris Van Dusen, produced by Shonda Rhimes et al., premiered on Netflix.
Callenbach, Ernest (1977), *Ecotopia: The Notebooks and Reports of William Weston*, New York: Bantam Books. (First self-published in 1975 as Banyan Tree Books.)
Clarke, Arthur C. (1949), 'The Lion of Comarre', *Thrilling Wonder Stories*, August, pp. 44–69.
Harris, Robert Dennis (2019), *The Second Sleep*, London: Hutchinson.
Joyce, James (^{3}2008), *Ulysses: The 1922 text*, ed. with an introduction and notes by Jeri Johnson, Oxford: Oxford University Press [1993].
La La Land (2016), U.S. musical romantic comedy-drama film written and directed by Damien Chazelle.
Leap Year (2010), U.S. romantic comedy film directed by Anand Tucker, written by Harry Elfont and Deborah Kaplan, and released in Ireland.
Longus [Λόγγος] (2004), *Daphnis & Chloe*, translated with an introduction and commentary by J. R. Morgan. Oxford: Oxbow Books. (Aries and Phillips Classical Texts.)
Nattel, Lilian (1999), *The River Midnight*, New York: Scribner.
Tokarczuk, Olga (2010), *Primeval and Other Times*, translated by Antonia Lloyd-Jones, Prague: Twisted Spoon Press.
Oh My Venus (2015), South Korean romantic comedy film directed by Kim Hyung-seok (김형석) and Lee Na-jeong (이나정), written by Kim Eun-ji (김은지), and aired by KBS and later on Netflix.

Rowling, Joanne (2006), *Harry Potter and the Half-Blood Prince*, London: Bloomsbury. (Volume 6 of the book series, first published in 2005.)
Sleepless in Seattle (1993), U.S. romantic comedy film directed and co-written by Nora Ephron, based on a story by Jeff Arch.
Szerb, Antal (2007), *The Pendragon Legend*, translated by Len Rix, New York: Pushkin Press. (Also as free digital resource.)
The Princess Weiyoung (2016), Chinese television series directed by Li Huizhu (李慧珠), written by Cheng Tingyu (程婷钰), and aired first on Dragon TV and Beijing TV, and later on Netflix.
Verne, Jules (2013), *20,000 Leagues Under the Seas: A World Tour Underwater*, translated and edited by Frederick Paul Walter, Albany/NY: State University of New York Press. (Also as free digital resource.)

8.3 Educational video

Kessler, Stephan (2021), *A Lecture on Happy Endings*, ten videos of a spring term course given at the University of Greifswald, free digital resource.

8.4 Bibliography

8.4.1 Printed tiles

Campbell, Joseph (2008), *The Hero with a Thousand Faces* [1949], 3rd edn., Novato/CA: New World Library. (Bollingen series 17.)
Creed, Barbara (1995), 'Horror and the carnivalesque', in Leslie Devereaux / Roger Hillman (eds.), *Fields of Vision: Essays in Film Studies, Visual Anthropology, and Photography*, Berkeley, Los Angeles & London: University of California Press, pp. 127–159.
Danto, Arthur C. (1985), *Narration and Knowledge (including the integral text of Analytical Philosophy of History)*, with an introduction by Lydia Goehr and a conclusion by Frank Ankersmit, New York: Columbia University Press.
Fleischer, Michael (1989), *Die sowjetische Semiotik: Theoretische Grundlagen der Moskauer und Tartuer Schule* [Soviet semiotics: theoretical foundations of the Moscow and Tartu schools], Tübingen: Stauffenburg Verlag. (Probleme der Semiotik 9.)
Forster, Edward Morgan (1990), *Aspects of the Novel* [1927], ed. by Oliver Stallybrass [1974], London et al.: Penguin Books.
[Fraj, Maks] Макс Фрай (2014), *Сказки старого Вильнюса III* [Fairy tales of old Vilnius, vol. 3], Санкт Петербург: Амфора.
—, — (2017), *Сказки старого Вильнюса VI* [Fairy tales of old Vilnius, vol. 6], Москва: АСТ.
—, — (2019a), *Сказки старого Вильнюса III* [Fairy tales of old Vilnius, vol. 3], Москва: АСТ.
—, — (2019b), *Сказки старого Вильнюса V* [Fairy tales of old Vilnius, vol. 5], Москва: АСТ.
Greimas, Algirdas Julien (1971), *Strukturale Semantik: Methodologische Untersuchungen* [Structural semantics: an attempt at a method], translated by Jens Ihwe, Braunschweig: Vieweg & Son. (Originally French, first published in 1966; English translation published in 1983.)
Hartmann, Karl (1980), *Atlas-Tafel-Werk zu Bibel und Kirchengeschichte: Karten, Tabellen, Erläuterungen, Bd. 2: Neues Testament und Geschichte der Kirche bis zu Karl dem Großen* [Infographics on the Bible and church history: maps, tables, explanations, vol. 2: New Testament and history of the church up to Charlemagne], Stuttgart: Quell Verlag.

Kahrmann, Cordula / Gunter **Reiss** / Manfred **Schluchter** (1991), *Erzähltextanalyse: Eine Einführung mit Studien- und Übungstexten* [Narrative text analysis: An introduction with study and exercise texts], 2nd edn., Frankfurt/M: Hain. (Athäneums Studienbuch: Literaturwissenschaft.)

Kermode, Frank (2000), *The Sense of an Ending: Studies in the Theory of Fiction* [1967], 2nd edn., with a new Epilogue, Oxford–New York et al.: Oxford University Press.

Kuhn, Annette (5 2018), 'Classic Hollywood narrative', in Pam Cook (ed.), *The Cinema Book*, 3rd edn. [2007], London & New York: The British Film Institute, pp. 45–48.

Lotman, Jurij [Юрий М. Лотман] (1977), *The Structure of the Artistic Text*, translated by Gail Lenhoff and Ronald Vroon, Ann Arbor: University of Michigan. (Michigan Slavic contributions 7. Originally Russian, published in 1971.)

[—, —] Юрий М. Лотман (1984), 'О семиосфере' [On semiosphere], *Труды по знаковым системам*, 17, pp. 5–23. (Acta et commentationes Universitatis Tartuensis 641.)

—, — [Юрий М. Лотман] (1990), *Universe of the Mind: A Semiotic Theory of Culture*, translated by Ann Shukman, introduction by Umberto Eco, London & New York: Tauris.

[—, —] Юрий М. Лотман (2010), *Семиосфера* [The semiosphere], Sankt-Peterburg: SPB.

MacDowell, James (2014), *Happy Endings in Hollywood Cinema: Cliché, Convention and the Final Couple*, 2nd edn., Edinburgh: Edinburgh University Press.

Marsch, Edgar (1983), *Die Kriminalerzählung: Theorie – Geschichte – Analyse* [The crime story: theory – history – analysis], 2nd edn., München: Winkler.

Neupert, Richard (1995), *The End: Narration and Closure in the Cinema*, Detroit: Wayne State University Press. (Contemporary film and television series.)

Simsone, Bārbala (2015), *Monstri un metaforas: Ieskats šausmu literatūras pasaulē* [Monsters and metaphors: an insight into the world of Horror literature], Rīga: Zvaigzne ABC.

Todorov, Tzvetan [Cvetan] (2 2018), *Einführung in die fantastische Literatur* [1976, Introduction to Fantastique fiction], übers. v. Karin Kersten, Senta Metz und Caroline Neubaur, Berlin: Klaus Wagenbach, 2013. (Originally French, first published in 1970; English translation published in 1973.)

White, Morton (1969), *Foundations of Historical Knowledge* [1965], New York: Harper & Row.

8.4.2 Digital tiles

Gustė (2014), 'Maksas Frajus: pseudonimo istorija' [Maks Fraj: the history of his pseudonym], post by 'Skaitytoja Gustė' on the blog of *'Nieko rimto' namai* [Publishing house 'Nothing serious'] at 30/04/2014.

Linder, Joachim / Claus-Michael **Ort** (2012), 'Zur sozialen Konstruktion der Übertretung und zu ihren Repräsentationen im 20. Jahrhundert' [On the social construction of infringement and its representations in the 20th century], in Joachim Linder / Claus-Michael Ort (eds.), *Verbrechen – Justiz – Medien: Konstellationen in Deutschland von 1900 bis zur Gegenwart* [1999], digital edn., Berlin: De Gruyter, pp. 3–80.

Romanenkova, Marina (2021), 'Эксперименты с памятью как способ вхождения в другую культуру (на материале книг Макса Фрая *Сказки старого Вильнюса*)' [Memory experiments as a way of entering another culture (based on Maks Fraj's *Fairy tales of old Vilnius*)], *Slavica Wratislaviensia*, 173 [2020], digital edn., pp. 127–135.

Russophone Literature in Latvia: Its Sociocultural Dimension and Vadim Vernik's *Gorlica*

An analysis
by Anna Stankeviča, Inna Dvorecka, and Jekaterina Gusakova
(Daugavpils)

Contributions to Baltic-Slavonic Relations in Literature and Languages: An Interdisciplinary Collection of Essays, edited by Stephan Kessler, Berlin: Logos Verlag, 2022, pp. 49–67.

Outline

Russophone literary works are in constant demand in the bookstores of Latvian cities. Therefore, in section 1, Latvian readers are described as the most avid. In 2018, 2,161 titles (1,578 original editions and 593 translated ones) were published in the Latvian Republic. Most of the publications were written in Latvian (1,126 titles), whereas books in either Russian or English were the next most common (116 and 117 titles, respectively). In Latvia's Russophone mass media, the Delfi portal holds the leading position, which distributes its content in different languages in parallel. Among the users of this multimedia platform, reviews of Russian literature on sale are in demand. Interviews with authors from Russia and with the ones who write in Russian regularly appear. Another area of acquaintance with Latvia's Russophone culture is film and theatre, which Delfi regularly reviews. These theatre and film reviews are also very popular with Delfi's readers. The context of the Russophone media in Latvia shows the coexistence of two cultural spheres in one national space. In section 2, the story *Горлица* [The Dove], written by the contemporary Latvian author Vadim Vernik, is used as an example of how the historical development of the Baltic region has resulted in multi-faceted Russian-Latvian cultural and literary ties. Latvia's Russophone literature is particularly complex and remains rather underinvestigated. *The Dove* is intriguing due to its orientation towards the broadest possible Russian-speaking audience — of both the Baltic states (Estonia is the central place in the story, although the narrator originates from Latvia) and Russia (the book has been presented in St. Petersburg and was nominated for an art prize there). In the current socio-cultural context, which rather often emphasises problems and conflicts on different levels (generational, gender, ethnic, racial), Vernik's story can be regarded as an attempt to contrast this with highly harmonious human relations.

Section one is written by Anna Stankeviča, Inna Dvorecka, and Ekaterina Gusakova, but section two by Anna Stankeviča and Inna Dvorecka.

Structure

1	Latvia's Russophone literature in sociocultural dimension	51
1.1	The circumstances: reading preferences and stakeholders	51
1.2	Russophone non-fiction	53
1.3	Russophone fiction and media	54
1.4	Conclusion	57
2	The phenomenon of Vadim Vernik's story *Gorlica* [The Dove] (variants of the opposition 'ours' vs 'theirs')	57
2.1	Aim of section, history of reception, and method of textual analysis	58
2.2	Vadim Vernik's *Gorlica* [The Dove] as formula fiction	59
2.3	Escapism as a way of constructing the fictional world of *The Dove*	61
2.4	Conclusion	63
3	**Overall Conclusion**	64
4	**Bibliography**	64
4.1	Printed titles	64
4.2	Digital items	66

1 Latvia's Russophone literature in sociocultural dimension

In very general terms, the cultural situation of today's Latvia can be characterised as follows: strong and progressively developing Latvian culture is dominant. At the same time, there are several weaker cultural flows — Russian, Polish, Belarusian, Ukrainian, or Jewish. Russian cultural societies and theatres have been working very actively in the Republic of Latvia. At universities, academic and professional Russian-medium programmes of philological, historical and cultural studies have been implemented.[1] The presence of communications and an intellectual environment is required for both the entire spiritual life of ethnic minority groups and the functioning of national cultural and educational institutions. One of the most important foundations of such kind of environment, by all means, is access to scientific, popular, reference, and children's literature and fiction in the respective language.

1.1 The circumstances: reading preferences and stakeholders

The problem of the functioning of the Russian segment in the context of the cultural process of Latvia has constantly been discussed in society over the past decades. Though Latvia's Russian culture is vital, stakeholders and scholars often put a question mark over its existence. Albeit Russian culture has historically been very fruitful in Latvia, it is not so productive in the last few years, and there is a discussion about its future development or even survival. Two opposed perspectives can be detected by, for example, the titles of published materials. On the one hand, we see boundless pessimism broadcast by some media that ask, 'There is Russian culture in Latvia, but no one needs it' (Anonymous 2013), or 'Who needs the Days of Russian Culture in Latvia?' (Gurin 2018). On the other hand, there are attempts to a balanced analysis of what is happening in the Republic, and the respective authors understand that Latvian culture should be developed at a large scale and the rights of the national minorities to realise their spiritual potential should be observed at the same time (Cheskin 2016). A collection of articles resulting from the investigations of Latvian scholars within the project *Ethnic and Narrative Diversity in Life Story Constructions in Latvia* is philosophically entitled 'We are all children of our time: the life stories of Russians in Latvia' (Zirnīte/Assereckova 2016). As the author of the foreword, Nadežda Pazuhina (Надежда Пазухина), says, the book gives 'a three-dimensional picture of the sociocultural experience of society' (Pazuhina 2016: 9). One of the most effective strategies for the internal harmonisation of Latvian society is creating a comfortable communication environment for each member of the society. That information, including fiction, is available in the native or any understandable language is one of the first conditions herein. A significant role in shaping the cultural milieu has one of the most popular Baltic electronic media, the Delfi portal, which distributes its contents multilingual. There is information in Russian along with Latvian, Lithuanian, Estonian news. Delfi's cultural policy is based

---

[1] Latvia's scientific community is actively involved in considering and discussing the formation of the cultural identity of Latvian society (Zelča 2018; Roskaša 2020; Lāce/Mazjāne 2020).

on existing artistic tastes and a desire to reflect new trends in the cultural and literary process.

Latvia can be called a reading country. When interviewed by Ekaterina Gusakova (Екатерина Гусакова), who is a journalist of the Delfi portal, the co-owner of the Polaris bookstore chain, Vasilyj Bystrov (Василый Быстров), has remarked that, in his view, in Latvia, there is a fashion for reading, and people of different ages and different nationalities are following this fashion. Indeed, statistical studies show that about 76 % of the population considers themselves reading, and only 23.5 % do not; 0.5 % find it difficult to answer. In the Latvian Republic, about 20 % of the population reads books every day or every two days. This ratio is characteristic of Latvians, Russians, and representatives of other ethnic groups (Laķe/Vinogradova/Baltskara 2018: 24). When discussing the issue in focus groups comprising teachers, students of the humanities, and members of cultural associations, it turns out that about one third visits libraries more or less regularly. The same number of respondents prefers exchanging books with friends and relatives; about half buy books. Similar results display the survey *Research on the Reading Preferences of the Residents of Latvia* conducted by specialists from the Latvian Academy of Culture in 2018 and commissioned by the Latvian Book Publishers Association. The study's respondents were selected proportionally according to five parameters (sex, age, nationality, region, and type of place of residence). In total, 1,611,326 people lived in the republic at that time. The respondents were 1010 residents of Latvia in the age from 15 to 77. Of these, 76 % consider themselves readers, 23 % as non-readers, and 0.5 % could not decide this question. Of the 768 respondents who said they were readers, 266 (34 %) prefer to read in Russian. Moreover, 42 % of Russian respondents and 49 % of the Latvian ones consider themselves to be book buyers in Latvia, 25 % of Russian and 35 % of Latvian respondents visit libraries, while 43 % of Russian and 30 % of Latvian respondents read books online. The e-book is also popular with Russian and Latvian respondents (19 % and 13 % respectively; Laķe *et al.* 2018: 56).

A peculiar situation evolved in the Latvian book market — shops that sell publications in Latvian and other languages of the European Union are trendy. However, Jānis Roze, the largest book-selling network in Latvia, deals with Russophone literature in a rather limited format. The leading player in this branch is the Polaris bookstore chain, which sells mainly Russophone books. This chain also has an online shop with the motto 'Don't hope to get rid of the book. Umberto Eco.' Worth highlighting is the Polaris's literary cafe, which is actively engaged in educational and awareness-raising events: it offers lectures on Russian literature, history, and culture, presents new books, organises concerts in the singer-songwriter's genre (*авторская песня*) and meetings to get in contact with Russophone authors from Russia and abroad. For instance, Denis Dragunskij (Денис Драгунский), Elena Katišonok (Елена Катишонок), Andrej Ivanov (Андрей Иванов), Evgenij Griškovec (Евгений Гришковец), Aleks Dubas (Алекс Дубас), Dmitrij Bykov (Дмитрий Быков), Igor Irteniev (Игор Иртениев), or Alla Bossart (Алла Боссарт), to mention just a few names that have appeared on the advertising posters of the cafe over the past two years.

Bystrov sees the work with Russophone literature in Latvia as his lifework; he is one of these enthusiasts, thanks to whom, after the collapse of the USSR, the Russian book trade in Latvia did not disappear, and, later, it did not have to start from scratch, as it happened with many other spheres of social life. Today, Russophone literature published in Latvia or abroad can be bought in the Polaris stores almost immediately after publication.

The paper aims to analyse the main components of the space of Russophone literature in Latvia: reader interests, book market, Russophone writing as such, opportunities and prospects, and the role of the media in these processes. When working on the material, cultural-historical, comparative, and statistical methods were used, as well as content analysis, interviews, questionnaires, and focus group discussions.

1.2 Russophone non-fiction

In Latvia, non-fiction (books that are based on facts) is the most demanded kind of literature. This category includes a wide range of products: dictionaries and encyclopaedias, cookbooks, handicrafts, popular science and educational literature, memoirs, essays, travelogues, books on psychology and personal growth, philosophy, political science, or the like. This increased interest in non-fiction manifests a pan-European and, more broadly, global trend. Modern sociologists associate this with the paradigm shift explained by Thomas Samuel Kuhn (1962) and Alvin Toffler (1980). The post-industrial world turns to a different artistic discourse, in which fiction takes a peripheral place (Gubin 2017). Statistical studies evidence the popularity of non-fiction in Latvia: to one extent or another, about 87 % of all Latvian readers are interested in factual literature; however, for many, these preferences do not exclude interest, for example, in fantasy or detective stories (Laķe/Vinogradova/Baltskara 2018: 36). The Latvian media also offer similar information. In an advertising article about the hottest offers in Latvian bookstores in March 2020, Marks Gurjevs (2019: para. 3) announces,

> And here are interesting non-fiction novelties: H. Murakami's confession book *Novelist as a Profession*, V. Ramakrishnan's *Gene Machine* on research into ribosomes, S. Gundry's *The Longevity Paradox*, I. Nikitchuk's *Restless Ukraine. History from Ancient Times*, *The Tenth Island* by D. Marcum, *Beautiful YOU* by beauty blogger K. Novikova, V. Istomin's *Not Boring Desserts*, *We Sew According to GOST* by the legendary dressmaker Z. Vysotskaya, Hatta, Y: *Japanese Knitting Stitches* (200 Stitch Patterns).

The consumer is offered non-fiction book products for every taste and request. Reviewing the Daugavpils Municipal Library, the *Daugavpils ziņas* portal speaks of Russophone literature that way:

> Readers preferred books on such vital topics as health, gender relations, psychology of happiness. The book by S. Hawking and L. Mlodinow *The Grand Design*, which make current scientific hypotheses about the secrets of the universe more accessible to the general public, can be considered a pearl amongst the five most-read non-fictional publications. (Gedzhune 2018)

As shown by a survey of library workers in Rīga and Daugavpils, such literature is in high demand among students and educated people, who are young and middle-aged. They consume books within the ongoing paradigm shift and their tastes are formed, among other things, as a response to the challenges of society. The next group of people interested in literary non-fiction is school youth. Many young people at the age of 15 or 16 already know the sphere of their future professional interests and are actively educating themselves. However, contemporary secondary school often fails to meet many of the intellectual needs of young people. The last, small, but very stable group is elderly readers, who have been admirers of one particular genre for several decades, such as memoirs, travelogues, or historical essays.

Bystrov notices that, according to long-term observations made by the bookstore workers, Russophone non-fiction is read not only by people for whom the Russian language is native but also, for example, by native speakers of Latvian. Statistical studies show that about 6 % of the native speakers of Latvian regularly read literature in Russian (Laķe/Vinogradova/Baltskara 2018: 66). Apparently, this is because Russophone non-fiction (including translations into Russian) is published in much larger volumes and on broader topics in Russia or Belarus, which have a larger book market than Latvia. Accordingly, copies from Russia or Belarus are more accessible and often cheaper than Russian originals from Latvia or their translations into Latvian. The most popular Russophone non-fiction in Latvia is with the titles of the Russian publishing houses ACT, Ad Marginem, Corpus, Манн, Иванов и Фербер, Бомбора, and Альпина нон-фикшн.

In 2018, 2,161 editions were published in Latvia, including 1,578 original works and 593 translations. In the same year, 479.9 thousand copies of fiction circulated, but 552.9 thousand copies of non-fiction. Most of the publications are in Latvian (1,126 nominations), followed by English- and Russian-medium books with 116 and 117 nominations, respectively (Latvijā 2018: 5). The statistics can be explained: Latvian is the official language of Latvia, but many residents also speak a second language, young people English, middle and older generations Russian. Therefore, books in Russian are in demand. Unfortunately, Russophone non-fiction is almost not published in Latvia. Vasilyj Bystrov states that good titles of non-fiction were published in tiny printings and only at the expense of the authors or private foundations. For example, the collective monograph of Marina Levina *et al.* (2010), *The Heritage of Religious Architecture and Art in Riga*, was translated into Russian and published by the Charitable Foundation of Cultural Heritage.

1.3 Russophone fiction and media

In a 2002 interview, Boris Ravdin (Борис Равдин), a Latvian cultural historian, reflects on the cultural process in Europe. He claims that there was Russophone literature in Latvia, and it would not matter whether or not it exists publicly (Borŝova 2002). He explains,

> There are no ideas that own the world today, and this is partly reflected in literature. It seems to me that in a crisis, it is precisely the peripheral cultures, if they can be called so, being not involved in the centrifugal forces, that are able to find their course for the sensation or even development of the literary process. We need to talk about some kind of world literary process, so whether it exists here is not the most important thing. A certain period of time must pass, and we will see who managed to reflect the movement of life in his work. The decline of literature? It cannot be, because every decline is evidence of a future rise. (Loc. cit.)

Eighteen years have passed since the moment these words were uttered, but even today, they provide the best description of the complex processes in the development and distribution of Russophone literature in the Latvian Republic as well as possible.

First, it should be noted that fiction is still popular. The aforementioned survey of the Latvian Academy of Culture shows that detective and crime novels are of the greatest interest to both Latvians and Russians in Latvia. Detective and crime novels are named among the preferred genres by 25 % of all respondents followed by historical novels (23 %), genre novels and romances (22 %), and fantasy literature (16 %). Poetry is read by just over 8 % of all respondents. At the same time, one can hardly speak about the absoluteness and persistence of these tendencies. Booksellers notice significant changes in the reading preferences that have recently been taking place: the dynamics of book sales indicate that the craze for mass literature (thrillers and so-called women's novels) no longer exists. For example, fifteen years ago, the Polaris bookstore chain sold Dar'â Doncova's (Дарья Донцова) novels in thousands of copies, but at present, 50–60 book copies of her new novels are hardly sold within two or three months.

Along with non-fiction, high-quality Russophone fiction is in demand. Focus group discussions show that there is a high demand for classic Russian literature and the nominees and laureates of Russian literary awards such as National Bestseller, Big Book, Book of the Year. The factors that increase interest in a particular literary text are, for example, an anniversary of a classic or a film adaptation. So, Guzel' Âhina's (Гузель Яхина) *Зулейха от-*

крывает глаза [Zulejha opens her eyes], published in 2015, experienced its peak popularity in Latvia in the spring of 2020, when an eight-episode television series based on this novel was released. The growing interest in classical literature sometimes has complex causal connections. Another peak of interest in classical literature falls in 2017. This year, the screen version of Lev Tolstoj's (Лев Толстой) novel *Анна Каренина* [Anna Karenina, 1875/77] directed by Karen Šahnazarov (Карен Шахназаров) was released. In the same year, Boris Èjfman's (Борис Эйфман) famous ballet known for his interpretations of Russian classical literature (*Onegin, The Idiot, The Brothers Karamazov, Master and Margarita*) was on tour in Rīga performing *Anna Karenina*. The Delfi portal published a large interview with the choreographer. One of the themes raised in this interesting conversation was about the role and place of classic Russian literature in the life of a modern person. When asked about the reason for the ongoing interest in theatre performing Russian literature, Èjfman explains,

> The value of the classic literature lies in its over-temporal relevance. In each of the books you have listed, you can find answers to many concerns of today's public life. But for me, it is more significant that all these works seek to unravel the mystery of the Russian soul. And the soul is that substance, which is beyond the control of political, economic and any other changes. (Hudenko 2017: para. 14)

Besides being a universal world of immersion in art and literature, theatre is also an important sphere for Latvia. The outstanding Russian theatre director Mark Rozovskij (Марк Розовский) called the theatre a version of literature (Rozovskij 2017). Latvian theatres regularly turn to classic Russian literature and contemporary Russian drama in their theatrical productions. In 2019, the Mihail Čehov Riga Russian Theatre received the prestigious state prize for staging Ivan Turgenev's (Иван Тургенев) *Муму* [Mumu, 1854] directed by Viesturs Kairišs. In recent years, Nikolaj Gogol''s (Николай Гоголь) *Ревизор* [The Government Inspector, 1842] has been staged twice, namely in the New Riga Theatre by the famous Latvian director Alvis Hermanis and in the Daugavpils Theatre by Olegs Šapošņikovs. For the Daugavpils performance, the play was transferred onto Latgale's soil.

The Daugavpils theatre especially loves classic Russian literature. The audience demonstrated mixed reactions to the interpretations of *Горе от ума* [Woe from Wit, 1825] based on the same-titled comedy of Aleksandr Griboedov (Александр Грибоедов), and of Nikolaj Ostrovskij's (Николай Островский) *Гроза* [The Storm, 1860] directed by the theatre director. However, Evgenij Švarc's (Евгений Шварц) *Голый король* [The Naked King, 1960] was greeted with enthusiasm, and the performance of a diptych, *Чайка* [The Seagull], based on the plays of Anton Čehov (Антон Чехов) and Boris Akunin (Борис Акунин) were sold out for months. A survey of booksellers and libraries in Daugavpils showed that the interest in texts of certain Russian authors is directly proportional to the inclusion of their works in the repertoire of the theatres in Latvia and the coverage and analysis of the performances by the media.

'There have always been Russophone writers in Latvia' is the title of an article (see Dmitriev 2014), which is a digest of well-known facts about 20th century Russophone literature and writers in Latvia until 2014. Yet, there has also been Latvian Russophone literature after 2014. A number of prominent, widely known names can be mentioned: Irina Cigaļska (1939–2021); a young poetess, writing under the pseudonym Ananastâ Ananasova (Ананастя Ананасова, b. 1992); Aleksandr Garros (Александр Гаррос, 1975–2017); Aleksej Evdokimov (Алексей Евдокимов, b. 1975), Vâčeslav Soldatenko (Вячеслав Солдатенко, 1969–2021; his pseudonym is Слава Се), or Aleks Dubas (Алекс Дубас, b. 1971), who is living both in Latvia and in Russia. These are not all: a whole galaxy of writers of regional importance is working. Characterising Latvia's Russophone literature, Vasilyj Bystrov considers the tendency a sad one that talented and bright writers were looking for a wider readership and opportunities to publish in large numbers, so they are either moving to Europe or Russia or living, as it has been mentioned above, 'in two homes.'

Russophone literature needs support, both material and informational. This also applies to Latvia's Russophone literature and any Russophone literature published outside that country. Bystrov names regular announcements, analytical materials, discussion notes on social networks as forms of informational support. He states that seven years of weekly posts on Instagram and Facebook, created by PR specialists and interested philologists on the order of Polaris, were giving positive results.

During the focus group discussion devoted to considering the issue of sources of information on Russophone literature in Latvia, the following nominations were most frequently mentioned: advice from a friend or relative; information on the network; electronic or paper media. Oleg Peka (Олег Пека), the Mix Media Group's programme director, who makes regular appearances on Radio Baltkom, was named an authoritative person in this area by literature teachers, humanities students, and members of the Russian cultural society in Daugavpils. Galina Ûzefovič (Галина Юзефович), the presenter of the Book Bazaar section on the Meduza website headquartered in Riga, and Andrej Šavrej (Андрей Шаврей), who writes for the LSM portal, were also named.

Most discussion participants specified the Delfi portal among Latvia's Russophone media. As the staff of the portal explained, the issues related to the cultural life in Latvia and abroad were of interest to the readers, but, if it can be defined that way, this interest was purely factual, and just a kind of light format aiming at information was needed, but not analyses and assessments. The professional scientific or critical literary review genre turns out to be unpopular among Delfi users, but reviews of books on sale are in demand. Regularly, in cooperation with the Polaris bookstore chain, a list of new products and bestsellers with small annotations is published on the media portal. This heading has the corresponding, telling name Observation Wheel. Practically every such review observes works of classic and contemporary Russian literature. So, in the October 2020 review, the readers were offered two novels of contemporary Russophone writers—*Симон* [Simon] written by Narinė Abgarân (Наринэ Абгарян), and *Одинокий пишущий человек* [A Lonely Writing Man] by Dina Rubina (Дина Рубина)—, two translated detective stories, and two thrillers. Six editions are addressed to children, including the Christmas gift edition for the little ones *Yolka, Cat and New Year*, and some classic Russian literature for children like the fairy-tale *Бобик в гостях у Барбоса* [Bobik visits Barbos] written by Nikolaj Nosov (Николай Носов). As usual, the non-fiction section is the one that is most fully represented by seven nominations that are very diverse thematically: forensics, medicine, epidemics and pandemics, the history of the creation of nuclear weapons, poisons and poisoners, and two historical works, including professor Nataliâ Basovskaâ's (Наталия Басовская) famous *Фееричная Франция* [Enchanting France]. It should be noted that some authors of Latvia's Russophone literature have recently been awarded extensive and detailed reviews. Among the most popular are Evgenij Vodolazkin (Евгений Водолазкин)—by the way, his best novels, *Лавр* [Laurus, 2012] and *Авиатор* [The Aviator, 2016], have been translated into Latvian—, Zahar Prilepin (Захар Прилепин), and Viktor Pelevin (Виктор Пелевин).

The Delfi platform regularly publishes interviews with Russian and Russophone authors and reviews of their lectures. It also reports on reading sessions with popular authors and laureates of literary awards. Among the latest interesting materials, there has been published reports on get-togethers with Aleksej Ivanov (18.04.2019), Slava Se (18.04.2019), and Evgenij Griškovec (08.01.2020). Judging by the number of comments, the information about Dmitrij Bykov's public lecture (02.12.2020) aroused great interest and ambiguous assessment among the readers. Bykov analysed the artistic process in Russia, arguing that the problems in modern Russian literature are directly related to the turbulence in Russian society. Surveys of the readers' opinion on the editorial policy of Delfi in the field of communication with Russophone writers, educational institutions, publishing houses, and book distribution networks show that, although a lot is being done, it would be advisable if there were more interest and activity from Delfi's journalist collective.

1.4 Conclusion

The development and dissemination of Russophone literature is an important condition for preserving and functioning Russian culture as a natural part of Latvia's culture. At present, those who wish to read Russian-language print media can use libraries and buy books, primarily in the specialised chain of the Polaris bookstores. Latvia's theatres of any language orientation demand Russian-medium plays. Original Russian literature is being translated into Latvian. Writers, who create their works in Russian, live and work in Latvia. One condition for the presence of the segment of Russophone literature in the culture of Latvia is full support from the media. The forms of communication in this area presented by modern media are diverse: advertising materials, presentations of new books, reviews, critical articles, discussions, interviews with Russophone writers and cultural figures. Almost all Russophone media in Latvia pay attention to this area of social life. The Latvian portal Delfi, which also publishes the materials in Russian, is one of the leaders in this area. However, as the opinion surveys among Russophone authors, specialists working in the field of the book trade, and librarians demonstrate, Latvia's society expects more interest and involvement in supporting and popularising Russophone literature from the media. In addition, the presented context of the Russophone media in Latvia reflects one of the levels of coexistence of two components in one cultural space.

2 The phenomenon of Vadim Vernik's story *Gorlica* [The Dove] (variants of the opposition 'ours' vs 'theirs')

Due to the peculiarities of historical development (changing borders of states and borderlines in Europe), the cultural space of the Baltic countries is multi-layered. One of the most complex segments of this cultural landscape is Russian culture and literature. Literary criticism has so far focused on literary phenomena of different periods — from the earliest literary evidence of Balto-Slavic cultural contacts up to the contemporary phenomena.[1]

Latvia's Russian literature is thematically diverse and multigenre. Translations of Russian literature into Latvian represent Russian literature in modern Latvia — with the 'dissemination leaders' being Evgenij Vodolazkin and Aleksandra Marinina (Александра Маринина) — and local Russian authors like the poets of the Orbita group, Slava Se, or Aleksej Evdokimov.

---

1   Among the fundamental studies, the following works should be noted: Abyzov (1993; 1999), Belobrovceva/Abyzov/Lavrinec (1996/2005), and Flejšman (1997).

2.1 Aim of section, history of reception, and method of textual analysis

The purpose of this article is to analyse the 'longer story' (*повесть*) *Горлица* [The Dove], published by the Riga writer Vadim Vernik (Вадим Верник) in 2017, that is a phenomenon of mass culture, with one of the main components of the artistic world being the opposition 'ours' vs 'theirs'. Vernik is an artist mosaicist from Rīga who evoked a lively response from the Russophone reading public in the Baltics. In 2018, *The Dove* received the prestigious Carskoe Selo art prize 'for the development of Russian literature outside Russia.' At the same time, the readers' reviews reveal a range of debatable issues related to the perception of the story. Consideration of text reference is one of these issues. As a rule, numerous responses of readers indicate that Vernik's text is most often perceived as a lifelike story that evokes some associations with what was experienced in the youth:

> Everything is beautiful—the turn of phrase and the plot—this love story conquers anyone who knows the thrill of youthful love, first mutual feelings, excitement and joy. (Kovalenko 2019)

> First, this is a well-written story, somewhat similar to the plot of the film *The Romance about Lovers*. Moreover, this is also a mysterious guess that our life indeed gives out such true-life plots that are 'beyond the control of our wise men.' (Šavrej 2017)

Several commentators display the opinion that there is a deep metaphysical subtext in the story, which makes it possible to see a 'novel-initiation', a 'novel-river' (*роман-река*), or 'the realisation of the archetype of Adam and Eve', in what has been written.

The second debatable issue is the interpretation of the sentimental component of the text. The author himself and numerous admirers of the story, as a rule, emphasise that *The Dove* is an example of high eroticism. However, some readers are sceptical about this benign assessment. In particular, the Latvian bookshop chain Polaris refused to distribute Vernik's story because the bookseller's experts consider it a pornographic text, and Polaris' trade policy does not allow to sell such literature.

These contradictions can be resolved by considering Vernik's *Gorlica* in the context of the phenomena of mass literature, specifically as an instance of a formulaic novel. The concept of formula was proposed by the American researcher of mass culture John Cawelti (1977), who believed that the modern mass reader is most appealed to books where the fictional world is given as a set or sequence of recognisable *formulae*, i.e. cultural clichés and archetypes. So, authors rely on such beloved structural patterns with high memorability. Thus, the formula novel is a kind of hybrid education that allows one to reinforce the existing interests of readers. The fictional world of the formula novel takes these interests and expectations into account. Even though the modern formula novel lacks artistic recognition, it is most often of good quality, a fact that fully applies to Vernik's *povest'*. It is worth recalling the term 'nobrow' here, that John Seabrook (2001) has introduced into cultural use. In its most general sense, *nobrow* means 'without hierarchy'—somewhat in between the highbrow and lowbrow statuses.[2]

For the study of the mass-cultural phenomenon of Latvia's Russophonic literature, the adequate methodology is interdisciplinary and based on contextual, intertextual, cultural-anthropological and philological approaches and sociolinguistic analysis. Only through interdisciplinarity, it is possible to extensively describe and interpret the features of the mass-cultural text and its functioning and perception in the complex socio-cultural context of the Baltic region.

---

2   The nobrow status has also been applied to Russian culture as such (see, for example, Černâk 2014).

2.2 Vadim Vernik's *Gorlica* [The Dove] as formula fiction

At the heart of the artistic world of Горлица, there is the story of love that struck two children — a boy and a girl; a love that became the highest happiness for a young man and a young woman and that ended, as is often the case in real life, by tragedy. The narration is conducted in the first person, and we learn that the protagonist-narrator is called Vadim, but his beloved is called the Girl throughout the entire story.

Vernik chooses a unique way of communicating with the audience. In the very introduction to the story, the author invites the reader 'to wrap oneself in a cosy blanket' and start reading, apparently subconsciously using the familiar formula of Russian mass culture when describing a cute intimate pastime. This is how an orientation towards the readership's expectations, familiar patterns, and semiotic norms is expressed, a device that is an important feature of the mass-cultural text (Temirbolat et al. 2016).

Vernik builds a sort of as familiar as unfamiliar fictional world, referring to the genre of formula fiction (in this case, the story). Let us turn to the main formula sets relevant to *The Dove's* story. The system of events in the story is par excellence — a love story that, according to the principles of organising the fictional world, goes back to two close artistic traditions: to the antique novel (the classic of the genre is *Ethiopic* by Heliodorus) and the 18th century's novel of sentimentalism which in modern mass culture has transformed into a mawkish-sentimental novel. At the centre of the antique novel, there was always the story of happy lovers separated by sudden circumstances, looking for each other for a long time and finding each other in the end.

The novel of sentimentalism, with some orientation towards this scheme, most often paid much attention to the obstacles and insurmountable circumstances rising in the path of those in love. Such a story often ended with the death of one of the lovers (cf. Johann Wolfgang von Goethe's *The Sorrows of Young Werther*, Jean-Jacques Rousseau's *The New Eloise*, or Nikolaj Karamzin's *Poor Liza*). The main semantic nodes of the plot of Vernik's *Dove* are a suddenly flared up feeling, forced parting, obstacles of all kinds (personal, social, criminal) that arise on the way, parting, a new meeting, reconciliation, beckoning happiness (the prospect of having a child and a wedding), and the tragic end (the death of the bride in a car accident). The last scene of the novel, of course, is aimed at a very sensitive reader: on a cold winter evening after the funeral, Vadim brings a bouquet of twenty white roses to the ruins of an old monastery that has been their favourite meeting place.

The development of a love story includes another important component, namely a sensual one. We would define this component of the fictional world as bodily redundancy, which is also a common technique of formula fiction. The world of the Girl and Vadim is sensually marked from the very beginning of their relationship by children's unconscious sexual play, all forms of bodily pleasures in youth, and the birth of family relationships. Perhaps the reader's impression of the narrator excessively focussing on the bodily component arises because the sexual marker (in its negative meaning as well) is almost dominant in the representation of almost all aspects of life. An incomplete list of sexual activities told in detail in the story is a gang-rape causing a serious illness of the Girl, an orgy during the army discharge, in which Vadim almost involuntarily participated, harassment, and rough self-pleasure. It seems that the artistic function of the narration's sexual aspect is not sufficiently motivated. Still, the function of a sexual marker in devising the entire structure of a formula text is indisputable. When analysing this structural feature, Cawelti (1977) says of the seeming paradox of most literary formulae, 'the fact that they are at once highly ordered and conventional and yet are permeated with the symbols of danger, uncertainty, violence, and sex' (Cawelti 1977: 16).

An equally important narrative component is the description of the protagonist's service in the Soviet army. In portraying this extremely unattractive reality, the author focuses on the cultural phenomenon of hack-and-slash, which is very important for the Russian art of the late 20th century. This is 'a wide layer of neo-naturalistic prose that opened the reader's eyes to the existence of homeless people, prostitutes, immigrants, army hazing, prison horrors and many other social phenomena' (Lipoveckij 1999: para. 7). Vernik describes in great detail the military service, whose absurdity and inhumanity literature and cinema have already well-comprehended: being on service, conscripts are bullied by 'established' soldiers, officers are tyrannic and cruel, and human dignity is constantly humiliated; there obtain domestic disorder, sexual violence, illness of soldiers, disgusting food, a show-off, and senselessness of existence. This undoubtedly gives Vernik's readership the expected feeling of resentment. However, this formula also includes facts of the opposite trend: despite all the killing factors, in the army, there is still a place for empathy, support, the friendship between young people who have fallen into the hardest troubles. The theme of the army brotherhood is also appreciated and widely developed by the modern Russian mass culture.

The next characteristic feature of *The Dove* that displays its formula fiction affiliation is a high degree of intertextuality. Undoubtedly, Vernik is a person well versed in world literature and, even broader, culture. His text is full of explicit and implicit quotations, associations, references to well-known texts. They are appropriate, most often demonstrative. This feature of mass literature has also been noticed by critics: 'It is easy and pleasant to play postmodern ping-pong with a humanitarian reader (you give him a quotation, he gives you a link)' (Arbitman 2001: 93).

In Vernik's *Gorlica*, one can conditionally distinguish two main groups of texts to which the author refers. First, the images of traditional culture. One of the most essential symbols of the story's fictional world is the dove itself. This literary image appears in the title but remains undeciphered almost until the conclusion. In one of the last scenes, the protagonist has a dream on the eve of the car accident in which his pregnant bride dies: 'I dreamed of a dove that fluttered up from a mountain ash branch and sat on my shoulder. And my beloved little girl, a maiden, then a young woman, appeared before my eyes' (Vernik 2017: 234). In Russian culture, the image of a dove is a symbol for a sacralised female gender, i.e. the world soul (Mekš: 2002). There are a number of literary texts where the image of a dove is marked with additional meanings of tragic love, e.g. the death of one of the lovers.[3] In the prophetic dream, the beloved girl treats the protagonist to berries of 'bright orange-red mountain ash'. The image of the mountain ash berries plays a suggestive role: in Russian traditional culture and folklore, the semantic cores of this mythologeme are holiness, sacredness, and female loneliness.[4] Traditional culture interprets the motive of treating mountain ash berries as a prediction of grief and tears. A prophetic dream, as well as the golden ring bought from a gipsy woman as an engagement ring that turned out to be a cheap fake—stamps, formulae prophesying trouble, which has many times been addressed by mass culture.

---

3 Evgenij Âblokov (2015) attributes the beginning of this literary tradition to Ivan Dmitriev's (Иван Дмитриев, 1760–1837) well-known sentimentalist poem *The gray dove is groaning* (1792).
4 'In ancient times, mountain ash was for people not just one of the trees in the forest. Mountain ash was considered as a holy tree.' (Makšanceva 2005: para. 5)

The second series of quotations is formed by classical culture. The story contains references to a wide range of pan-European and national heirlooms, accentuating certain facets of the narrative's historical timeframe. For example, the most cloudless, full of hope time in lovers' relationship correlates with the famous canvas of the early Renaissance, namely Sandro Botticelli's *Primavera* [Spring, ca. 1480]. The chapter preceeding the first night meeting of the lovers (one of the most sensual scenes of the story) is called 'The smell of Antonovka', which introduces the context of Russian literature, namely Ivan Bunin (Иван Бунин, 1870–1953) with his sensual and, at the same time, tragic understanding of love, which is clearly visible in his short story collection *Тёмные аллеи* [Dark Avenues, 1943]. The collection's nostalgic retrospective and the fatal doom of love find an echo in Vernik's story.

Along with the previously mentioned traditions of the Greek novel and sentimentalism, the paradigm of romanticism is essential for the imaginary world of Vernik's *Dove*. His references to romanticism comprise both individual symbolic texts and entire genres (for example, the legends of Old Tallinn, i. e. fairy-tale images, are associated with the tradition of national romanticism). One of the key literary quotations of *Gorlica* is George Sand's (1804–1876) novel *La Comtesse de Rudolstadt* [The Countess of Rudolstadt, 1842/44], which the Girl reads on the eve of her date in a bathhouse. Vernik's heroine writes a farewell letter, even quoting the novel of George Sand. Sand's heroine is a musician, the fact that Vernik uses for an entire series of quotations with reference to music: both at the plot level (the heroine of the story also takes up music) and at the level of intertextual ties. Musical quotations (words and tunes to songs) accompany the character-narrator in the most important, turning points of the narration and create an appropriate emotional background. Thus, the main musical accompaniment is the song *Девонька* [My Girl] composed by Pëtr Lešenko (Пётр Лещенко), a famous singer, whose peak of popularity came in the 1920s and 1930s, but who also enjoyed unofficial fame in the Soviet post-war space. This is the favourite song of the main heroine's grandfather; Vadim recalls it after the death of his beloved, which is how the story ends. Other songs and verses also adjoin this series. They concern different aspects of love and friendship. For instance, during the lover's breakup, a depressing rock ballad sounds in the consciousness of the protagonist; it is 'I want to be with you' (*Я хочу быть с тобой*) performed by the 1980s cult rock band Nautilus Pompilius. Before leaving the army, the soldiers who have become friends sing the well-known lyric song about friendship 'You and me, we are together' (*Ты да я, да мы с тобой*).

2.3 Escapism as a way of constructing the fictional world of *The Dove*

Besides the obligatory love-erotic and hack-and-slash (noir) components, formula fiction is also distinguished by how it constructs the fictional world. Formula texts avoid mimesis, i. e. they avoid real problems of any kind. Instead, their most important tool is escapism. Cawelti (1977) calls it the creation of a slightly modified, imaginary world. Vernik transfers the action to the mid-1980s. In today's socio-cultural context, which often accentuates the problems and conflicts of interpersonal communication at various levels (generational, gender, ethnic, racial), Vernik's story can be viewed as an attempt to oppose extremely harmonious human relations — between representatives of different nationalities, different generations, but above all between two people in love. The Baltic world built by the writer is an absolute idealisation. There are no ontological contradictions in this world, and there are no strangers. It is the world of ours, the loved ones, relatives.

In this context, the solution of the national paradigm is exciting. On the one hand, a multicultural component is essential for *The Dove*: the love story is developing in Estonia — the lovers are a local girl and a boy who came from Latvia for the summer. However, he was also born in Estonia and was named after the Russian officer who saved his grandmother during the blockade of Leningrad. Later, when describing the army life, other peoples of the Soviet Union are mentioned, like Lithuanians, Ukrainians, Georgians, or residents of the Central Asian Union republics.

On the other hand, despite the multinational composition of the system of characters in the story, the lack of national identity, characteristic of the Soviet space, eliminates the possibility of acute conflicts and misunderstandings between different national groups. The national cultural tradition is presented superficially (at the level of personal names and names of famous brands — the main character brings a herbal schnapps, Rīgas Balzāms, from Latvia; in Estonia, he and his beloved girl drink Vana Tallinn liqueur) and does not play any role in the development of *Gorlica's* storyline.

In addition, there are no other conflicts in the world of Vernik's story, neither of social affiliation nor age or gender. Two generalising formulae determine the features of interpersonal communication in the story. The first formula marks how the narrator perceives the Girl's relatives: 'The brother was like everyone else, handsome, cheerful and kind' (Vernik 2017: 116). The second appears in the army context: 'And yet, I was lucky to have good people nearby' (Vernik 2017: 203). The communication experience described in the story is generally favourable. Significantly, the second phrase was said about the image of the army. In the presence of a hack-and-slash context (hazing, physical and moral violence, a dangerous opportunity to get to Afghanistan), the dark side of the army life mentioned above remains on the narrative periphery. As a rule, the army life's dark side happens somewhere near, but the protagonist is not involved. In the city where Vadim is serving, soldiers are well-liked. Women treat them to pies, girls treat them to ice cream and write love notes. Despite the exhausting physical activity, the army did help the young soldiers. Everyone got fit, more challenging, and more energetic. It turns out that you can learn a lot from the 'established' ones; there may be honest and fair commanders (even a seemingly cynical commander with rude humour, who insults soldiers, turns out to be preparing them for further service and testing their strength and loyalty to their word). In the end, the army turns out to be a positive experience for the protagonist: it does not break, but rather strengthens him physically and spiritually, allowing him to understand himself better. Even the guardhouse, where he ends up getting as a punishment and where soldiers are systematically beaten and humiliated, according to Vadim, i.e. the narrator himself, becomes 'a necessary bitter pill' (Vernik 2017: 195) in a crisis, since it coincides with the news of a break up with his beloved.

The idealisation of the depicted world is most clearly manifested in the central plotline concerning the lovers. Their love is described as a bright, all-embracing feeling that reveals the best in man, the highest manifestation of beauty and harmony of being. Despite the tragic dénouement, the very love feeling that arose just between children grows more substantial and develops the couple further being young adults, is not associated with something dark or problematic. The Dove is not a story of unhappy, unrequited or forbidden love. On the contrary, everyone around the lovers supports them. The feeling grows naturally and organically, without overcoming challenging obstacles. First of all, the lovers are supported by their families. The Girl's grandfather invites Vadim to celebrate the New Year so that the lovers re-meet there. Despite her grumbling and anxiety, the Girl's grandmother calls the couple 'the doves', referring to the image in the story's title. Even though the relatives constantly become casual witnesses of the lovers' intimacy, this fact soon turns into the subject of good jokes. The friends also actively develop the lovers' relationship—they arrange dates, pass news, and maintain these contacts. Finally, even occasional passers-by admire the beautiful couple and its love.

Although the sensual-erotic aspects of the lover's relationship and their excessive intimacy are represented in detail, Vadim's and the Girl's feelings are portrayed as sublime and pure. It is no coincidence that the primary literary quotation is the novel by George Sand, which assigns primary importance to such significant categories of romanticism as loyalty, sacrifice, and spiritual nobility. Despite bold experiments in the sensual sphere, the characters promise each other to keep their virginity until the wedding. The protagonist correlates his love for the Girl to such concepts as the soul, i.e. the mysteries of life. Through his love for her, he perceives himself and life in general. Therefore, one of the key terms of the story that occurs in conversations with the Girl's grandfather, who embodies the archetype of a wise old man, is 'initiation'—a test associated with comprehending the hidden meaning of being (the alchemy motive supports this in the story). In addition, secrets are the keyword in a children's conversation with their parents. Interestingly, this is the story's only dialogue written in Estonian, emphasising its esoteric meaning. The parents twice become accidental witnesses of Vadim's and the Girl's love: both times, it happens on the ruins of an old monastery. The first time during the marriage proposal, the second when Vadim brings a bouquet of twenty roses after the death of his beloved.

At last, even terrible circumstances (the gang rape and the fatal accident in which the Girl dies) still cannot destroy the love of both characters though they were deeply traumatised. The terrible external circumstances are a faceless dark force that remains outside the framework of the narration: in both cases, the protagonist learns about the terrible events from someone post factum. In this sense, the death of his beloved, which, of course, becomes a great shock for the protagonist, is quite natural in the context of the *Dove's* time structure. It allows the author to close the story in an idealised past and to create a world similar, but not in congruence with reality. In the historical aspect, it is significant that the narration interrupts at Perestrojka, when fundamental changes begin in the space described. However, as he admits himself, the protagonist-narrator missed these changes as he was serving in the army at that time. He also rejects the offer to join the 'brigade', i.e. a criminal gang that is a sign of the new era—the 'freewheeling 90s'—that characterises criminalisation, racketeering, and other recognisable attributes. When the new page of the big history has been opend, the protagonist finds himself 'out of the way' (Vernik 2017: 206). Moreover, at the Dove's conclusion, a pre-war song of Pëtr Lešenko sounds (the hero-narrator hears the song on the radio, and fragments of the lyrics are quoted), and finally, it transfers everything depicted into a retro context with its nostalgic melancholy (Guffey 2006).

2.4 Conclusion

Vernik's story is a vivid example of a mass cultural text in the Russophonic literature of Latvia, for it is formula fiction. This structural framework is associated with options for solving the opposition 'ours' vs 'theirs'. First, the inclusion of a wide range of quotations and the focus on the frequently excessive number of plot formulae recognisable by the mass consciousness make the text as open as possible for the 'stranger's word', which, accordingly, maximises its potential readership. Secondly, the resolution of the opposition 'ours' vs 'theirs' at the plot level is also subordinated to this pragmatic aspect. On the one hand, Vernik creates a multicultural world encompassing the multinational space of the Soviet Union of the 1970s and 1980s and, first of all, the Baltic area since *The Dove's* action is primarily set in Estonia. At the same time, national diversity is declared schematically and superficially; it is conflict-free because national differences do not affect interpersonal communication in any way, but love and friendly or constructive professional relationships dominate. The opposition 'ours' vs 'theirs' is practically eliminated at the national and sociocultural levels — representatives of various nationalities, generations, or genders almost always find a common language. Although the world of strangers bursts into this idealised world created by the author and plays a fatal role in the fate of the characters (its representatives perform physical, sexual, and moral violence), it remains faceless and peripheral since it does not violate the inner beauty of the harmonious human relations depicted. Moreover, it becomes the feature that separates the fictional world from reality.

3 Overall Conclusion

Russophone literature in Latvia is at an essential stage in its development. On the one hand, it can be said that many people in the country read in Russian and Russian books are in demand. On the other hand, the number of authors living in Latvia who write in Russian decreases. Many authors who are popular among Russophone readers are starting to publish in Russia, and this is due to the larger number of readers and consequently more extensive circulation. It seems that in the coming years, this tendency will persist: Russophone books, both in their original language and in translations into Latvian, will be represented in the Latvian book market; new talented authors writing in Russian will not appear often.

4 Bibliography

4.1 Printed titles

[**Abyzov**, Jurij] Юрий Абызов (1993/99), ed., *От Лифландии – к Латвии: Прибалтика русскими глазами* [From Livonia to Latvia: The Baltics through Russian eyes], 2 vol., Москва: Аркаюр, Рига: Insight.

[**Arbitman**, Roman] Роман Арбитман (2001), '7,62: модел для разборки?' [7.62: a model for dismantling?], *Л-критика: Ежегодник Академии русской современной словесности* 2, pp. 93–97.

[**Belobrovceva**, Irina / Jurij **Abyzov** / Pavel **Lavrinec**] Ирина Белобровцева / Юрий Абызов / Павел Лавринец (1996/2005), eds., *Балтийский архив: Русская культура в Прибалтике* [The Baltic archive: Russian culture in the Baltics], 3 vol., Tallinn: Avenarius, Rīga: Daugava, Vilnius: Русские творческие ресурсы Балтии.

Cawelti, John (1977), *Adventure, Mystery and Romance: Formula Stories as Art and Popular Culture*, Chicago: University of Chicago Press.

[**Černâk**, Marija] Мария А. Черняк (2014), 'Новейшая литература и вызовы массовой культуры: к вопросы о синтезе "высоких" и "низких" жанров' [Current literature and the challenges of mass culture: regarding the synthesis of 'high' and 'low' genres], *Вестник Нижегородского университета* 2, pp. 340–346.

Cheskin, Ammon (2016), *Russian-Speakers in Post-Soviet Latvia: Discursive Identity Strategies*, Edinburgh: Edinburgh University Press; also via DOI.

[**Flejšman**, Lazar / Ûrij **Abyzov** / Boris **Ravdin**] Лазар Флейшман / Юрий Абызов / Борис Равдин (1997), *Русская печать в Риге: из истории газеты "Сегодня" 1930-х годов* [The Russian press in Riga: A history of 'Segodnâ' in the 1930s], 5 vol., Stanford: Stanford University.

Guffey, Elizabeth (2006), *Retro: The Culture of Revival*, London: Reaktion Books.

Heilman, Robert B. (1975), 'Escape and escapism: varieties of literary experience', *The Sewanee Review* 83:3, pp. 439–458.

Henning, Bernd / Peter **Vorderer** (2001), 'Psychological escapism: predicting the amount of television viewing by need for cognition', *Journal of Communication* 51:1, pp. 100–120; also via DOI.

Konzack, Lars (2018), 'Escapism', in Mark J. P. Wolf (ed.), *The Routledge Companion to Imaginary Worlds*, New York–London: Routledge, Taylor & Francis, pp. 246–255.

Kuhn, Thomas S. (1962), *The Structure of Scientific Revolutions*, Chicago: University of Chicago Press.

Laķe, Anda / Līga **Vinogradova** / Elīna **Baltskara** (2018), *Pētījums par Latvijas iedzīvitāju grāmatu lasīšanas paradumiem* [A study on the book-reading habits of Latvian residents], Rīga: Latvijas Kultūras akadēmijas Zinātniskās pētniecības centrs.

Levina, Marina / Janis **Zilgalvis** / Agrita **Tipane** / Dace **Choldere** / Vita **Banga** (2010), *Наследие сакрального искусства и архитектуры Риги* [The heritage of sacred art and architecture in Riga], Rīga: Neputns.

[**Lipoveckij**, Mark] Марк Н. Липовецкий (1999), 'Растратные стратегии, или метаморфозы "чернухи"' [Wasteful strategies, or the metamorphosis of hack-and-slash], *Новый мир* 11; also via internet.

[**Makšanceva**, Nataliâ] Наталия В. Макшанцева (2005), 'Концепт "рябина" в русском языковом сознании' [The concept of mountain ash in Russian language consciousness], in *Язык – культурные концепты – текст*, Нижний Новгород: NGLU, pp. 78–86.

[**Mekš**, Èduard] Эдуард Б. Мекш (2002), 'Мифологический архетип в искусстве и жизни (Всеволод Иванов и Варлам Шаламов)' [Mythological archetype in art and life (Vsevolod Ivanov and Varlam Šalamov)], *Русская литература* 2, pp. 226–234.

[**Pazuhina**, Nadežda] Надежда Пазухина (2016), 'Предисловие' [Foreword], in Māra Zirnīte / Marija Assereckova (eds.), *Все мы дети ... / Visi esam ...* [We are all children ...], see below, pp. 5–9.

Roskoša, Antra (2020), *Kultūras idenitāte Latvijas daudzkultūru sabiedrības kontekstā* [Cultural identity in the context of Latvian multicultural society], Daugavpils: DU apgāds Saule.

Seabrook, John (2001), *Nobrow: The Culture of Marketing, the Marketing of Culture*, New York: Vintage Books.

Toffler, Alvin (1980), *The Third Wave*, New York: William Morrow & Company.

[**Vernik**, Vadim] Вадим Верник (2017), *Горлица* [The Dove], Rīga: IU Kultūras dialogs.

Zelče, Vita (2018), *Latvijas mediju vides daudzveidība* [Diversity of the Latvian media environment]. Rīga: LU apgāds, 551 p.

Zirnīte, Māra / Marija **Assereckova** (2016), eds., *Все мы дети своего времени: истории жизни русских в Латвии / Visi esam sava laikmeta bērni: krievu dzīvesstāsti Latvijā* [We are all children of our time: life stories of Russians in Latvia], Rīga: Институт философии и социологии ЛУ.

4.2 Digital items

[**Âblokov**, Evgenij] Евгений А. Яблоков (2015), *Мистерия анатомического театра (рассказ "Голубь и горленка" – возвращаясь к теме "Платонов – Заболоцкий")* [An anatomical theatre mystery (the story of 'The Dove and the Cutthroat' goes back to Platonov's and Zabolockij's topic)], via link.

Anonymous (2013), 'Автор 40 книг: русская культура в Латвии есть, но она никому не нужна' [Author of 40 books: there is a Russian culture in Latvia, but nobody needs it], about the author Daliâ Truskinovskaâ, *Freecity.lv*, 22/01/13, via link.

[**Borŝova**, Katerina] Катерина Борщова (2002), 'Кому нужна русская литература Латвии?' [Who needs Latvia's Russian literature?], *Delfi*, via link.

Daugavpils ziņas, the *Daugavpils ziņas* portal.

Delfi, the *Delfi* portal.

[**Dmitriev**, Mart] Март Дмитриев (2014), 'В Латвии всегда были русские писатели!' ['There have always been Russian writers in Latvia!'], *Газета 7 суперсекретов* 31, 31/07/14, via link.

Gedžūne, Inga (2019), 'Самые читаемые книги в Латгальской Центральной библиотеке за 2018 год' [The most read books in the Latgalian Central Library in 2018], *Daugavpils ziņas*, 18/01/19, via link.

[**Gubin**, Dmitrij] Дмитрий Губин (2020), *Как Хокинг и Докинз победили Толстого и Достоевского* [How Hawking and Dawkins beat Tolstoj and Dostoevskij], lecture on You Tube, via link.

[**Gurin**, Aleksandr] Александр Гурин (2018), 'Кому нужны Дни русской культуры в Латвии?' [Who needs Days of Russian Culture in Latvia?], *Совет общественных организаций Латвии*, 13/11/18, via link.

Gurjevs, Marks (2020), *Interesantas grāmatas 7. martā* [Interesting books at March 7], advertisement in the Polaris bookstore, via link.

[**Hudenko**, Kristina] Кристина Худенко (2017), 'Руки прочь от нашего гения: Борис Эйфман о народных критиках, тайнах русской души и Марисе Лиепе' [Keep your hands off our genius: Boris Èjfman on people's critics, the mysteries of the Russian soul, and Māris Liepa], *Delfi*, 02/02/17, via link.

[**Kovalenko**, Diana] Диана Коваленко (2019), 'Отзывы о книге "Горлица", Вадим Верник' [Reviews of Vadim Vernik's 'The Dove'], *LitRes*, via link.

Lāce, Agnese / Madara **Mazjāne** (2020), *"Ebreji", "romi", "cilvēki ar invaliditāti"? Praktiski padomi iekļaujošai un cieņpilnai valodai mūsdienās* ['Jews', 'Roma', 'people with disabilities'? Practical tips for today's inclusive and respectful language], via link.

Latvijā (2020), *Latvijā izdotās grāmatas un brošūras* [Books and brochures published in Latvia], official statistical matters, via link.

McGarry, Kassie (2017), 'Psychology of Pop Culture: Escapism', *Psychological Mindset: Blog of Observational Psychology*, via link.

Polaris bookstore, the Polaris bookstore chain's online shop.

[Rozovskij, Mark] Марк Розовский (2017), 'Литература – ето канон, а театр – ето всегда версия' [Literature is the canon, but theatre is always a version], *Читаем вместе: Навигатор в мире книг*, 01/02/17, via link.

[Šavrej, Andrej] Андрей Шаврей (2017), 'О чем вещает "Горлица" писателя Вадима Верника' [What does writer Vadim Vernik's 'Gorlica' talk about], *Rus.lsm.lv: Латвийские общественные СМИ*, 18/11/17, via link.

Temirbolat, A. B. / S. D. **Daribaev** / R. S. **Imakhanbet** / A. A. **Ospanova** / A. A. **Ospanova** (2016), 'Influence of Mass Literature on the Readers Consciousness', *Global Media Journal*, via link.

Latvian Concept of Linguistic Integration

A contribution to language policy research
by Sergei Kruk (Rīga)

Outline

The Soviet Union changed the ethnic composition of Latvia's population, and as a consequence, Latvian was losing its position in many spheres of public communication. To raise the profile of Latvian, scholars and policymakers have promoted a policy of coercive linguistic integration since the 1990s. Besides the communicative function, this political concept attributes the function of social cohesion to language. This function has not been exposed in academic literature. Contextual analysis of propositions about linguistic integration reveals a legacy of Romantic notions on language maintenance as if a shared language would consolidate individuals into a nation. Proponents of linguistic integration assumed that individuals were not cooperative beings, and for the sake of social cohesion, had to follow a mandatory monolinguistic norm, which enables the nationwide transmission of thoughts; a common language delimited ethnic boundaries and conveyed the favoured ethnic group's worldview, which is fixed in and mediated by texts. Linguistic integration is expected to provide the inclusion of other ethnicities. Nevertheless, the scholars fail to distinguish language from ethnicity, which remains a salient tool of ethnic categorisation. Beliefs in social homogeneity and language as being a strong and transparent semiotic code underpin the concept of linguistic integration.

Acknowledgement

The research received the financial support of the Latvian National Research Programme VPP Interframe-LV.

Structure

1	Introduction	71
2	Language teaching: positive motivation vs legal coercion	72
2.1	The policy document *Integration of Society in Latvia*	73
	2.1.1 Communicative function … 73 — 2.1.2 Expressive function … 73 — 2.1.3 Social cohesion … 73	
3	Conflating language and group	74
4	Top-down communication	75
5	Neglecting individual agency	76
6	Linguistic integration: strong code and homogeneous society	79
7	Conclusion	81
8	Bibliography	82
8.1	Printed titles	82
8.2	Digital titles	86

1 Introduction

The encyclopedic 475-page book *The Latvian Language*, written by twenty famous linguists, begins with the following statement:

> Why was language so important for the consciousness, history and fateful turning points of the Latvian people? Apparently, because it is the principal element unifying the Latvian nation—multicoloured, torn by contradictions and directed to individualism. Like the folk-song language united Latvians in their diversity. (Veisbergs 2013: 13)

The identification of a language with a people is an idea penned by the Romantic philosopher Johann Gottfried Herder in the eighteenth century, and it is still popular. In the middle of the 20th century, the ethnic revival once more associated ethnic identity with language policy. Newly emerging post-colonial states conflated the ethnic sense of self with political decisions about language use. The potential of language in differentiating ethnic groups was demonstrated after the fall of the communist multilingual states. For example, in the Balkans, public debates concentrated on the role of language in the struggles of cultural affirmation and territorial separation and on the standardisation of languages guided by the idea of differentiation from the neighbouring peoples. The conflation of languages and ethnicities can be found in the political and media discourses of the Western democracies, too (Blommaert/Verschueren 1992; Conte/Giordano/Hertz 2002; Daskalov/Marinov 2013; García 2012; Nunberg 1989).

The commonplace discourse does not explain how the semiotic system 'language' consolidates speakers in large groups. In Latvia, academia supports the Romantic idea, so this country is of particular interest for research. Latvian scholars are active public communicators. They have participated in shaping and implementing the official language policy and claim to have worked out its theoretical substantiation (see Druviete 2018b: 10). Moreover, after the dissolution of the Soviet Union in 1991, public necessity provoked a paradigmatic shift. The difference of languages attested to the fundamental difference between the ethnic groups, thereby supporting claims to statehood and exclusion of ethnic others from the polity. The restored Republic of Latvia counted 48 % of the population as non-titular; many had little or no knowledge of Latvian (see Schmid 2008; Vihalemm/Hogan-Brun 2013, on the language situation). Restoring the interwar Citizenship law in 1991, the Republic of Latvia denied political rights to 700,000 out of 2.6 million residents—mostly those who settled in Soviet Latvia in 1940–1991. These second-class citizens, referred to as *nepilsoņi* 'non-citizens', were called upon to acquire Latvian citizenship, for which several conditions had to be met. Thus, language acquisition became a *conditio sine qua non* of naturalisation.

Demanding that Russians speak Latvian, ethnic Latvians strived to see their linguistic rights respected in the public sphere. Two approaches to language training emerged in the 1990s. A group of scholars and educators working with the National Program for Latvian Language Training supported the principle of smooth progress and development of teaching tools adapted to the needs of professional target groups. In contrast, officials of the State Language Center and sociolinguists of the University of Latvia insisted that legal coercion and juridical pressure on business were more effective motivators. This process, known as 'linguistic integration of society' by Ina Druviete (2013: 412), the Minister of Education and Science of the Republic of Latvia in 2004–2006 and 2014, was also expected to increase social cohesion. Here, the concept of language as a tool integrating people across ethnic boundaries requires a theoretical revision of the notion inspired by Herder that language was a separator of ethnic groups. How do scholars explain the causality between switching languages and social integrity? My contribution systematises the arguments I found in relevant policy documents and academic and popular articles sampled by the keywords 'linguistic integration', 'social integration', 'language policy', and 'language and society' in the catalogue of the Latvian National Library.

Language policy is a very sensitive topic. Druviete declares that its theoretical discussion was impossible because 'each country represents a unique case where linguistics and sociolinguistics go their own way' (2018b: 10). However, the discussion is possible on a meta-discursive level. The task of my paper is to find out the analytical logic of propositions regarding linguistic integration.

2 Language teaching: positive motivation vs legal coercion

In the early 1990s, the Latvian government expected Latvian Russians to learn Latvian rapidly under legal pressure. The development of relevant laws and the supervising functions were assigned to the State Language Center, set up by the Ministry of Justice in 1992. The centre worked out several language levels and proficiency tests for the professions, established attestation commissions responsible for the language exams, and implemented a language inspection to control the use of Latvian in business. However, no methodological and pedagogical means were provided to make Latvian accessible for learning. 'Instead, the Latvians [were] keeping their language as a secret code in a golden cage ... 153,000 persons passed the language proficiency tests [in 1992/93], but the language situation changed very little. The result was a deep disappointment on both sides' (Priedīte 2002: 2, 4).

In 1994, the government asked the United Nations Development Program (UNDP) to help elaborate and implement language training. An institution called National Program for Latvian Language Training (the National Agency for Latvian Language Training since 2004) was founded in 1996 with the financial and expert support of the UNDP, EU Phare Program, and various donor states. The head of the institution, DPhil and language educator Aija Priedīte, is a Diaspora Latvian who re-emigrated to Latvia after the Soviet Union fell apart. Voluntaryism, gradualness, and succession were the main teaching principles promoted by Priedīte (2004: 7). The National Program's goal was to develop students' communication skills about professional issues in natural settings. A team of Latvian language educators implemented the student-centred teaching methods appropriate for specific target groups: schoolteachers, medical personnel, and policemen. Education experts were developing a method of teaching Latvian as a second language—prior to this, it was taught as a mother tongue to non-natives. Among the methodological novelties were play and interactive tools for various occupational groups to evolve their conversational skills in informal and formal settings. A bilingual weekly issued by the language educators helped to learn patterns of public communication. Positive stimulation of non-native speakers to learn Latvian was the absolute criterion of education (Priedīte 1998, 2003, 2005; Latviešu valodas 2004; Latviešu valodas 2008).

2.1 The policy document *Integration of Society in Latvia*

Striving to join the European Union, Latvia succumbed to Brussels's demand for the concession of political rights to the disenfranchised Slavic origin residents labelled 'non-citizens'. The policy document *Integration of Society in Latvia* approved in 2001 claimed that the disenfranchised people lacked sociality and set cultural socialisation as a precondition for access to political rights. The policymakers provided no explicit definition of the integration process and the indicators of its final result. Contextually, the word 'integration' refers to social interaction (mutual understanding, cooperation, democratic and consolidated civil society, common fundamental values), relations with state authorities (shared state, loyalty), welfare (recognition of the fact that personal wellbeing depends on the future, stability, and security of the state), and the use of Latvian (willingness to adopt the official language, respect for the language and culture of minorities). The role of language is described vaguely: it is an instrument of integration, one among the preconditions of integration, a base for mutual understanding and cooperation (Sabiedrības integrācija 2001: 4, 11, 51). Propositions with the word 'language' correspond to communicative and expressive functions outlined by the scholars of language policy (e. g., Réaume/Pinto 2012).

2.1.1 Communicative function

The titular population, the Latvians, have a right to use their native language in public settings; therefore, Russian-speakers should learn Latvian to communicate with public institutions and customers of their business; a common language enables access to shared values and information indispensable for democracy and participation in polity. The incentives are positive motivation and the legal injunction to use Latvian, *inter alia*, in specified public settings. The policy document suggests enhancing the inter-ethnic networks, promoting discussions about various political and social issues in a friendly informal environment. However, a priority given to top-down communication makes the official language a tool for the state-sponsored refinement of the population. 'Many Latvians failed to find their role in democracy because their state, political and legal awareness was inappropriate'; therefore the government should educate people and deliver 'quality information' (Sabiedrības integrācija 2001: 18).

2.1.2 Expressive function

The policy document contends that language is a distinctive mark of identity and affiliation for Latvians; it guarantees to maintain their traditions, lifestyle, identity, and ethnic spirit. In using Latvian, non-natives can gain the confidence of ethnic Latvians. The expressive function of Russian for local Russians is relegated to the spheres of their traditional culture and family.

2.1.3 Social cohesion

The School of Sociolinguistics institutionalised at the University of Latvia advanced the third function: social cohesion. Ina Druviete, the leading scholar promoting this function, was an active politician — in 2002–2014 she was a Member of Parliament, in 2004–2006 and 2014, she took up the post of Minister of Education. While for the National Programme/Agency, gradualness and positive stimuli were the primary teaching principles, the opponents argued that legal coercion was the only effective instrument (Blinkena 1999; Druviete 2012c). They treat post-Soviet Latvia as being disintegrated across the ethnolinguistic boundary, and therefore the task of language policy is to build up a 'homogenous society' (Joma 2007: 326). For political stability, linguistic integration had to bring about the results as soon as possible. Vineta Poriņa (2009), referring to Abraham Maslow's hierarchy of needs, even proposed to deprive the Russian-speaking population of basic needs (e.g., denying service to Russian-speaking clients in grocery shops) to compel them to learn Latvian. The National Programme/Agency for Latvian Language Training worked in 'politicised and antagonistic circumstances' (Hogan-Brun et al. 2009: 95) until it was disbanded in 2009. The antagonism was so tense that scholarly publications pass over the efforts and experience of Priedīte's institution in silence.

3 Conflating language and group

The conflation of a language with a social group is the foundation of coercive linguistic integration. The idea can be traced back to the 18–19th-century national romantics who believed that social cooperation was possible among individuals possessing common traits of character. The identification of the ethnocultural community with language made of the latter a perfect instrument of socialisation binding individuals into a homogenous group. Latvian proponents of linguistic integration apply this formula to pluralist societies taking no notice of its logical inconsistency. On the one hand, they argue that language acquisition enables minorities to participate in a democratic political community on equal rights with the ethnic majority. On the other hand, they define the political community in terms of primordial ethnocultural identity thus restricting access to the polity.

Druviete (2010b: 156) describes the mechanism of linguistic group consolidation in vague generalities: 'Latvian language, as a standardised state language guarantees: 1) the unity of the Latvian nation [orig. *latviešu nācija* 'nation of ethnic Latvians'], 2) the integration of Latvian society, 3) [...] it is a value that has been polished and cherished for more than 400 years, which guarantees the nation's right to existence.' The distinction between the first and the second outcome of group consolidation is a circumstance worth noting. It means that the shared language does not consolidate political nations across ethnic boundaries. Druviete defines the word 'national' in ethnic terms rather than as a phenomenon of political organisation of society (Druviete 2010b: 177 and 2018b: 8; Baltiņš/Druviete 2017: 143). Nevertheless, the interrelations between linguistic and ethnic identity remain unclear. In different papers or even in the same paper, both are conflated to a different degree: linguistic identity has been defined as 'a stable component' (Druviete 2004), 'the most important component' (2012a), 'an integral component' (2018a), 'a considerable component' (Baltiņš/Druviete 2017: 46), 'the foundation' (Druviete 2012a) of ethnic/national identity, and even as one that 'can hardly be distinguished from ethnic identity' (2005: 51). Druviete's doctoral student Poriņa (2009) totally conflates both identities. Failing to make a distinction between the structure of the natural world and semiotics of the natural world, she treats linguistic categories as tantamount to the relations between 'things' in the real world. Social categorisation expressed in language is misunderstood as an ontological categorisation dictated by the unique living conditions of ethnic groups. Based on the above, Poriņa concludes that a language is an important tool of ethnic categorisation because ethnic groups consolidate their boundaries by language. A mismatch between linguistic and ethnic identity should be avoided. Other ethnicities should revive their primordial Ukrainian, Tatar, Armenian etc. identities and use the language of ancestors rather than Russian in the family. Political identity could only follow the primordial one: 'ethnic groups missing a linguistic identity threaten the Latvian political nation' (Poriņa 2009: 134). Poriņa contends that the re-ethnicisation of Latvian society creates new barriers for communication, and it is the function of Latvian to overcome them and shape civil society. Her idea has a clear scope. Russian is the lingua franca for individuals from different regions of the Soviet Union who have moved to Latvia; Poriņa seeks to minimise the use of Russian in the private spheres, i. e. in family and inter-ethnic contacts. Poriņa's ontological structuralism cannot explain how the existing and revived distinctive linguistic worldviews of ethnic groups will result in the universalism of modern democracy.

4 Top-down communication

The formula 'societal integration through Latvian' was promoted by the first-ever *Official Language Policy Guidelines 2005–2014*. The expression can mean both the result and the process: an integrated society is a Latvian-speaking one, as well as, only individuals speaking Latvian can learn the values of democracy indispensable for integration into society. An explicit definition of the term 'integration' is missing in the Guidelines. However, its purport can be inferred from a description of 'social disintegration':

> In the absence of a quality linguistic means of communication, some groups of Latvian society can gradually choose the information space of global subculture and other states as an identity component. This would have made the social disintegration of society possible. Any society split into linguistic and communicative aspects will negatively affect the attraction of investments, thus reducing economic growth potential. (Valsts valodas 2005–2014: §2.8)

The Guidelines' concern is the transborder Russian television channels available on Latvian cable networks. The policymakers maintain that foreign media nurture political disloyalty among the Russian-speaking population. Linguistic integration is purported to make respective Latvian media content that the Latvian television disseminates accessible. The argument was elaborated by sociolinguists Kertu Kibermane, Gunta Kļava, Linda Lauze and Kristīne Tihomirova in their 2014 monograph studying television broadcasts. The authors promote the model of top-down mass media communication controlled by the state. They refer to the paper 'Media and Democracy' written by media sociologist Leo Bogart (1998) and expect it to provide liberal arguments supporting the non-liberal communication model. However, the four authors misread Bogart's text and thus misunderstand his arguments: they omit several statements and, being biased, insert new ones between the source's propositions. Let us analyse a paragraph in detail that the four authors did not put in quotation marks, but a closing footnote suggests that they have borrowed the entire argument from Bogart's contribution. Here, the fragment is quoted in extenso from the English edition; words abandoned in the Latvian book are underlined, insertions are in square brackets.

> Media are instruments, they can serve different ends. They are indispensable to a democratic society [needs media pluralism and diversity] because they make information available to all social levels and in all its geographical corners. They are essential as critics [criticise] of government, as investigators [and investigate] of wrongdoing, as advocates of good as well as not-so-good causes. They are a forum for discussion and debate [about the topics indispensable for society]. They create and define the separate constituencies whose compromise make democracy work. At the same time by creating [In this way] common experiences, [of the society is being created] offering shared symbols and giving the public a sense of contact with its leaders, they offer a constant reminder of [which at the same time creates and maintains] national identity. (Bogart 1998: 11, compared with Kibermane et al. 2014: 7)

The omitted fifth and edited sixth sentences alter the role of media in a pluralist society substantially. Bogart says media 'remind' about national identity rather than 'create' it; media give the individual a sense that his/her experience is also shared by others, and create separate constituencies (rather than unity) that seek a compromise between their plural interests. In the Latvian interpretation, the mere fact of disseminating information creates the national identity; given this, the authors justify more robust government control of broadcasting. Boggart discusses mass media because they enable an exchange of opinions between different interest groups in a pluralistic democracy. In contrast, in the view of Kibermane et al., mass media deliver information consolidating the nation. In the context of their book, the words 'media pluralism and diversity' refer to a wealth of media institutions but not to the media's content. Nevertheless, the authority should control the extent of the diversity of communication channels. Paraphrasing another argument of Bogart, the four sociolinguists create this statement: 'However, the existence of an advanced and diverse media system [and political freedom automatically] does not guarantee that it will serve democracy [democratic system]' (Bogart 1998: 11, compared with Kibermane et al. 2014: 7). Bogart suggested that the increase in numbers of commercial TV stations and online platforms in the 1990s had not increased quality information being provided, whereas the four Latvian sociolinguists conclude that the freedom to communicate is not a value *per se* and therefore the government should adopt a mass media law based on an ethnic, national ideology that aims to minimise the availability of the Russian language on TV screens, regardless of whether it concerns Russia's transborder or locally produced channels. 'It is especially important to attract the minority audience to watch television in Latvian to promote the integration of society', contend Kibermane et al. (2014: 66). The authors dismiss multilingualism of the public sphere. According to the Official Guidelines, the values appropriate for Latvia's democracy can be communicated in Latvian only: 'The Latvian language is one of the elements uniting society which ensures the strengthening of the Constitutional democratic values for the sustained development of the Latvian state' (Valsts valodas 2021–2027: §2.2).

Neglect of feedback is not only a feature of linguistic integration: by and large, the Latvian government does not recognise bottom-up communication as a political communication channel. The *Official Language Policy Guidelines for 2021–2027* drafted by the Ministry of Education and Science do not reflect upon the critical perception of the minority school reform (enacted in 2018) by minorities and avoids naming the Russian-speaking population at all (Valsts valodas 2021–2027). The most recent policy documents, the *National Development Plan of Latvia for 2021–2027* and the *Cohesive and Active Civil Society Development Guidelines for 2021–2027*, stress the importance of active civil society but do not guarantee it a say in politics. The main instrument increasing activism is paternalist top-down communication, teaching participation skills in voluntary work, fostering a feeling of belonging, and delivering information about values. The government does not envisage feedback channels, e.g., public opinion research and public broadcasting media, as being indispensable for political decision-making in a pluralist society.

5 Neglecting individual agency

The National Programme/Agency for Latvian Language Training stressed the importance of teaching colloquial language to facilitate everyday communication. The educators respected the needs, resources, and capacity of individual students. In contrast, the government's linguistic integration places the highest priority on certain group interests. The integrative capacity is reduced to standard ('literary', 'quality') Latvian language (Druviete 2013: 412; see also 2006, 2012b, 2018c). Two recognised Latvian linguists, Jānis Rozenbergs (1995) and Valentīna Skujiņa (2000, 2001, 2003), argue that standard Latvian is a systemic and perfect code. Words denoting reality phenomena and the logical grammar structure permitted the transmission of thoughts. According to Blinkena (2000, 2009), perfect command of the linguistic standard enables readers to retrieve the communicated values from texts, and subsequently, the received values form the spiritual life and sensual world of readers. According to the proponents of linguistic integration, these characteristics of the linguistic standard enable the function of social cohesion.

> In several social classes, language presents itself as a form of code, the key to which is not always known to outsiders of these groups. Therefore, each group that is conscious of its national belonging, and of its main and primary indicator being its language, thus strives to create such a unified form of its language that contains the best of all its forms of expression. This is all the more necessary, if a person desires to save its national identity. (Druviete 2010b: 155)

Policymakers picked this idea up in the Official 2015–2020 Guidelines: standard language unites ethnic Latvians across dialects and idiolects maintaining Latvia's territorial integrity (Valsts valodas 2015–2020: 17). Since speaking the linguistic standard is concomitant to preserving the nation's collective identity, subjective motives for using Latvian were beyond the interest of researchers. A national sociolinguistic survey of Latvian-speakers conducted in 2004 (N = 1004, the sample includes 63% ethnic Latvian and 37% minority respondents) surprised scholars. Latvia's population conceived ethnic identity and language contrary to the academia's expectations, which Sarma Kļaviņa (2007: 87) regrets. Less than half (41%) of the respondents agreed that language was the main feature of ethnicity; every fourth (23%) respondent named birthplace as the most important criterion for ethnic identity (Ernstsone/Joma 2005: 41–42); no correlation data with socio-demographic parameters are available in the survey report. Another survey revealed that two out of three Latvians were reluctant to speak Latvian with Russians even if their interlocutors had a good command of Latvian (Druviete 2010b: 176).

Keeping this empirical evidence in mind, Druviete (2018b) admitted that language was not the foundation of identity and acknowledged the social variance of language use. She explained that the choice of linguistic codes is a factor of individual agency: in concrete circumstances of interaction, interlocutors assume certain identities, demonstrating their position in the social structure. As a matter of fact, this is only a declaration. Referring to a government policy document, Druviete gives the homogenising definition of national identity that places a priority on primordial ethnocultural characteristics as the criteria of a group membership. As a result, Druviete's list of social variances of language use worthy of sociolinguistic study does not include interethnic contact situations. The sociolinguist does not address the questions of the expressive function of Russian for Russian-speakers and subjective strategic reasons of language shift in contacts between Latvians and Russians.

As reagards Latvian-speakers, Druviete introduces the notions of a subjective language attitude and symbolic value of language as mediators between ethnic and linguistic identity. The aim is to safeguard the mutual causality of the identities, which has not been corroborated empirically. '[E]xactly the subjective factor viz. language attitude does not allow one to recognise the Latvian ethnolinguistic vitality as matching the situation of language competition' (Druviete 2016: 32; 2018b: 58). Symbolic value as a mediator between subjective linguistic attitude and supposedly objective ethnic identity is to legitimise the control of language use. Defining symbolic value, Druviete quotes the sociolinguist John Joseph:

> Since language and the nation are conceptually so closely bound together, it is not surprising that the politics of language choice [...] rarely depend on purely 'functional' criteria, such as what language will be most widely understood. The symbolic and emotional dimensions of national identity are crucial, and language policies that ignore them prove dysfunctional in the long run. (Quotation in Druviete 2018 b: 8; English original in Joseph 2006: 24)

Joseph uses the adjective 'symbolic' several times in his book, but he never clarifies the meaning. Contextually, it could refer to a subjective emotional evaluation of the mother tongue by the linguistic minority when the majority language enjoys an instrumental value. Joseph contends that a majority that drafts language policy should respect a minority language that for the latter is a sensitive part of its identity. The idea formulated in the policy document *Integration of Society in Latvia*, that Latvian has an emotional value for its native speakers, is congenial to this understanding of symbolic value even if the document reversed the majority-minority position. The present-day ethnic Latvian majority perceives its language emotionally as a guarantee of identity and lifestyle, and the former majority of Russian-speakers should acknowledge this emotional importance to pave the way to mutual trust (Sabiedrības integrācija 2001). So far, symbolic value has an affinity to the expressive function.

Druviete abandons the emotional dimension. In place of the subjective evaluation, she proposes an objective collective symbol defined as 'reflection of reality in a socially salient unit with traditionally encoded meaning which has consolidated in people's consciousness and creates the foundation of ethnic group and state identity' (Druviete 2013: 393). Language is placed among the legally defined symbols of the state such as the flag, coat of arms and anthem, and this 'implies its learning and usage, and recognition in the hierarchy of languages' (Druviete 2010 b: 163). The objective symbol fills the gap between two subjective phenomena: 'language attitude and awareness of identity' (Druviete 2018 b: 9). The appeal to the collective ethnic identity is expected to reinforce language's symbolic value, subsequently improving language attitude (Druviete 2018 a: 61). The practical mechanism of attitude change is not addressed in the paper.

The concept of linguistic integration builds clear cut boundaries between ethnic and linguistic groups. The empirical sociolinguistic research is underpinned by methodological collectivism, too. Survey questionnaires categorise the respondents by ethnicity, mother tongue and the language spoken at home, and they only allow one choice at a time (cf. Ernstsone/Joma 2005; Druviete 2012 c; Lauze 2016). Nonetheless, the uneven geographical distribution of ethnicities causes a different intensity of linguistic contacts in Latvia's communicative settings. The share of interethnic marriages in Latvia is considerable. From 1970–2019, every fifth ethnic Latvian married another ethnicity; among ethnic Russians, the share of mixed marriages varied between 36–46 % (Krastiņš 1998: 2; Central Statistical Bureau 2020: 52). Sociolinguists do not apply inferential statistics methods to identify peculiar properties of language use shared by individuals living and working in a heterogeneous social environment.

The intended homogenisation of ethnic and linguistic groups explains the disregard of student-centred teaching methods. Proponents of coercion neglected improving language teaching, as a policy analyst observed (Diatchkova 2005). Still in 2013 sociologists revealed that bilingual education in preschool educational institutions lacked a methodological foundation (Kļave/Šūpule/Bebriša 2013). They observed that teachers missed special pedagogical training and skills and had no elementary audiovisual supportive toolkits. Any methodology of teaching in the intercultural environment was missing despite the country's heterogeneity. An overly complicated study programme neglected the basic conversational needs of children in everyday contact situations. The sociologists warned that the coercive approach cultivated a negative attitude towards Latvian among children and their parents. Lastly, the proponents of coercive linguistic integration recognised the importance of positive incentives and student-orientated teaching methodology (Kibermane/Kļava 2016: 121; Valsts valodas 2015–2019: 6), although they eschewed mentioning the groundwork laid by the National Pro-gramme/Agency for Latvian Language Training.

6 Linguistic integration: strong code and homogeneous society

Druviete (2018b: 10) claims that sociolinguists have elaborated the theory of language policy and that the concept of linguistic integration 'had been widely discussed in countless publications' (Druviete 2010b: 156). Nevertheless, the explicit theoretical framework can be found neither in a voluminous edition of her collected papers (Druviete 2010a), nor in other monographs either discussing the role of language in society (Baltiņš/Druviete 2017) or reviewing the domestic trends of language research (Druviete/Veisbergs 2018). The encyclopaedic edition *Latvian Language* does not include a single paragraph about linguistic integration (Veisbergs 2013). The titles of several academic and popular contributions of Druviete (2000, 2011, 2018a, 2018b) promise to elaborate on both concepts, 'linguistic identity' and 'integration'. However, the author changes the topic, in fact, and switches to linguistic ecology, juridical protection of 'small' languages, and coercive language teaching methods.

Context analysis of propositions about linguistic integration points to the Romantic notion of language as Johann Georg Hamann and Johann Gottfried Herder have proposed, and William von Humboldt has elaborated later (cf. Brown 1967; Formigari 2004; Forster 2011; Kļaviņa 1999; Underhill 2009). The central argument of this notion is that language was an intellectual attribute of a nation possessing 'collective subjectivity', and persons could only realise themselves through membership in the ethnic-national whole. Additionally, a 'developed' (i.e. standard) language that has evolved in the specific environment of an ethnic group is conceived of as a fully organised, systemic and perfect whole. Since language is closely connected to cognition and thought, individuals perceive the external world and think about it through and by their language. Since languages differ by their structures, the linguistic communities have different worldviews. To summarise the argumentation of the Romantic paradigm, language plays a crucial role in the organisation of societies because linguistic behaviour correlates with non-linguistic behaviour.

It is not the task of this paper to trace the historical roots of linguistic thought in Latvia. The Romantic paradigm is used here as a heuristic tool helping to explain the logic of linguistic integration: the standard language permits the impeccable top-down transmission of the nation's worldview, which enables individuals to subdue their subjectivities to the nation's collective characteristics. This is the precondition of social relationship and cohesion.

Discussing media communication, Kibermane et al. (2014) suggest causality between speaking Latvian and being a liberal democrat. Since democracy envisages participation in and responsibility for decision-making, it would be reasonable to enable as many feedback channels as possible to maintain political balance in a pluralist society. Even in the context of paternalist character change, it would be more effective to inculcate the values of democracy in any language convenient for the audience. The rejection of the locally produced Russian-language broadcasts as a channel of political communication only makes sense in the linguistic relativism paradigm. If languages create distinctive worldviews, citizens speaking different languages will disagree on many issues, and their society will fall apart. The conflation of language and worldview makes multilingualism a problem, because it is impossible to describe the local reality in a foreign language adequately. It goes without saying that the ethnic majority holds a homogenous worldview. Powerful media effect theory which dates back to the 1920s, underpins the effectiveness of top-down communication. Known as the hypodermic needle model, it contends that media content is injected into the receiver's consciousness and accepted entirely. The audience is treated as a passive and helpless homogenous mass of people manipulated by strong communication stimuli creating behavioural effects (McQuail 2005; Baran/Davis 2014).

Imagining societies as ethnolinguistically homogenous entities, the sociolinguists do not study the mixed identities and varieties of social contact situations — this is the main epistemological problem of research and policymaking. Language conceived of as a consolidator of society does not accommodate the individual agency of language users who are expected to follow the rules of the standard language. A duty to safeguard the collective identity outweighs the pragmatic goals of interlocutors in concrete events of social interaction. Rigid categorisation of respondents by ethnicity and mother-tongue in the surveys does not admit mixed and fluid identities. Belief in the deductive method downplays the importance of inductive, empirically-based thought. Neglect of inferential statistics does not permit sociolinguists to find out the regularities of diverse linguistic practices.

Empirical inductive sociology disproves the thesis that linguistic integration is the precondition for social relationships. Surveys of interethnic contact situations demonstrate that the basis for mutual trust develops in banal everyday cooperation on issues of mutual interest rather than within the framework of state-planned integration activities, which places the hypothetically alienated individuals in artificial conditions of interaction (Birka 2014; Kalniņa/Sūna 2008; Kļave/Šūpule/Bebriša 2013; Rungule/Koroļova/Sniķere 2008; Tabuns 2010). Language use patterns in Baltic countries depend on the intensity of interethnic contact. Geographical, economic, educational, and personal factors create a scale of identity types with blurred boundaries; interlocutors are constantly negotiating and constructing their identities (Ehala 2013: 101). Pragmatism, interactionism, and linguistics of enunciation (Benveniste 1974; Culioli 1991; Goffman 1974; Gumperz 1989; Hymes 1972) have shown the importance of the communication situation and communicators' identity in discourse. Variants of native and foreign languages are symbolic resources permitting interlocutors to manage their identities and represent their concept of the situation. Linguistic integration, on the contrary, envisages abstract speakers in ideal context-free situations who use standard language in the referential function. Emphasising the role of the standard, the Latvian scholars misrepresent the experience of those non-titular speakers who sufficiently command colloquial, professional, or regional variants of the official language.

Latvian scholars who publish in English point out the long-term dysfunctionality of coercion and paternalism (Dilans 2009; Priedīte 2005). The belief that rapid linguistic integration will grant minority people a new perception of selfhood adequate for the new political conditions neglects the expressive function of Russian. Despite the growth of Latvian language proficiency, we witness a demonstrative Russian monolingualism in informal settings such as a private business, media consumption and shopping practices. The phenomenon can be interpreted as a response to symbolic power inherent to the coercive practices of integration. Russian-speakers give up on the public Latvian-language television exactly because the broadcaster ignores the identities and agenda of the multicultural society, as audience research reveals (Juzefovičs 2017). Lacking micro-level studies of individual language use practices in natural settings, the officials treat such behaviour as an expression of disloyalty.

The proponents of linguistic integration do not distinguish between language and ethnicity. Ethnicity remains a salient feature of group identification and promotes the us/them division despite language acquisition. The increase in official language proficiency does not correlate with a substantive admission to public and political life. Jobs in the public sector are much less accessible to other ethnicities: 23 % of ethnic Latvians are employed in state-financed organisations; among minorities, the share is 12 % (SKDS National representative survey, September 2020, N = 1003). Minorities are underrepresented in government institutions (Volkov 2013). Since the launch of the integration process in 2001, only two politicians of Slavic origin have held a Cabinet position. Political parties representing the interests of ethnic minorities have not been admitted to the government coalitions since 1991. Ethnic minorities are kept at bay from decision-making, even on issues concerning their private life such as choosing the language of education (Diatchkova 2005; Ozolins 2019). Their interests and opinions are underrepresented in public television LTV-1 programming (Kibermane et al. 2014; Juzefovičs 2017). The grievances are canalised in rare mass action such as protests against the 2004 and 2018 educational reforms or the referendum on Russian as a second state language in 2012. However, even this feedback channel is discredited: the social movements are portrayed as subversive acts abetted by the Kremlin (cf. Veisbergs 2018; Ozolins 2019). In 2014, the Parliament institutionalised the priority of Latvian ethnicity in the Constitution Preamble.

7 Conclusion

Despite the currency of the notion of linguistic integration, scholars and policymakers have proposed no viable definition of the term. Contextual analysis of the scholarly papers and policy documents suggests that integration is understood as social homogeneity that should be achieved by forcing individuals to use an extremely standardised semiotic code. Nevertheless, the society is not homogeneous and the code is not strong. Individuals use linguistic resources in the ongoing identity construction and presentation process in a de facto heterogeneous society. The theoreticians that promote linguistic integration neglect day-to-day social reality and variability intrinsic to semiotic codes. These sociolinguists still do not provide for the mixed ethnic and/or linguistic identities in their surveys of language use today. Since ethnicity remains a salient feature of social categorisation, linguistic integration per se cannot provide for inclusion in the polity.

What sort of linguistic policies would be preferable for Latvia? The conflation of language and social cohesion eventuates in disrespect of pluralism: the fact of speaking Russian is interpreted as an unwillingness to accept the common good formulated by the public authorities. Language acquisition cannot transform values and interests, however. Common good policies need compromises that can be achieved in communication about the plural concepts of what is good. The idea of a paternal state that distributes the common good to its citizens and non-citizens allows language policymakers to define language acquisition as the precondition for access to the public sphere. However, individuals can survive pursuing their vested interests, even without collective approval: reliance on closed social structures and informal economy is an established practice in Latvia (Cimdiņa 2012; Vasiļjeva 2016). By neglecting feedback in the Russian language the government narrows down the potentialities of pragmatic decision-making in the sphere of the economy, thus increasing institutional distrust and social tension that is opposite to the ideal of coercive linguistic integration.

8 Bibliography

8.1 Printed titles

Baltiņš, Māris / Ina **Druviete** (2017), *Ceļavējš cilvēku ciltij: Valoda sabiedrībā* [Tail-wind for a human tribe: Language in society], Rīga: Latviešu valodas aģentūra.

Baran, Stanley J. / Dennis K. **Davis** (2014), *Mass Communication Theory: Foundations, Ferment and Future*, Stamford/CT: Cengage Learning.

Birka, Ieva (2014), 'Krievvalodīgās kopienas piederības izjūta' [The feeling of belonging among Russian-speakers], in Juris Rozenvalds / Aija Zobena (eds), *Daudzveidīgās un mainīgās Latvijas identitātes*, Riga: LU Akadēmiskais apgāds, pp. 79–93.

Benveniste, Emile (1974), *Problèmes de linguistique Générale, Tome 2*, Paris: Gallimard.

Blinkena, Aija (1999), 'Valsts valodas prestižs – intergācijas pamats' [The prestige of the national language is the basis for integration], *Latvijas Vēstnesis*, April 22, p. 7.

Blinkena, Aija (2000), 'Humanitārā izglītība un latviešu valoda' [Liberal education and Latvian language], *Latvijas Universitātes Zinātniskie Raksti* 624, pp. 5–15.

—, — (2009), 'Esiet viens, un būsiet stipri!' [Be alone and you'll be strong!], *Valodas prakse: vērojumi un ieteikumi* 4, pp. 5–12.

Blommaert, Jan / Jef **Verschueren** (1992), 'The role of language in European nationalist ideologies', *Pragmatics* 2:3, pp. 355–375.

Bogart, Leo (1998), 'Media and democracy', in Everette E. Dennis / Robert W. Snyder (eds.), *Media and Democracy*, New Brunswick–New Jersey: Transaction Publishers, pp. 3–11.

Brown, Roger Langham (1967), *Wilhelm von Humboldt's Conception of Linguistic Relativity*, The Hague: Mouton.

Central Statistical Bureau of Latvia (2020), *Demogrāfija / Demography*, Riga: Central Statistical Bureau of Latvia.

Cimdiņa, Ausma (2012), 'Lauku dzīves racionalitāte un kultūrsociālā iesaknotība' [Rationality of rural life and socio-cultural rootedness], *Akadēmiskā Dzīve* 48, pp. 35–45.

Conte, Édouard / Christian **Giordano** / Ellen **Hertz** (2002), 'La globalisation ambiguë', *Études Rurales* 163/164, pp. 9–24.

Culioli, Antoine (1991), *Pour une linguistique de l'énonciation, Tome 1: Opérations et représentations*, Paris: Ophrys.

Daskalov, Roumen Dontchev / Tchavdar **Marinov** (2013), eds., *Entangled Histories of the Balkans, vol. 1: National Ideologies and Language Policies*. Leiden–Boston: Brill.

Diatchkova, Svetlana (2005), 'Ethnic democracy in Latvia', in Sammy Smooha / Priit Järve (eds.), *The Fate of Ethnic Democracy in Post-Communist Europe*, Budapest: Open Society Institute, pp. 81–114.

Dilans, Gatis (2009), 'Russian in Latvia: an outlook for bilingualism in a post-Soviet transitional society', *International Journal of Bilingual Education and Bilingualism* 12:1, pp. 1–13.

Druviete, Ina (2000), 'Valodas politikas loma sabiedrības integrācijas procesā' [The role of language policy in societal integration], in Elmārs Vēbers (ed.), *Integrācijas un etnopolitika*, Rīga: LU Filozofijas un socioloģijas institūts, pp. 184–198.

—, — (2004), 'Mūsu valoda – Latvijas vai Eiropas savienības identitātes daļa?' [Is our language a part of a Latvian or an EU identity?], *Lauku Avīze*, October 11.

—, — (2005), 'Lingvistiskās identitātes daudzveidīgie aspekti' [The manifold aspects of linguistic identity], in Andrehs Veisbergs / Māris Baltiņš / Daiga Joma / Jānis Valdmanis (eds.), *Latviešu valoda – robežu paplašināšana*, Rīga: Valsts Valodas komisija, pp. 51–60.

—, — (2006), 'Valodas attīstība un standartizācija: valsts vai sabiedrības atbildība?' [Language development and standardization: the responsibility of the state or society?], *Vārds un tā pētīšanas aspekti* 10, pp. 161–168.

—, — (2010a), *Skatījums: valoda, sabiedrība, politika* [A viewpoint: language, society, politics], Rīga: LU Akadēmiskais apgāds.

—, — (2010b), 'Latvian language as the official language: as a symbol, as a form of communication, or the foundation for statehood', in Ausma Cimdiņa (ed.), *Latvia and Latvians*, Rīga: Zinātne, pp. 145–182.

—, — (2011), 'Valsts valodas integratīvā un ekonomiskā vērtība' [The integrative and economic value of the national language], *Vārds un tā pētīšanas aspekti* 15:2, pp. 97–106.

—, — (2012a), 'Latviešu valoda kā nacionālās identitātes pamats: Ata Kronvalda ieguldījums mūsdienu skatījumā' [Latvian as the basis of national identity: the contribution of Ata Kronvalds to the modern perspective], in *Valoda laikā un kultūrtelpā*, Rīga: Zinātne, pp. 37–40.

—, — (2012b), 'Literārā valoda latviešu valodas paveidu sistēmā' [The literary language in the system of Latvian varieties], in *Literārā valoda (standartvaloda) vēsturiskā, normatīvā un sociolingvistiskā skatījumā*, Rīga: LU Latviešu valodas institūts, pp. 15–16.

—, — (2012c), ed., *Valodas situācija Latvijā: 2004–2010* [The language situation in Latvia 2004–2010], Rīga: Latviešu valodas aģentūra.

—, — (2013), 'Valodas situācija un valodas politika' [The language situation and the language policy], in Andrejs Veisbergs (ed.), *Latviešu valoda*, Rīga: LU Akadēmiskais apgāds, pp. 393–414.

—, — (2016), 'Latviešu valoda pasaules sociolingvistisko procesu kontekstā' [Latvian in the context of international sociolinguistic processes], in Linda Lauze (ed.), *Valodas situācijas Latvijā 2010–2015*, Rīga: Latviešu valodas aģentūra, pp. 11–34.

—, — (2018a), 'Language as national identity: thirty years after the re-establishment of Latvian as the official state language', in Ina Druviete (ed.), *Nacionālās identitātes sociolingvistiskie aspekti*, Rīga: LU Latviešu valodas institūts, pp. 45–62.

—, — (2018b), 'Identitāte, valoda, valodas politika' [Identity, language, language policy], in Ina Druviete (ed.), *Nacionālās identitātes sociolingvistiskie aspekti*, Rīga: LU Latviešu valodas institūts, pp. 7–20.

—, — (2018c), 'Valoda stereotipu spogulī' [Language in the mirror of stereotypes], *Valodas prakse: vērojumi un ieteikumi* 13, Rīga: Latviešu valodas aģentūra, pp. 5–17.

—, — / Andrejs **Veisbergs** (2018), 'Latviešu valoda 21. gadsimtā' [Latvian in the 21st century], in Tālavs Jundzis / Maija Kūle / Ojārs Spārītis / Andrejs Vasks / Guntis Zemītis (eds.), *Latvija un latvieši*, vol. 1, Rīga: Latvijas Zinātņu Akadēmija, pp. 222–254.

Ehala, Martin (2013), 'Russian-speakers in the Baltic countries: language use and identity', in Virve-Anneli Vihman / Kristiina Praakli (eds.), *Negotiating Linguistic Identity: Language and belonging in Europe*, Bern: Peter Lang, pp. 89–110.

Ernstsone, Vineta / Daiga **Joma** (2005), *Latviski runājošo Latvijas iedzīvotāju lingvistiskā attieksme un valodu lietojums* [The linguistic attitude of and language use by ethnic Latvians], Rīga: Valsts valodas aģentūra.

Formigari, Lia (2004), *A History of Language Philosophies*, Amsterdam: John Benjamins Publishing Company.
Forster, Michael N. (2011), *German Philosophy of Language From Schlegel to Hegel and Beyond*, Oxford: Oxford University Press.
García, Ofelia (2012), 'Ethnic identity and language policy', in Bernard Spolsky (ed.), *The Cambridge Handbook of Language Policy*, Cambridge: Cambridge University Press, pp. 79–99.
Goffman, Erving (1974), *Frame Analysis: An Essay on the Organisation of Experience*, New York–Evanston et al.: Harper & Row.
Gumperz, John (1989), 'Contextualisation cues and metapragmatics: the retrieval of cultural knowledge', in C. Wiltshire/B. Music/R. Graczyk (eds.), *CLS 25: Papers from the Parasession on Language in Context*, Chicago: University of Chicago Press, pp. 10–35.
Hogan-Brun, Gabrielle / Uldis **Ozoliņš** / Meilutė **Ramonienė** / Mart **Rannut** (2009), *Language Politics and Practices in the Baltic States*, Tallinn: Tallinn University Press.
Hymes, Dell H. (1972), 'On communicative competence', in J. B. Pride/Janet Holmes (eds.), *Sociolinguistics: Selected Readings*, Harmondsworth: Penguin, pp. 269–293.
Joma, Daiga (2007), 'Latvijas iedzīvotāju attieksme pret izglītības reformu (1998–2004)' [The attitudes of Latvia's population towards the education reform of 1998–2004], in Daiga Joma (ed.), *Latviešu valoda 15 neatkarības gados*, Rīga: Zinātne, pp. 309–326.
Joseph, John E. (2006), *Language and Politics*, Edinburgh: Edinburgh University Press.
Juzefovičs, Jānis (2017), *Broadcasting and National Imagination in Post-Communist Latvia: Defining the Nation, Defining Public Television*, Bristol–Chicago: Intellect.
Kalniņa, Anita / Laura **Sūna** (2008), 'Kultūra un sabiedrības integrācija' [Culture and the social integration], in Leo Dribins (ed.), *Sabiedrības integrācijas tendences un prettendences, Latvijas un Igaunijas pieredze: Etnisko attiecību aspekts*, Rīga: LU Filozofijas un socioloģijas institūts, pp. 71–84.
Kibermane, Kertu / Gunta **Kļava** / Linda **Lauze** / Kristīne **Tihomirova** (2014), *Valodas ideoloģija un plašsaziņas līdzekļi (televīzija)* [Language ideology and mass media (TV)], Rīga: Latviešu valodas aģentūra.
—, — / Gunta **Kļava** (2016), 'Valsts valodas lietojums sociolingvistiskajās jomās' [The use of the national language in sociolinguistic spheres], in Linda Lauze (ed.), *Valodas situācijas Latvijā 2010–2015*, Rīga: Latviešu valodas aģentūra, pp. 93–122.
Kļave, Evija/Inese **Šūpule**/Iveta **Bebriša** (2013), *Etniski heterogēnas pirmsskolas izglītības iestādes* [Ethnically heterogeneous preschool educational establishments], Rīga: Latviešu valodas aģentūra.
Kļaviņa, Sarma (1999), 'Plašs un dziļš skats uz valodu' [A broad and profound view on language], *Kentaurs* 21:18, pp. 4–9.
—, — (2007), 'Latviešu lingvistiskā identitāte kā piederība un patība zem svešu varu sloga un savā valstī' [Latvian linguistic identity as belongingness and identity under foreign rule and in the own state], in Janīna Kursīte (ed.), *Kultūra un vara*, Rīga: LU Akadēmiskais apgāds, pp. 83–91.
Krastiņš, Oļģerts (1998), 'Jauktās laulības kā problēma tautai un ģimenei' [Mixed marriages as a problem for the nation and the family], *Latvijas Vēstnesis*, October 21, p. 2.
Lauze, Linda (2016), ed., *Valodas situācijas Latvijā 2010–2015*, Rīga: Latviešu valodas aģentūra.
McQuail, Denis (2005), *Mass Communication Theory*, London: Sage Publications.
Nunberg, Geoffrey (1989), 'Linguists and the official language movement', in *Language* 65:3, pp. 579–587.

Ozoliņš, Uldis (2019), 'Language policy, external political pressure and internal linguistic change: the particularity of the Baltic case', in Sanita Lazdiņa / Heiko F. Marten (eds.), *Multilingualism, Language Contact and Majority–Minority Relations in Contemporary Estonia, Latvia and Lithuania*, London: Palgrave, pp. 29–55.

Poriņa, Vineta (2009), *Valsts valoda daudzvalodīgajā sabiedrībā: individuālais un sociālais bilingvisms Latvijā* [The national language in a multilingual society: individual and social bilingualism in Latvia], Rīga: LU Latviešu valodas institūts.

Priedīte, Aija (1998), 'Latviešu valodas apguves valsts programmas nozīme sabiedrības integrācijā' [The Latvian Language Training Programme's role in the social integration], in Elmārs Vēbers (ed.), *Pilsoniskā apziņa*, Rīga: LU Filozofijas un socioloģijas institūts, pp. 165–175.

—, — (2003), 'The evolutionary process of laws on the State language, education, and naturalisation: a reflection of Latvia's democratisation process', *Mercator Working Papers* 12.

—, — (2005), 'Surveying language attitudes and practices in Latvia', *Journal of Multilingual and Multicultural Development* 26:5, pp. 409–424.

Réaume, Denise / Meital **Pinto** (2012), 'Philosophy of language policy', in Bernard Spolsky (ed.), *The Cambridge Handbook of Language Policy*, Cambridge: Cambridge University Press, pp. 37–58.

Rozenbergs, Jānis (1995), *Latviešu valodas stilistika* [The stylistics of Latvian], Rīga: Zvaigzne ABC.

Skujiņa, Valentīna (2000), 'Lai valoda izdzīvotu – tā ir rūpīgi jākopj' [For a language to survive, it must be carefully nurtured], *Latvijas Vēstnesis*, 12 July.

Skujiņa, Valentīna (2001), 'Nacionālās valodas noturīguma pamati gadsimtu gaitai' [Fundamentals of the persistence of the national language over the centuries], *Linguistica Lettica* 8, pp. 9–15.

—, — (2003), 'Vārda semantika objektīvā un subjektīvā skatījumā [The semantics of the word from an objective and subjective point of view], *Linguistica Lettica* 12, pp. 147–155.

Rungule, Ritma / Ilze **Koroļeva** / Sigita **Sniķere** (2008), 'Jauniešu iekļaušanās analīze identitātes un līdzdalības diskursu kontekstā' [Analysis of youth inclusion in the context of identity and participation discourses], in Leo Dribins (ed.), *Sabiedrības integrācijas tendences un prettendences, Latvijas un Igaunijas pieredze: Etnisko attiecību aspekts*, Rīga: LU Filozofijas un socioloģijas institūts, pp. 37–54.

Schmid, Carol L. (2008), 'Ethnicity and language tensions in Latvia', *Language Policy* 7:1, pp. 3–19.

Tabuns, Aivars (2010), 'Identity, ethnic relations, language and culture', in Nils Muižnieks (ed.), *How Integrated is Latvian Society?*, Rīga: University of Latvia Press, pp. 253–278.

Underhill, James W. (2009), *Humboldt, Worldview, and Language*, Edinburgh: Edinburgh University Press.

Vasiļjeva, Sanita (2016), 'Sociālais kapitāls un krīzes pārvarēšanas stratēģijas' [Social capital and crisis resolution strategies], in Sergejs Kruks (ed.), *Ekonomiskā krīze Latvijā: "veiksmes stāsta" pēcgarša*, Rīga: Rīgas Stradiņa Universitāte, pp. 125–151.

Veisbergs, Andrejs (2013), ed., *Latviešu valoda* [Latvian language], Rīga: LU Akadēmiskais apgāds.

—, — (2018), 'Language planning in Latvia as a struggle for national sovereignty', in Ernest Andrews (ed.), *Language Planning in the Post-Communist Era*, London: Palgrave MacMillan, pp. 219–240.

Vihalemm, Triin / Gabrielle **Hogan-Brun** (2013), 'Language policies and practices across the Baltic: processes, challenges and prospects', *European Journal of Applied Linguistics* 1:1, pp. 55–82.

[**Volkov**, Vladislav] Волков, Владислав (2013), 'Демография русского населения Латвии в XX–XXI веке' [The demography of Latvia's Russian population in the 20th/21st c.], in Вадим Полещук (ed.), *Этническая политика в странах Балтии*, Москва: Наука, pp. 177–196.

8.2 Digital titles

Cohesive and active civil society development guidelines for 2021–2027, *Saliedētas un pilsoniski aktīvas sabiedrības attīstības pamatnostādnes 2021.–2027. gadam*, draft, 2020, online resource.

Latviešu valodas apguves valsts programma, *Gada pārskats 2003* [Annual Report 2003], 2004, digital resource.

Latviešu valodas apguves valsts aģentūra, *Gada pārskats 2007* [Annual Report 2007], 2008, digital resource.

National Development Plan of Latvia for 2021–2027, digital resource.

Priedīte, Aija (2002), 'Latvian language acquisition — a fight with myths, stereotypes and prejudices', *Noves SL. Revista de Sociolingüística*, Winter 2002, digital edn.

—, — (2004), 'Izaicinājumi un izmaiņas LVAVP darbības vidē 2003. gadā' [Challenges and changes in the operating environment of LVAVP in 2003], in Marija Golubeva (ed.), *Latviešu valodas apguves valsts programma. Gada pārskats 2003*, Rīga: LVAVP, pp. 6–7, digital edn.

Sabiedrības integrācija Latvijā [The societal integration in Latvia], 2001, digital resource.

Valsts valodas politikas pamatnostādnes 2005.–2014. gadam [National language policy guidelines for 2005–2014], 2005, digital resource.

Valsts valodas politikas pamatnostādnes 2015.–2020. gadam [National language policy guidelines for 2015–2020], 2015, digital resource.

Valsts valodas politikas pamatnostādnes 2021.–2027. gadam [National language policy guidelines for 2021–2027], 2020, digital resource.

Zur Integration slawischer Verben und verbaler Wortbildungselemente im Lettgallischen

Ein Beitrag zur Kontaktlinguistik
von Nicole Nau (Poznań)

Outline

As a result of prolonged language contact, Latgalian shows considerable material and structural borrowings from Slavic languages (Russian, Belarusian, Polish) and has developed techniques for their integration and use. Based on material from spoken and written Latgalian from the late 19th to the 21st century, this study highlights four techniques for the integration of verbs and verbal derivational affixes: the use of inflected Russian verb forms in the speech of bilinguals, the integration of Slavic verbal stems into the Latgalian lexicon, the development of a verbal derivational suffix on the base of borrowed stems, and the borrowing of verbal prefixes. The first two phenomena illustrate that nonce borrowings differ from stable ones, while the latter corroborate a distinction between direct and indirect borrowing of affixes. In addition, the borrowed affixes are shown to have pragmatic functions that are more important than their notional and structural functions. They can flag a multilingual identity and mark Latgalian as different from Standard Latvian.

Danksagung

Für hilfreiche Kommentare zu diesem Aufsatz danke ich Kirill Kozhanov, Peter Arkadiev und ganz besonders Björn Wiemer. Stephan Kessler danke ich für seine Anregungen zum Kürzen der ersten Fassung und sein Engagement für diesen Sammelband.

Gliederung

1	Einführung	89
2	Integration beim Sprechen: Code-Switching und Ad-hoc-Entlehnung	90
3	Integration verbaler Stämme und (Re-)Analyse von wortbildenden Suffixen	94
4	Entlehnte Präfixe	98
5	Zusammenfassung der Ergebnisse	103
6	Nachweise	104
6.1	Sprachen und Abkürzungen in den Glossen	104
6.2	Quellen	105
	6.2.1 Gedruckte Titel ... 105 — 6.2.2 Digitale Titel ... 105	
6.3	Verwendete Literatur	105
	6.3.1 Gedruckte Titel ... 105 — 6.3.2 Digitale Titel ... 109	

1 Einführung

Das im Osten Lettlands gesprochene Lettgallische hat seit jeher in engerem Kontakt zu slawischen Sprachen gestanden als die westlichen und mittleren Dialekte des Lettischen.[1] Slawische Lehnwörter sind daher eines der Merkmale, die Lettgallisch vom Standardlettischen unterscheiden, und ihre Rolle für die Standardvarietät des Lettgallischen wird oft diskutiert. Auf der einen Seite lehnen viele Sprachpfleger Slawismen ab, auf der anderen Seite benutzen insbesondere jüngere Sprachaktivisten bewusst slawische Modelle, um ihre Sprache auszubauen und den Abstand zum Lettischen zu betonen. Die Anzahl an Slawismen schwankt stark sowohl im mündlichen Sprachgebrauch als auch in geschriebenen Texten verschiedener Autoren. Es ist daher im Allgemeinen schwer zu bestimmen, welche Elemente Teil des Sprachsystems des Lettgallischen sind und welche kurzlebige spontane Entlehnungen. Im vorliegenden Beitrag werden verschiedene Resultate von Sprachmischung untersucht, und zwar von Code-Switching über Ad-hoc-Entlehnungen bis hin zu etablierten Lehnwörtern. Dabei beschränke ich mich auf die materielle Übernahme von einzelnen Wörtern, Stämmen und Affixen im Verbalbereich und gehe der Frage nach, wie solche Elemente beim Sprechen und Schreiben ins Lettgallische integriert werden und was ihre Verwendung auszeichnet. Die Ergebnisse dieser Studie zeigen zum einen die Besonderheiten materieller Entlehnungen von Verben und ihren Bestandteilen im Gegensatz zu anderen Wortarten, zum anderen die Relevanz struktureller Ähnlichkeit zwischen Modell- und Replikasprache für einzelne Prozesse der Integration.

Ostlettland gehört zu einem Areal, in dem sich seit Jahrhunderten slawische und baltische Sprachen treffen und gegenseitig beeinflussen (dazu siehe Wiemer 2003, 2004, 2013; Wiemer et al. 2014; Nau 2012). Zu verschiedenen Zeiten, in verschiedenen Lebensbereichen (z. B. bei nachbarschaftlichen Kontakten, im Handel, in der Verwaltung, in der Kirche, im Bildungsbereich) und für verschiedene Mundarten des Lettgallischen spielten jeweils Varietäten des Russischen, Belarussischen oder Polnischen eine größere oder kleinere Rolle. Im Ergebnis ist oft nicht auszumachen, welches die Modellsprache eines Lehnwortes war. Ich spreche daher hier allgemein von slawischen Lehnwörtern und versuche nicht, die Modellsprache näher zu identifizieren, wenn diese nicht offensichtlich Russisch, Belarussisch oder Polnisch ist.

Im Verlauf des 20. Jahrhunderts hat Russisch die anderen slawischen Sprachen in Ostlettland weitestgehend verdrängt, während Polnisch und Belarussisch heute nur noch von kleinen Minderheiten gesprochen werden und keinen Einfluss mehr auf das Lettgallische ausüben (zum Belarussischen in Lettgallen siehe Jankowiak 2009; zum Polnischen Kuņicka 2016). Die Sprecher des Lettgallischen – d. h. etwa 32 % der Einwohner des Verwaltungsbezirks Lettgallen und etwa 164 Tsd. Personen in ganz Lettland (Census 2011) – sind überwiegend dreisprachig mit Lettgallisch, Standardlettisch und Russisch (zur sprachlichen Situation in Ostlettland und der soziolinguistischen Situation des Lettgallischen siehe Šup-

---

[1] »Lettisch« wird als Überbegriff für verschiedene mündliche und schriftliche Varietäten verwendet (ISO 639-3 Kode LAV), kann aber auch im Kontrast zu Lettgallisch (LTG) nur die lettische Standardsprache und die westlichen Dialekte (LVS) meinen.

linska/Lazdiņa 2009; Lazdiņa et al. 2011; Marten/Lazdiņa 2016; zur Sprachstruktur des Lettgallischen siehe Breidaks 2006; Nau 2011; Arkadiev et al. 2015).

Aus vielen verschiedenen Sprachkontaktsituationen ist bekannt, dass Verben sich anders verhalten als Substantive und andere Inhaltswörter. Verben werden generell seltener entlehnt, was sich teilweise dadurch erklären lässt, dass das Verb z. B. durch Kongruenz und Rektion enger mit der Satzstruktur verbunden ist. Dies erschwert die Integration in eine andere Sprache insbesondere bei struktureller Verschiedenheit (vgl. Winford 2003: 51–53; Matras 2007: 48–49; Muysken 2013: 207–208). In der Lehnwortforschung sind Verben erst seit etwa fünfzehn Jahren in das Zentrum des Forschungsinteresses gerückt (Wichmann/Wohlgemuth 2008; Wohlgemuth 2009; Alexiadou 2017; Dux 2017; Forker 2020). Smetonienė (2015a, 2015b) untersucht in ihrer Dissertation slawische Lehnverben in altlitauischen Texten; nicht wenige der von ihr aufgeführten Verben finden sich auch im Lettgallischen, insbesondere in älteren Texten, in denen der polnische, belarussische und teilweise litauische Einfluss stärker sind als der russische. Die Dissertation von Kožanov (2015) und weitere Arbeiten des Autors sind Sprachkontakterscheinungen im Bereich der Verbalpräfixe im slawisch-baltischen Kontaktgebiet gewidmet. Zu Slawismen im Lettgallischen gibt es bisher erstaunlich wenig Arbeiten; hervorzuheben sind einige kürzere Beiträge von Rēķena (enthalten in Rēķena 2008), in denen auch auf Verben und verbale Affixe eingegangen wird. Speziell mit der Integration von slawischen Verben in einen lettgallischen Dialekt befasst sich Leikuma (1982).

Dem vorliegenden Aufsatz liegt eine breite, ›dynamische‹ Auffassung von Entlehnung zugrunde, entsprechend der Definition von *borrowing* in Windford (2010):

> To summarize, borrowing can be defined as the transfer of linguistic materials from an SL [source language] into an RL [recipient language] via the agency of speakers for whom the latter is the linguistically dominant language, in other words, via RL agentivity. (Winford 2010: 172)

Andere Definitionen beschränken den Terminus auf Fälle, in denen das übernommene Material Teil des Sprachsystems geworden ist, d. h. Entlehnung wird aus diachroner Perspektive betrachtet (z. B. bei Backus/Dorleijn 2009). Winfords Definition schließt dagegen Ad-hoc-Entlehnungen ein und umgeht so das von vielen Forschern als unlösbar angesehene Problem der kategorischen Unterscheidung von Entlehnung und Code-Switching (siehe z. B. Matras 2009: 110–114; Bullock/Toribio 2009: 5; Muysken 2013). Dass Entlehnung ein aktiver Prozess ist, wird in der Sprachkontaktforschung insbesondere in den Arbeiten von Yaron Matras betont (2009; 2015: 51–53).

Im folgenden Abschnitt 2 werden mögliche Unterschiede zwischen Code-Switching und Ad-hoc-Entlehnungen diskutiert, ausgehend von Beispielen aus Aufnahmen gesprochener Sprache. Das Material für die Abschnitte 3 und 4 entstammt dagegen schriftlichen Quellen: Wörterbüchern, Glossarien, dem Korpus »MuLa« und der Märchensammlung von Ulanowska (2011 [1895]). In Abschnitt 3 wird die Entlehnung von verbalen Stämmen besprochen sowie die Ausbreitung des aus Lehnverben herausgelösten Suffixes *-av-*. Das Thema von Abschnitt 4 sind die materiell aus dem Slawischen entlehnten Präfixe *pad-*, *pro-* und *roz-*. Die Ergebnisse der Abschnitte 2–4 werden im abschließenden Abschnitt 5 zusammengefasst.

2 Integration beim Sprechen: Code-Switching und Ad-hoc-Entlehnung

Allgemein bezeichnet Code-Switching die Verwendung von zwei Sprachen oder sprachlichen Varietäten innerhalb eines Redebeitrags, während bei Entlehnung eine Sprache durch Elemente einer anderen bereichert wird. Die Unterscheidung ist unproblematisch, wenn ganze Sätze oder längere Phrasen in einer anderen Sprache geäußert werden (*alternational code-switching*). Ein typischer Kontext für ein solches »Umschalten«[1] ist die Redewiedergabe. Es können aber auch nur einzelne Wörter in einer anderen Sprache geäußert, d. h. »eingeschaltet« werden (*insertional code-switching*). Ausschnitt (1) zeigt beide Fälle. Die Grundsprache ist Lettgallisch. In Zeile (1c) gibt der Sprecher die Äußerung eines anderen auf Russisch wieder, in Zeile (1b) schaltet er ein russisches Verb in einen lettgallischen Satz ein.

(1) a. *nu vot* (1,8)   *tod* (0,8)
        'also (1,8)   dann (0,8)'

    b. **оформляет**   *jau*   *jis*
        prepare(IPF).NPST.3SG already   3.NOM.SG.M
        'fertigt er schon den Antrag an'

    c. **орден получить тебе надо** (0,8)
        '»du musst einen Orden bekommen«'

    d. *nu vot jis te*
        'also er'

    e. *maņ pīroksta vysu vysu tā*
        'schreibt mir alles, alles so auf/ein'

(Sprecher M104-1928-Andrupene, in TriMCo Corpus[2])

Ausschnitt (1) ist Teil einer Erzählung darüber, wie der Sprecher zu Sowjetzeiten bedrängt wurde, in die Partei einzutreten. Im Laufe seiner Erzählung verwendet der Sprecher mehrfach Russisch für die Wiedergabe von Dialogen mit Parteifunktionären. In dem Teil der Erzählung unmittelbar vor Ausschnitt (1) wird jedoch eine Begegnung mit dem Parteisekretär (ohne direkte Rede) ganz auf Lettgallisch wiedergegeben. Zum Code-Switching kommt es hier erst, als der Sprecher einen bestimmten Begriff sucht (die Pausen in Zeile 1a zeugen von Wortfindungsproblemen) und das passende Verb zuerst auf Russisch findet (*оформлять* 'in rechtskräftige Form bringen; Formalitäten vollziehen'). Er verbindet es in seiner russischen Flexionsform mit einem lettgallischen Pronomen, kombiniert also die Grammatik zweier Sprachen. Der folgende Satz (1c) ist die Rede des Parteisekretärs, durch Prosodie und eben den Sprachenwechsel als Redewiedergabe gekennzeichnet. In (1d) setzt der Sprecher zu einer neuen Beschreibung der Situation an, wobei er diesmal das lettgallische Verb *pīraksteit* 'jemanden einschreiben, registrieren (u. a.)' verwendet.

Die Beispiele in (1) weisen Merkmale auf, die nach Auer (1998: 3) das prototypische Code-Switching charakterisieren. Das Gespräch wird prinzipiell auf Lettgallisch geführt, und die Verwendung des Russischen stellt eine Abweichung von der Sprachwahl dar und ist dadurch bedeutsam: Sie repräsentiert »das Andere« (*code-switching signals 'otherness'*, Auer 1998: 3). Die russische Sprache ist in diesem Teil des Gesprächs mit sowjetischer Administration und der kommunistischen Partei assoziiert. Während der Sprecher von den verschiedenen Begebenheiten in diesem Zusammenhang erzählt, ist Russisch immer neben Lettgallisch aktiviert: Der Sprecher befindet sich im bilingualen Modus. Das Einsetzen

---

1 Auer (1998: 9) nennt die von Stolt (1964) gebrauchten Termini »Umschaltung« und »Einschaltung« als deutsche Entsprechungen von *alternational* und *insertional code-switching*. Die deutschen Termini mögen ungewöhnlich sein, scheinen mir aber sehr nützlich.
2 Zum TriMCo-Corpus siehe Wiemer et al. (2019). Der lettgallische Teil dieses Korpus wird zurzeit in das neue Korpus des gesprochenen Lettgallisch aufgenommen; dieses soll ab Herbst 2022 online zur allgemeinen Verfügung stehen.

einer einzelnen russischen Flexionsform in eine lettgallische Konstruktion ist jedoch ungewöhnlich und scheint auf Verben beschränkt zu sein. Einzelne Substantive, die in einen lettgallischen Satz in mündlichen oder schriftlichen Texten eingeschaltet werden, erhalten in der Regel eine lettgallische Kasusendung, seltener erscheinen sie in einer aus lettischer Sicht unflektierten Form (dies betrifft vor allem Substantive, die auf einen Vokal außer -a enden, wie z. B. *metro*). Der Fall, dass ein russisches Substantiv mit seiner russischen Kasusendung eingeschaltet würde, ist mir bisher noch nicht begegnet.

Russische Verbformen finden sich nicht nur im typischen Code-Switching. Ausschnitt (2) stammt aus einem Märchen, das während einer ethnographischen Expedition 1973 aufgezeichnet wurde. Der Sprecher ist 1892 geboren und ein beliebter Märchenerzähler, der gewöhnt ist, dieselben Märchen auf Lettgallisch und Russisch zu erzählen.[3] In seiner Erzählung sind relativ viele etablierte slawische Lehnwörter zu hören, zumeist Adverbien und Funktionswörter wie *patom* 'dann, darauf' in (2a). Slawischstämmige Substantive, ganz gleich, ob sie allgemein übliche Lehnwörter oder Ad-hoc-Entlehnungen aus dem Russischen sind, erscheinen in seiner Rede mit einer lettgallischen Kasusendung. Russische Verben werden jedoch mit ihrer russischen Flexionsendung verwendet. Dabei kann der Stamm phonetisch und morphologisch mehr oder weniger adaptiert sein. So enthält die Aufnahme das russische Verb *освободить* 'befreien' einmal in der Vergangenheitsform mit der Aussprache [asvabaˈdzil], was der russischen Aussprache in der Region entspricht. Die Futurform *atsvabadiš* in (2e) zeigt zwar dieselben phonetischen Merkmale (Endbetonung, Akanie und Dz-Kanie), aber das russische Präfix *o-* [a] wurde durch das baltische Präfix *at-* ersetzt.

(2) a. *a   patom   iz-leis-s-i   uorā*
       but   then   PVB-creep-FUT-2SG   out
       'doch dann kriechst du heraus'

   b. *i   jū   pošu   redzie-s-i*
      and   3.ACC.SG   self.ACC.SG   see-FUT-2SG
      'und siehst sie [= die Prinzessin]'

   c. *da-sa-runuo-s-i*
      PVB-RFL-talk-FUT-2SG
      'du verständigst dich [mit ihr]'

   d. *tev   i   augļu   ī-dū-s*
      2SG.DAT   ADD   fruit.GEN.PL   PVB-give-FUT(3)
      'und sie gibt dir von den Früchten'

   e. *i   tu   jū   **at-svabadz-iš**   nu   tīnis*
      and   2SG.NOM   3.ACC.SG   PVB-free(PFV).NPST-2SG   from   there.GEN.SG
      'und du **befreist** sie von dort'

(Sprecher Pēteris Janušenoks, in Garamanta)

Handelt es sich in (2e) noch um Code-Switching? Ein wesentliches Merkmal des von Auer (1998) aufgestellten Prototyps fehlt: In der Märchenerzählung lässt sich keine funktionale Motivation für die Verwendung russischer Wörter ausmachen – Russisch hat hier keine Signalwirkung, repräsentiert nicht ›das Andere‹ und keine mit dem Russischen assoziierten Situationen. Die russischen Verben sind auch nicht prosodisch hervorgehoben, und es gibt keine Anzeichen, dass sie das Resultat von Wortfindungsschwierigkeiten wären. Die Sprachmischung in dieser Aufnahme entspricht eher dem von Auer (1998) aufgestellten

---

3   Handschriftlich notierte Informationen über den Sprecher sind hier archiviert (die Seite, die der Link ansteuert, und die folgende Seiten). Die Aufnahme, aus der Ausschnitt (2) stammt, ist hier zugänglich.

Typ *Language Mixing (LM)*. Allerdings gehört zu Auers (Proto-) Typ LM eine hohe Frequenz von Elementen der zweiten Sprache, bis hin zu Situationen, wo nicht eindeutig zu bestimmen ist, welches die Grundsprache der Rede ist. In den mir vorliegenden Beispielen ist das nicht der Fall, es werden nur gelegentlich einzelne russische Verben in eine ansonsten eindeutig lettgallische Rede eingesetzt. Ich sehe diese Beispiele daher als Ad-hoc-Entlehnungen an. Die Grenze zwischen Code-Switching und Ad-hoc-Entlehnung ist fließend, und die Einschaltung einzelner russischer Verben kann mehr oder weniger einer dieser Kategorien zugeordnet werden.

Die Ersetzung des russischen Präfixes *o-* [a] durch *at-* wurde vermutlich durch die lautliche Ähnlichkeit begünstigt. Hinzu kommt, dass es im Gemeinlettischen bereits ein etabliertes Lehnwort LTG *atsvabynuot*, LVS *atsvabināt* 'befreien' gibt, an das sich der Sprecher vielleicht in diesem Moment erinnert und das er mit dem russischen Wort fusioniert. Dieses Lehnwort enthält außer dem Präfix *at-* noch das lettische Kausativsuffix, das auch zur Ableitung von Verben aus Adjektiven gebraucht wird (LTG *-yn-*, LVS *-in-*), und das stammbildende Suffix LTG *-uo-*, LVS *-ā-*, so dass nur die Wurzel *-svab-* noch ein (ursprünglich) slawisches Element ist. In Abschnitt 3 wird näher auf stammbildende und stammerweiternde Suffixe eingegangen. Hier ist es dagegen wichtig festzuhalten, dass diese Elemente nicht bei Ad-hoc-Entlehnungen russischer Verben beim Sprechen verwendet werden. Bei Substantiven ist das anders; z. B. kann ein russisches Substantiv sofort mit einem lettgallischen Diminutivsuffix verbunden werden, wie in *doč-eit-e* 'Töchterchen' (vgl. RUS дочь, доч-ка 'Tochter'). Bei der Ad-hoc-Entlehnung von Verben wird in diesen Beispielen dagegen die Technik verwendet, die in Wohlgemuths (2009) Typologie *paradigm insertion* heißt: Ein Wort wird mit Flexionsendungen entlehnt und kann dadurch potentiell in der Replikasprache ein Paradigma bilden, das von dem heimischer Wörter abweicht. Wohlgemuth (2009: 119) spricht auch die Schwierigkeit an, zwischen Verbintegration bei Entlehnung und Code-Switching zu unterscheiden. In dem von ihm angeführten Beispiel aus dem Ajia Varvara Romani argumentiert er für Entlehnung, da er es für unwahrscheinlich hält, dass nur Verben, nicht aber Substantive und andere Wörter in ihren Flexionsformen Teil von Code-Switching sind. Wie oben gezeigt, werden auch im Lettgallischen Verben anders behandelt als Substantive. Jedoch scheint das nicht mit anderen Kriterien, nach denen Code-Switching und Entlehnung unterschieden werden, zusammenzufallen. Vielmehr ist im Lettgallischen Paradigm Insertion eine Technik sowohl im Code-Switching als auch bei Ad-hoc-Entlehnung von Verben in der Rede bilingualer Sprecher. Die Anwendung dieser Technik wird durch den hohen Grad an Zweisprachigkeit von Sprechern und Hörern ermöglicht und vielleicht durch strukturelle Ähnlichkeiten der beteiligten Sprachen begünstigt. Diese Ähnlichkeiten betreffen jedoch die Konstruktion, den Satzbau, nicht die Verbformen selbst, bei denen sich die Realisierung der Kategorien Tempus, Aspekt und Person stark unterscheidet.

Im Lettgallischen bleibt Paradigm Insertion auf die spontane gesprochene Sprache beschränkt und führt nicht zu einer Subklassenbildung im Lexikon, wie sie vor allem aus Varietäten des Romani belegt ist (Hancock 1992; Friedman 2008; Matras 2015; allgemein zu Lehnwörtern als Subklassen innerhalb des Flexionssystems einer Sprache vgl. auch Nau 1995: 68–76). Etablierte Entlehnungen, die Teil des überindividuellen Sprachsystems sind, zeigen hingegen andere Techniken der Integration, die im folgenden Abschnitt 3 beschrieben werden.

3 Integration verbaler Stämme und (Re-)Analyse von wortbildenden Suffixen

Unter den Slawismen sind Substantive um vieles zahlreicher als Verben, jedoch ist die Zahl entlehnter Verben (oder, vorsichtiger formuliert, von Verben mit einer entlehnten Wurzel) nicht unerheblich und auf jeden Fall groß genug, um einige Tendenzen der Integration zu erkennen. Die meisten dieser Verben sind vor dem 20. Jahrhundert ins Lettgallische gekommen. Polnisch, Belarussisch und russische Dialekte haben lange Zeit die Vorbilder geliefert, die russische Standardsprache gewann erst gegen Ende des 19. Jahrhunderts einen stärkeren Einfluss und hat nach und nach die anderen slawischen Modellsprachen verdrängt. Allerdings wählen einige heutige Sprachenthusiasten manchmal bewusst polnische Vorbilder zur Prägung von Neologismen oder reaktivieren aus dem Polnischen stammende Lehnwörter, während moderne Russizismen kein hohes Prestige haben. Wie bereits in der Einleitung bemerkt, ist die Modellsprache eines entlehnten Verbs oft nicht zu bestimmen. Wenn hier zu den lettgallischen Beispielen parallele Wörter aus einer slawischen Sprache in ihrer heutigen Standardvarietät genannt werden, bedeutet das nicht, dass diese Wortform das Modell war.

Als Untersuchungsmaterial für diesen Abschnitt habe ich 50 unpräfigierte Verben aus Wörterbüchern und Korpora zusammengestellt. Dazu kommen präfigierte und reflexive Verben mit denselben Stämmen. Das Material erlaubt keine quantitativen Analysen, enthält jedoch die am weitesten verbreiteten und über einen längeren Zeitraum belegten Verben. In die Sammlung wurden keine Verben aufgenommen, die auch im Standardlettischen belegt sind und daher zu einer älteren Schicht von slawischen Entlehnungen gehören.

Verben mit slawischem lexikalischem Material finden sich im Lettgallischen in verschiedenen semantischen Bereichen. Die große Mehrheit bezeichnet menschliche Tätigkeiten, vor allem geistige und soziale. Die größte Gruppe in meinem Material ließe sich mit »soziale Beziehungen und Transaktionen« überschreiben. Dazu gehören u. a. *darāvuot* 'schenken', *dzekavuot* 'danken', *targavuot* 'handeln', *targavuotīs* 'feilschen', *žabravuot* 'betteln', *žīčeit* 'borgen', *pazvoleit* 'erlauben', *kiravuot* 'leiten, beherrschen; beaufsichtigen', *sporeitīs* 'streiten', *gasteit* 'zu Gast sein; Gäste bewirten', *služeit* 'dienen; in Diensten stehen', *ženeit* 'verheiraten' und *ženeitīs* 'heiraten'. Zu dieser Gruppe könnte man im weiteren Sinne auch Verben zählen, die mentale Einstellungen bezeichnen oder aus dem religiösen oder übersinnlichen Bereich stammen: *ļūbēt* 'lieben, mögen', *vīrēt* '(jemandem) Glauben schenken, vertrauen', *spadzeivuotīs* 'hoffen, erwarten', *spovedeitīs* 'beichten', *(iz)spovedēt* 'die Beichte abnehmen', *iz-pokotovuot* 'sühnen', *čaravuot* 'zaubern' und andere.

Eine kleinere Gruppe bezeichnet Tätigkeiten aus den Bereichen Haushalt und Handwerk, z. B. *beļavuot*, *belēt* 'tünchen', *budavuot* 'bauen', *maļavuot* 'malen, färben', *prasavuot* 'bügeln', *tarkavuot* 'reiben', *žareit* '(Fleisch) braten, grillen'. Manche Stämme haben mehrere Bedeutungen, von denen in einzelnen Dialekten oder bei einzelnen Sprechern nicht alle gebräuchlich sind. Dies kann darauf hindeuten, dass sie mehrfach entlehnt wurden. Die Wurzel *-pruov-* findet sich in Verben mit den Bedeutungen 1. 'in eine bestimmte Richtung lenken, schicken' (vgl. RUS направить) und 2. 'ausbessern' (vgl. POL *po-prawić*, RUS исправить). Daneben gibt es eine homonyme Wurzel mit der Bedeutung 'Versuch', die auf eine gemeinlettische Entlehnung aus Niederdeutsch *prove*, *proven* zurückgeht. Verben mit dieser Wurzel bilden den Infinitiv mit *-ē-* (*pruovēt*, *papruovēt* 'versuchen'), während Verben mit der slawischen Wurzel eher *-ei-* als stammbildendes Element verwenden: *aiz-pruoveit* 'wegschicken', *sa-pruoveit* 'ausbessern, reparieren'; siehe Beispiele (3–4). Wie aus diesen

Tabelle 1. Stammbildende Elemente im Lettgallischen (Konjugationsklasse II)

Stamm	*uo*-Klasse	*ei*-Klasse	*ē*-Klasse
Infinitivstamm (ST1)	-uo-	-ei-	-ē-, alterniert mit -ā-
Präsensstamm (ST2)	-oj-	-ej-	-ej-
Präteritumstamm (ST3)	-uoj- oder -ov- [1]	-ej-	-ēj-, -ie- [2]

Beispielen ersichtlich ist, tragen Präfixe zur Disambiguierung bei, allerdings ist das nicht immer der Fall.

Zur Integration von Lehnverben verwendet das Lettgallische überwiegend nur eine der von Wohlgemuth (2009) unterschiedenen vier Hauptstrategien, die direkte Integration (*direct insertion*), bei der ein Verb abgesehen vom stammbildenden Element ohne ein weiteres Suffix die Flexionsstämme bildet. Viel seltener ist indirekte Integration (*indirect insertion*), bei der ein zusätzliches Suffix hinzugefügt wird. Da beide Techniken auch zur Ableitung von Verben aus Wörtern mit entlehnter oder ererbter Wurzel verwendet werden, ist oft nicht zu entscheiden, was zuerst entlehnt wurde, ein Verb oder ein anderes Wort, von dem das Verb dann abgeleitet wurde. Diese Frage ist aber aus rein synchroner Sicht nicht wichtig (vgl. Pakerys 2014, der für Lehnverben im Litauischen argumentiert, dass Derivationsbeziehungen synchron erkennbar und beschreibbar seien).

Ein lettisches Verb benötigt drei potentiell unterschiedliche Stämme, um alle Flexionsformen zu bilden: je einen Infinitiv-, Präsens- und Präteritumstamm. Je nachdem, welche dieser Stämme einen stammbildenden Vokal enthalten, werden in der lettischen Grammatiktradition drei Klassen (›Konjugationen‹) unterschieden. Lehnverben im Lettgallischen gehören immer zur zweiten Klasse, bei der alle Stämme ein stammbildendes Element haben, das aus einem Vokal oder Diphthong allein oder in Verbindung mit j oder v besteht; siehe Tabelle 1. Bei der Integration slawischer Verben wird der stammbildende Vokal auf der Basis des Verbalstamms in der Modellsprache ausgewählt. Auf diese Weise werden genetisch bedingte Ähnlichkeiten zwischen den Sprachen ausgenutzt und auch verstärkt. Prinzipiell gibt es drei Möglichkeiten: -*uo*-, -*ei*- und -*ē*- (im Infinitiv), allerdings fallen die beiden letzteren in vielen Dialekten zusammen oder vermischen sich (d.h. der Infinitivstamm wird nach einer anderen Klasse gebildet als der Präteritumstamm; der Präsensstamm ist in beiden Klassen gleich). Tabelle 1 zeigt die Formen des stammbildenden Elements in den drei Stämmen; in einigen Mundarten gibt es weitere Varianten. Die Beispiele (3–6) aus dem Korpus MuLa illustrieren verschiedene Verbformen im Kontext.

(3) *Jumtā viejs izruovs lelu caurumu,*
    vajag   **sa-pruov-ei-t**.
    be_need.PRS.3   PVB-mend-ST1-INF
    'Der Wind hat ein großes Loch aus dem Dach gerissen, wir müssen es **reparieren**.'

(4) *Vysus radinīkus – lobpruoteigi voi nalabpruoteigi –*
    jī   *beja*   **aiz-pruov-ej-uš-i**   *iz*   *cytom*   *vītom.*
    they   be.PST.3   PVB-send-ST3-PST.PA-PL.M   to   other.DAT.PL.F   place.DAT.PL
    'Alle Verwandten hatten sie – freiwillig oder unfreiwillig – an andere Orte **weggeschickt**.'

---

1   Dialektale Variation, beide Varianten im Standard akzeptiert; *uo* wird auch *ō* geschrieben.
2   Dialektale Variation, im Standard -*ē*- in der dritten Person, -*ie*- in den anderen Personen.

(5) Moš atvedi Pīteri pi plāšnīcas,
    lai   drusku   **ap-čarav-oj**
    so_that a_bit   PVB-hex-ST1(PRS.3)
    'Vielleicht bringst Du Pīters mal zu einer Wunderheilerin, damit sie ihn ein bisschen **behext**.'

(6) Bess   jiusus   **čarav-uoj-s?**
    devil.NOM.SG   2PL.ACC   hex-ST3-PST.PA.SG.M
    'Hat euch der Teufel **verhext**?'

(Korpus MuLa)

Ganz allgemein entspricht in der Bildung des Infinitivstamms LTG -ei- oder -ē- slawischem -i- und -y- (z. B. LTG ļūbeit oder ļūbēt 'lieben, mögen', vgl. RUS любить, POL lubić; LTG lečeit oder lečēt 'ärztlich behandeln', vgl. POL leczyć), LTG -uo- slawischem -a- (z. B. spadzeivuotīs 'hoffen, erwarten', vgl. POL spodziewać się 'erwarten', BEL спадзявацца 'hoffen'; vgl. Endzelīns (1971 [1899]). Der Stammvokal kann allerdings auch dialektal variieren, innerhalb eines Dialekts schwanken und im Laufe der Zeit wechseln. Zum Beispiel findet sich bei Jūrdžs (1999 [1916]) spuor-**uo**-t-īs 'streiten', Lukaševičs (2011) verzeichnet spuor-**ei**-t-īs (auch sporeitīs), vgl. RUS спорить 'streiten', BEL спрачацца); im ältesten erhaltenen lettgallischen Buch, Evangelia toto anno (2004 [1753]) wird für 'beichten' spoveid-**uo**-t-īs verwendet, in Ulanowskas Märchensammlung (2011 [1895]) kommt (iz)spoved-**ē**-t für 'die Beichte abnehmen' vor, und im Korpus MuLa gibt es einen Beleg für spoved-**ei**-t-īs 'beichten'. Generell scheint es eine Tendenz zu geben, -ei- zu bevorzugen, wenn nicht -avuo- vorliegt. Diese These müsste allerdings noch gründlich empirisch überprüft werden. In Mundarten tritt auch -ā- als Stammvokal auf, so in dzekavāt, dzekovāt 'danken', Präteritumstamm dzekav-av- (vgl. BEL дзякаваць, POL dziękować) bei Ulanowska (2011 [1895]) und Reķēna (1998). In der von Leikuma (1982) beschriebenen Mundart von Izvalta ist bei entlehnten Verben, die im Infinitiv auf -uot enden, das stammbildende Suffix im Präteritum immer -av-, während bei ererbten Verben sowohl -av- als auch -ov- gebraucht werden, z. B. LTG mozg-**av**-u oder mozg-**ov**-u 'ich wusch', aber nur sortav-**av**-u 'ich sortierte' (Leikuma 1982: 56). Dies weist darauf hin, dass Lehnverben im Bewusstsein der Sprecher eine eigene Klasse bilden, obwohl sich die Flexion ansonsten nicht von der heimischer Verben unterscheidet.

Es ist wahrscheinlich, dass die meisten slawischen Lehnverben im Lettgallischen direkt als Verben entlehnt und nicht aus zuvor oder gleichzeitig entlehnten Wörtern anderer Wortart abgeleitet wurden (abgesehen von Verben auf -avuot, zu denen ich unten komme). Insbesondere zu den Verben auf -eit oder -ēt gibt es selten ein morphologisch einfacheres anderes Lehnwort. Eher finden sich Substantive, die aus den Verben abgeleitet sind, wie LTG ļūbesteiba 'Liebe' aus ļūbēt 'lieben' oder truceklis 'Gift' aus trucēt/truceit 'vergiften'. Bei den deutschen Lehnwörtern im Gemeinlettischen oder im Standardlettischen allein ist das anders, dort finden sich häufiger Paare wie LAV prov-e 'Versuch', prov-ēt 'versuchen', die entweder auf eine Ableitung des Verbs oder auf eine parallele Entlehung von Verb und Substantiv hinweisen. Auch bei den lettgallischen Verben auf -uot (außer -avuot) habe ich nur wenige solche Paare gefunden. Lukaševičs (2011) führt z. B. LTG kukar-uot 'kochen' (neben kukar-s 'Koch') und dzjubk-uot 'schnäbeln' (neben dzjubk-a 'Schnabel') auf. Das oben erwähnte LTG spoved-uot/spoved-ēt/spoved-eit 'die Beichte abnehmen' (mit Reflexivmarker: 'beichten') steht synchron in einer Ableitungsbeziehung zum Substantiv spoveds 'Beichte', aber ob es historisch daraus abgeleitet oder gesondert als Verb entlehnt wurde, lässt sich nicht mehr feststellen.

Eine besondere Gruppe bilden Verben, die auf -avuot enden. Sie sind sehr zahlreich und häufiger als die anderen Lehnverben mit einem Substantiv assoziiert. Dabei kann aus synchroner Sicht eine eindeutige Ableitungsrichtung Substantiv → Verb bestehen, z. B. prā-

cavuot 'mühevoll arbeiten, sich abrackern' (auch 'arbeiten' allgemein) und *prāca* '(schwere) Arbeit, Mühsal'; *prasavuot* 'bügeln' und *prasa* 'Bügeleisen', *tarkavuot* 'reiben' und *tarka* 'Reibe', *parādavuot* 'Ordnung schaffen' und *parāds* 'Ordnung'. In anderen Fällen liegen Substantive vor, die offensichtlich zu dem Verb gehören, ohne dass eine formale Ableitungsbeziehung besteht, z. B. *ratavuot* 'retten' und *ratunka* 'Rettung', *strugavuot* 'hobeln' und *strugans* 'Hobel'. Es liegt daher nahe, dass Sprecher das Element -*av*- vor dem stammbildenden Element als verbbildendes Suffix interpretieren.[3] Ähnliches wurde auch für litauische Dialekte beschrieben (Wiemer 2009; Kožanov 2015: 275–276). Dabei stellt sich die Frage, zu welchem Grad dieses Suffix zu einem produktiven Wortbildungselement geworden ist und sich von Vorbildern der Modellsprache gelöst hat. In litauischen Dialekten ist nach Ansicht Kožanovs die Produktivität von -*av*- gering: Fast alle Belege können als materielle Entlehnungen des Verbs angesehen werden. Wenn das Suffix mit einer baltischen Wurzel verbunden wird, dann ist diese in der Regel mit der slawischen Wurzel eines Modellworts etymologisch verwandt und daher lautlich ähnlich, z. B. LIT *žiem-av-oti* 'überwintern', vgl. BEL *зім-ав-аць*, RUS *зим-ов-ать* (Kožanov 2015: 276), d. h. diese Verben sind teilangepasste materielle Entlehnungen. Wiemer (2009) führt jedoch an, dass das Suffix -*av*- in litauischen Inseldialekten auf slawischem Sprachgebiet auch in litauischen Verben auftritt, deren Wurzel keine lautliche Ähnlichkeit mit einem slawischen Verb hat.

Auch im Lettgallischen ist das Suffix -*av*- im Bewusstsein der Sprecher zunächst mit Slawismen assoziiert. Seine Funktion ist eher pragmatisch als grammatisch: Es signalisiert ein slawisches Lehnwort, und damit auch einen Unterschied zum Standardlettischen. In dieser Funktion kann es von kreativen Autoren auch mit nicht-slawischem Material verbunden werden. Eine Brücke dafür bilden Internationalismen wie *drukavuot* 'drucken', *planavuot* 'planen'. Im 18. und 19. Jahrhundert kamen Internationalismen überwiegend aus dem Polnischen und Russischen ins Lettgallische, während sie im westlichen Lettisch, aus dem sich das Standardlettisch entwickelte, zumeist ein deutsches Vorbild hatten. Dadurch stehen lettgallischen verbalen Internationalismen auf -*avuot* standardlettische Internationalismen mit einfachem stammbildenden Element gegenüber: LVS *drukāt* 'drucken', *plānot* 'planen'. Nach der Gründung der lettischen Republik 1918 wurde allmählich Standardlettisch die wichtigste Modellsprache für Lettgallisch, und viele Internationalismen wurden angeglichen, d. h. die entsprechenden Verben verloren das Element -*av*- (LTG *drukuot*, *planuot*). Im heutigen Lettgallisch sind verbale Internationalismen mit und ohne -*av*-freie Varianten. Dabei erscheinen die Formen mit diesem Suffix vor allem in Texten von Autoren, die sich bemühen, den Abstand des Lettgallischen zum Lettischen zu markieren, darunter humoristische Texte. Ein Beispiel mit dem Verb LTG *lak-av-uot* (als Variante des häufigeren *lak-uot*) 'lackieren' ist Beispiel (7).

(7) čūkstu   vīn   grūzeit   mōk   i   nogus   **lakavōt**
    buttocks.ACC.SG only   wiggle.INF   can.PRS.3   and   nail.ACC.PL   varnish.INF
    'kann nichts als mit dem Hintern wackeln und die Nägel **lackieren**'

(8) juos   malnī   moti   pi   sakneitem   izavēre
    3.GEN.SG.F   black.NOM.PL.M.DEF   hair.NOM.PL   at   root.DIM.DAT.PL   PVB.RFL.look.PST.3
    nadaudz   **sa-sa-spek-av-uoj-uš-i**
    NEG.much   PVB-RFL-grease-SUF-ST3-PST.PA-PL.M
    'ihre schwarzen Haare sehen an den Wurzeln etwas **angespeckt** aus'

(MuLa)

---

3   Endzelīns' (1979 [1927]) Hypothese, dass das Suffix -*av*- in Verben nicht aus dem Slawischen stammt, sondern aus heimischen Substantiven, ist für das Lettgallische abzulehnen; siehe dazu schon Reķēna (2008 [1967]): 119).

In Beispiel (8) hat der Autor die nominale Wurzel *spek-* (ein altes Lehnwort aus Deutsch *Speck*) mit LTG *-av-uo-* kombiniert. Eine standardlettische Entsprechung dieser kreativen Bildung wäre *no-speķ-uo-t-ies* 'fettig werden, (Fett)flecken bekommen'.

Dieses Beispiel zeigt, dass das Suffix möglicherweise beginnt, produktiv zu werden, auch wenn es dafür bisher nur wenige Belege gibt. Die Herauslösung der Sequenz *-av-uo-* aus dem Kontext slawischer Entlehnungen und ihre Verwendung mit Elementen anderer Provenienz ist ein typisches Beispiel für indirekte Suffixentlehnung, wie sie aus vielen Sprachen und Kontaktsituationen bekannt ist. Seifart (2017) stellt quanitative Kriterien auf, nach denen entschieden werden kann, ob ein Affix auf diese Art oder direkt entlehnt wurde; die derzeit verfügbaren Korpora des Lettgallischen schränken die Anwendung dieser Kriterien leider ein. In Hinblick auf Wohlgemuths (2009) Typologie der Integration entlehnter Verben stellen die lettgallischen Verben auf *-avuot* ein kleines Paradox dar. Bei den aus slawischen Sprachen entlehnten Verben handelt es sich um direkte Integration, denn es wird ja kein wortbildendes Element hinzugefügt. Dennoch enthalten diese Verben ein innerhalb der Replikasprache interpretierbares, produktives Derivationssuffix, was sie wie das Ergebnis indirekter Integration aussehen lässt.

Die Technik der indirekten Integration mit einem heimischen Suffix wird bei der Integration slawischer Verben ins Lettgallische nicht genutzt. Das ist insofern bemerkenswert, als im Standardlettischen die Integration von Verben mit dem Kausativsuffix *-in-* eine wichtige Rolle spielt, ebenso im Litauischen (Pakerys 2013; Kožanov 2015: 375–375). Im heutigen Lettgallischen finden wir, vermutlich nach standardlettischem Vorbild, neue internationale oder englische Lehnverben mit diesem Suffix, aber kaum Slawismen.

4 Entlehnte Präfixe

Im Baltischen sind wie im Slawischen Präfixe das wichtigste verbale Wortbildungsmittel. Sie haben lexikalische und deiktische Bedeutungen und drücken Aktionsarten aus. Eine rein perfektivierende Wirkung ist selten. Das Inventar ist etwas kleiner als etwa im Russischen oder Polnischen: Das Standardlitauische hat zwölf, das Standardlettische elf Verbalpräfixe. In Tabelle 2 sind die standardlettischen Präfixe mit ihren lettgallischen Entsprechungen aufgeführt. Für einen Vergleich der Inventare baltischer und slawischer Sprachen siehe Kožanov (2015: 25–30) und Kožanov (2016: 364).

Ein weiteres wichtiges verbales Wortbildungselement ist der Reflexivmarker. Im Standardlettischen erscheint dieser immer am Ende einer Verbform, im Lettgallischen und Litauischen wird er vor den Stamm gesetzt, wenn das Verb präfigiert ist (Tmesis). Dabei hat er je nach Dialekt die Form *-sa-* oder *-za-*. Wenn das Präfix auf *z* endet, fusioniert es mit dem Reflexivmarker. Beispiele aus dem Lettgallischen: *dūt* 'geben', *deve* 'gab', *dūt-īs* 'sich begeben', *devē-s* 'begab sich', *at-dūt* 'zurückgeben', *pa-sa-dūt* 'sich ergeben', *pa-sa-deve* 'ergab sich', *iza-dūt* 'gelingen', *iza-deve* 'gelang', etc.

Weitere Präfixe im Lettgallischen, die keine Entsprechung im Standardlettischen haben, sind entweder aus dem Slawischen entlehnt oder verdanken ihre Erhaltung indirekt slawischem Lehneinfluss. Dies sind: *da-* 'hin; (bis) zu; hinzu', *pad-/pod-* 'unter; heran, herbei' *pro-* 'vorbei; entlang; durch' und *roz-* 'durch; auseinander; zer-, ver-, ent-'. Bei *da-* und *pro-* ist bis heute umstritten, ob es sich um materielle Entlehnungen oder um nur im Osten des lettischen Sprachgebietes erhaltene ererbte Morpheme handelt, während *pad-/pod-* und *roz-* allgemein als Entlehnungen angesehen werden. Diese Unterscheidung ist für den Ausbau der lettgallischen Standardsprache bedeutsam. Das Präfix *da-*, das auch in einigen

Tabelle 2. Gemeinlettisches Inventar an verbalen Präfixen

Standardlettisch	Lettgallisch	Lokale oder lokaldeiktische Bedeutung
aiz-	aiz-	'hinter; weg, ab'
ap-	ap-	'herum'
at-	at-	'her; hin'
ie-	ī-	'hinein, herein'
iz-	iz-	'hinaus, heraus; weg', LTG auch 'hinauf'[1]
nuo-	nū	'hinunter, herunter'
pa-	pa-	'unter'
pār-	puor-	'über; hinweg'
pie-	pī	'an; (hin)zu'
sa-	sa-	'zusammen'
uz-	(uz-)[1]	'hinauf, herauf'

nicht-lettgallischen Mundarten des Lettischen belegt ist, wird von den meisten lettgallischen Sprachpflegern als ererbtes Präfix angesehen und daher für den Standard akzeptiert – im Gegensatz zum Litauischen, wo *da-* als Slawismus und daher nichtstandardsprachlich gilt. Zu diesem Präfix und den Streit um seine Herkunft im Lettgallischen und Litauischen siehe Reķēna (2008 [1967]), Breidaks (2007a [1969]; 2007b [1972]), Wiemer (2009) und Kožanov (2013; 2015: 293–311; 2014). Umgekehrt wird LTG *pro-* nur von wenigen als ererbte Entsprechung von Litauisch *pra-* angesehen (so Breidaks 2007a [1969]). Dagegen spricht jedoch die Form *pro-* (nicht *pra-*) und das Fehlen des Präfixes in denjenigen Mundarten, die den meisten Kontakt mit dem Litauischen hatten. Das einzige im ganzen lettgallischen Sprachgebiet verbreitete Verb, das mit *pro-* oder *pra-* beginnt, ist *propuļt/prapuļt* 'verschwinden; zugrunde gehen'; es wird jedoch nicht als präfigiert analysiert, da es kein einfaches **puļt* gibt. Wenn es ein Relikt aus einer Zeit ist, in der es im Gemeinlettischen noch ein Präfix *pra-* gab, so muss diese Zeit sehr weit zurückliegen.[1]

Formal verhalten sich die entlehnten Präfixe genau wie heimische. Sie werden häufig mit dem Reflexivmarker kombiniert, wobei *roz-* mit *-sa-* zu *roza-* verschmilzt (analog zu *iza-* und *aiza-*). Interessant ist, dass nur bei einem dieser vier Präfixe Vokalschwankungen zu beobachten sind, die auf unterschiedliche Modellsprachen oder auf Alternationen innerhalb einer Modellsprache hinweisen können: bei *pad-/pod-*. Die anderen drei kommen nur in einer Form vor (*da-, pro-, roz-*), unabhängig davon, wie der Vokal im slawischen Modellwort realisiert wird. Dies zeugt davon, dass sie als Präfixe einen Platz im lettgallischen System haben.

Nach den von Seifart (2015) aufgestellten Kriterien können die entlehnten Präfixe (ob nun zwei, drei oder alle vier) als direkte Entlehnungen klassifiziert werden, denn es gibt zumindest im heutigen Lettgallischen keine entlehnten präfigierten Verben, in denen das Präfix als solches hätte analysiert und abgetrennt werden können – so, wie das Suffix *-av-* in entlehnten Verben erkannt werden konnte. Die Präfixe *da-, pad-, pro-* und *roz-* werden fast ausschließlich mit ererbten Verben oder mit bereits gut integrierten Lehnwörtern kombiniert. Gardani (2021) hat kürzlich, wie bereits einige vor ihm, die Möglichkeit einer direkten oder unvermittelten Entlehnung (in seiner Terminologie *immediate borrowing*)

---

1 Das Präfix *uz-* ist in vielen Varietäten des Lettgallischen mit *iz-* zusammengefallen.

von Affixen und die Berechtigung von Seifarts Opposition angezweifelt. Seiner Ansicht nach verlangt die Übernahme eines Affixes immer ein komplexes Modell, d.h. ein vollständiges Wort, aus dem das Affix herausgelöst wird (Gardani 2021: 142). Meines Erachtens schließt die Erfordernis einer Analyse aber direkte Übernahme nicht aus. Indirekte (lexikalisch vermittelte) Entlehnung liegt vor, wenn das komplexe Wort Teil der Replikasprache ist, und sei es nur im Idiolekt eines Sprechers. Im klassischen Fall der indirekten Affixentlehnung ist das Modell bereits in die Replikasprache integriert und seine Zerlegung erfordert keine Kenntnis der Modellsprache. Bei direkter (unmittelbarer) Affixentlehnung zerlegen Zweisprachige hingegen ein modellsprachliches Wort und übernehmen einen Bestandteil in die Replikasprache, während andere Bestandteile mit bereits vorhandenem Material gleichgesetzt, d.h. übersetzt werden. Beispielsweise kann nach einem polnischen Modellwort *roz-bić* 'zerschlagen' direkt ein gleichbedeutendes lettgallisches *roz-sist* gebildet werden. Dies ist ein mögliches Szenario, das das Fehlen von mit ihrem Präfix entlehnten Verben erklären würde. Seifarts (2015) Unterscheidung erscheint mir daher angemessen, zumal er sie nicht kategorisch auffasst, sondern als Pole einer Skala. Wenn die Übernahme slawischer Präfixe ins Lettgallische (und ähnlich ins Litauische) ganz am ›direkten‹ Pol dieser Skala liegt, so wird das nicht nur durch die verbreitete Zweisprachigkeit, sondern auch durch verschiedene sprachinterne Faktoren begünstigt:

1. Die slawischen Verbalpräfixe haben eine hohe Tokenfrequenz und sind leicht abtrennbar, sie können daher schon bei geringerer Kenntnis der Sprachen erkannt werden;
2. slawische und baltische Sprachen haben ähnliche Systeme, so dass Präfixe leicht als solche indentifiziert und integriert werden können.

Die materielle Entlehnung gleich mehrerer Präfixe bestätigt die in Seifarts (2017) empirischer Studie von Affixentlehnung in hundert Sprachen festgestellte Tendenz, dass Affixe häufiger in kleinen Gruppen entlehnt werden als einzeln. Arkadiev/Kozhanov (Ms.) streichen heraus, dass Litauisch und Lettgallisch dieselben Präfixe aus dem Slawischen entlehnt haben (wobei sie *da-*, *pad-/pod-* und *roz-* nennen, aber nicht *pro-*). Sie begründen dies damit, dass die entlehnten Präfixe Lücken im baltischen Präverbsystem füllen; so auch Kožanov (2015: 341). Dies mag ein begünstigender Umstand sein, aber zumindest im Lettgallischen ist die Situation komplizierter. Die in Spalte 3 von Tabelle 2 gegebenen Übersetzungen geben nur einen kleinen Teil der Bedeutungen wieder, in denen die Präfixe gebraucht werden, und es gibt diverse Überschneidungen. Auch die entlehnten Präfixe haben mehrere Bedeutungen und sind nicht klar gegeneinander und gegen die anderen Präfixe abgegrenzt, insbesondere in ihren nicht-lokalen Bedeutungen. Vor allem für *roz-* und *pro-* gilt, dass sie gerade durch ihre Polysemie so gut ins lettgallische System passen und von manchen Sprechern mehr aus stilistischen Gründen verwendet werden als aus Mangel an Ausdrucksmitteln. Unabhängig davon, ob diese Präfixe durch Entlehnung in die Sprache gekommen oder Reflexe ererbten Materials sind, werden sie von heutigen Sprechern mit Slawismen assoziiert und können als Marker des Abstands zum Standardlettischen verwendet werden.

Bei der Verwendung der Präfixe *roz-*, *pro-* und *pad-/pod-* im Lettgallischen liegt häufig eine genaue semantische Entsprechung zu einem slawischen Modellwort vor, die sich nicht unmittelbar aus der Bedeutung von Verb und Präfix ergibt. Viele der Belege im Korpus MuLa scheinen Ad-hoc-Bildungen zu sein, bei denen ein heimisches Verb, das dem slawischen semantisch entspricht, mit dem Lehnpräfix, das dem des Modellworts materiell entspricht, kombiniert wird. Oft ist nicht zu bestimmen, ob es sich um ein Wort handelt, das mehreren Sprechern geläufig ist, oder eine spontane Bildung. In Beispiel (9) sind die Verben LTG ***pro-***

sa-runuot 'sich verplappern' und ***roz-lerkšēt*** 'ausplaudern' belegt.² Das erste wurde auch in anderen Quellen gefunden, das zweite könnte spontan nach Russisch ***раз-болта-ть*** 'ausplaudern' gebildet worden sein. Die verbreitete Zweisprachigkeit und die Ähnlichkeit der Systeme machen solche Bildungen in jedem Fall verständlich.

(9) Čut **na-pro-za-run-ov-i** par tū viersi. Tev
 almost NEG-PVB-RFL-speak-ST3-2SG about DEM.ACC.SG bull.ACC.SG 2SG.DAT
 vusu **roz-l̦erkš-ie-t** vāg.
 all.ACC.SG PVB-babble-ST1-INF necessary
 'Jetzt hättest du dich beinahe wegen dem Bullen **verplappert**. Du musst immer alles **ausplaudern**.'

(MuLa, Danskovīte)

Beispiel (9) stammt aus einer Komödie. Die Stücke der Autorin Danskovīte (mit bürgerlichem Namen AnitaLočmele) werden vorwiegend von Laientheatern aufgeführt. Sie sind in Mundart geschrieben und enthalten viele Slawismen, insbesondere kleine Wörter (Adverbien, Interjektionen, Partikeln) wie *čut* + Negation 'fast' in Beispiel (9), sowie eben die Präfixe *pro-* und *roz-*. Diese Präfixe sind in der Mundart gebräuchlich, ihre Häufigkeit in den Texten von Danskovīte ist jedoch auffällig: Sie sind Stilmittel zur Kennzeichnung des ›einfachen‹ Menschen vom Land, zugleich ein Merkmal, das den lettgallischen Dialekt von der lettischen Standardsprache unterscheidet. Als solche werden sie von verschiedenen Autoren eingesetzt. Die Bildungen mit *pad-/pod-*, *pro-* und *roz-* sind allen Sprechern verständlich, werden aber nicht von allen gebraucht. Diese Präfixe haben daher einen besonderen Status im Sprachsystem. In stilistisch neutraler Sprache kommen sie kaum vor, und sie sind auch selten in Wörterbüchern aufgeführt. Das umfangreiche Wörterbuch von Bērzkalns (2007) enthält nur ein einziges Verb mit einem dieser drei Präfixe: LTG *pro-sal̦t* 'erkälten'. Dieses Verb wurde bisher in keiner anderen Quelle gefunden. Auch in Leikuma (2013) ist nur ein solches Verb enthalten und als mundartlich gekennzeichnet: LTG *pro-spiel̦uot* 'verspielen'; es ist aber auch anderswo belegt. Das Wörterbuch von Lukaševičs (2011), in dem viele Slawismen aufgeführt sind, enthält ein Verb mit *pro-* (nämlich LTG *pro-laist* 'begleiten; nicht bemerken, sich entgehen lassen'), drei Verben mit *pod-* (*pod-īt* 'herangehen', *pod-saceit* 'vorsagen' und das in russischer Form angegebene und im Lettgallischen nicht analysierbare *podjegoritj* 'betrügen'), aber keines mit *roz-*, obwohl in Texten des Autors verschiedene Verben mit diesem Präfix zu finden sind. Dies ist ein weiteres Indiz dafür, dass mit *roz-* präfigierte Verben häufig ad hoc gebildet und nicht als feste Bestandteile des Wortschatzes angesehen werden.

Um ein besseres Bild von der Verbreitung und Verwendung der drei Präfixe zu erhalten, habe ich in verschiedenen schriftlichen Quellen nach Belegen gesucht und diese in einem elektronischen Wörterbuch zusammengestellt.³ Es wurden nur Verben aufgenommen, deren Stamm auch unpräfigiert vorkommt, d. h. nicht die oben erwähnten *podjegoritj* 'betrügen' und *propul̦t* 'verschwinden' (letzteres ist in allen Quellen belegt). Die Sammlung umfasst 124 Verben; die Anzahl der in den einzelnen Quellen gefundenen Verben ist auf der folgenden Seite in Tabelle 3 zu sehen. Dabei handelt es sich um Lexeme (Types). Zur Tokenfrequenz komme ich im Anschluss zu sprechen. Die Werte in Tabelle 3 belegen zwar eine relativ große Zahl an Verben mit *roz-* in Texten, aber dennoch enthält keines der Wörterbücher auch nur ein Verb mit diesem Präfix. Verben mit *pad-/pod-* sind wenig belegt in

---

2 Die in (9) belegte Infinitivform *rozl̦erkšiet* zeigt eine mundartliche Form des stammbildenden Suffixes und mit der Verwendung von *l̦* vor *e* eine Abweichung von der Standardorthographie.
3 Frei zugänglich unter diesem Link.

Tabelle 3. Anzahl belegter Verblexeme mit den Präfixen LTG *pad-*, *pro-* und *roz-*

Wörterbücher	pad-/pod-	pro-	roz-
Bērzkalns (2007)	0	1	0
Leikuma (2013)	0	1	0
Lukaševičs (2011)	2 (*pod-*)	1	0
Glossare			
Jūrdžs (1999 [1916])	0	6	7
Kursīte/Stafecka (2003)	0	2	3
ADT	5 (2 *pad-*, 3 *pod-*)	5	8
Korpora			
Ulanowska (2011 [1895])	5 (*pad-*)	2	21
MuLa2012	15 (überwiegend *pod-*)	25	44
Alle Quellen (Lexeme)	25	31	68

älteren und mundartgeprägten Quellen, finden sich aber etwas häufiger in den neueren Texten, die im Korpus MuLa enthalten sind.

Nur zwanzig der 124 gefundenen Verben (16 %) sind in mehr als einer der acht Quellen belegt: Fünf Verben fanden sich in drei der Quellen und fünfzehn in zwei. Zu den in drei oder zwei Quellen belegten Verben gehören präfigierte Formen frequenter Bewegungsverben wie LTG *īt* 'gehen' (*proīt* 'vorbeigehen', *rozaīt* 'auseinandergehen', *padīt* 'herangehen'), *skrīt* 'rennen' (*proskrīt* 'vorbeirennen', *rozskrīt* 'hindurchrennen; vorbeirennen; losrennen'), *krist* 'fallen' (*prokrist* 'hindurchfallen', *rozkrist* 'hindurchfallen; zerfallen') und *dzeit* 'treiben, jagen' (*prodzeit* 'vertreiben, fortjagen', *rozdzeit* 'verjagen, vertreiben; antreiben'). Hier haben die Präfixe lokale Bedeutungen, und die Zusammensetzungen sind transparent. Auffällig ist auch die Bedeutungsüberlappung von Präfigierungen mit *pro-* und mit *roz-*, die beide 'hindurch' und 'fort, los' bedeuten können.

Im Korpus »MuLa2012« sind 80 der 124 gefundenen Verben belegt, davon werden 60 nur von einem Autor gebraucht, und meist nur ein einziges Mal (53 Verben). Diese Zahlen zeigen, dass die Präfixe LTG *pad-/pod-*, *pro-* und *roz-* produktiv sind und dass vermutlich viele Ad-hoc-Bildungen darunter sind, die, wie oben beschrieben, unmittelbar einem slawischen Modell folgen können. Nur acht Verben werden im Korpus von drei und mehr Autoren gebraucht. Darunter sind wieder Bewegungsverben, in denen das Präfix lokale Bedeutung hat und die Bildung transparent ist (*proīt* 'vorbeigehen', *probraukt* 'vorbeifahren', *prodzeit* 'verjagen', *rozplēst* '(Arme, Beine) auseinanderbreiten, (Mund, Augen) aufreißen'), aber auch solche, bei denen ein slawisches Modell offensichtlich ist: *roz-stuosteit* 'erzählen' (LTG *stuosteit* bedeutet bereits 'erzählen') nach RUS *рас-сказать/рас-сказывать* 'erzählen', und LTG *pod-turēt* 'unterstützen; erhalten' (mit LTG *turēt* 'halten'), nach RUS *под-держать/под-держивать* 'unterstützen' und vielleicht auch POL *pod-trzymać/pod-trzymywać* 'aufrechterhalten'. Das Verb LTG *podturēt* 'unterstützen' ist mit insgesamt fünfzehn Belegen von fünf verschiedenen Autoren eines der am besten belegten der untersuchten Verben im Korpus MuLa. Allerdings ergibt eine nähere Analyse der Belege, dass ein großer Teil davon aus demselben Kontext und von jungen Autoren stammt, die untereinander bekannt sind und sich sprachlich gegenseitig beeinflussen (sie gehören zu einem sozialen Netzwerk innerhalb der Sprachgemeinschaft). Das Verb LTG *probraukt* 'vorbeifahren u. a.' hat nur fünf Belege, die aber von fünf verschiedenen Autoren aus unterschiedlichen Kontexten stammen, was ihm einen festeren Platz in der gesamten Sprachgemeinschaft attestiert.

5 Zusammenfassung der Ergebnisse

In dieser Arbeit wurden vier verschiedene Phänomene untersucht, die die Integration entlehnten Materials im verbalen Bereich betreffen: Die Einfügung russischer flektierter Verbformen in eine lettgallische Konstruktion während des Sprechens, die Eingliederung slawischer Verbalstämme in den Wortschatz, die Entwicklung eines Verbalsuffixes -av- und die Verwendung slawischer Präfixe. Es handelt sich um vier verschiedene Techniken, sodass diese kleine Studie einen guten Einblick in die vielfältigen Aspekte materieller Entlehnung gibt. In jedem der Bereiche zeigte sich zudem, wie die strukturelle Nähe der beteiligten Sprachen zum einen die Techniken der Integration begünstigt, zum anderen durch die Entlehnungen noch zunimmt. Ferner wurden Spezifika der Integration verbaler Elemente deutlich, im Unterschied zu Entlehung von Substantiven.

In Abschnitt 2 wurde die Integration kompletter russischer Verbformen in eine lettgallische Äußerung beschrieben. Diese Technik liegt auf einem Kontinuum zwischen Code-Switching und Entlehnung. Die Integration russischer Flexionsformen wurde nur bei Verben beobachtet, während einzelne Substantive mit lettgallischen Kasusaffixen versehen werden. Ähnliche Satzkonstruktionen im Russischen und Lettgallischen machen die Integration leichter: An einer bestimmten Stelle im Satz wird z. B. »ein Verb im Infinitiv« oder »eine Futurform der zweiten Person Singular« verlangt, und der mehrsprachige Sprecher kann diese aus seinem Repertoire auswählen. Im Lettgallischen tritt diese Technik nur bei Ad-hoc-Entlehnungen auf. Dies könnte der erste Schritt zu einer Subklassenbildung im Flexionssystem sein, wie sie in einigen wenigen, besonders intensiven Kontaktsituationen dokumentiert ist (Wohlgemuth 2009; Matras 2015). Im Lettgallischen bleibt es bei diesem ersten Schritt. Es wäre interessant zu untersuchen, ob und wie häufig diese Technik heute auch von jüngeren Sprechern verwendet wird, beispielsweise im Slang, jedoch ist dafür bisher kein geeignetes Untersuchungsmaterial vorhanden.

Die dauerhafte Entlehnung verbaler Stämme wurde in Abschnitt 3 besprochen. Zu ihrer Integration in das lettgallische System ist die Allokation in eine Stammklasse erforderlich, für die das slawische Modell einen Hinweis gibt: Je nach Modell wird ein stammbildendes Element mit hinterem Vokal oder Diphthong (Slawisch a, o, Lettgallisch uo, selten ā) oder mit vorderem Vokal (Slawisch u, ы, e, Lettgallisch ē oder ie) gewählt. Die Verwendung eines zusätzlichen Ableitungssuffix (wie im Standardlettischen -in-) ist in slawischen Lehnverben im Lettgallischen kaum belegt. Ein solches Ableitungssuffix hat sich jedoch aus dem bereits integrierten Material entwickelt: Durch die Häufigkeit entlehnter Verben auf -avuot (mit -uo- als stammbildendem Suffix und -t als Infinitivendung) sowie der gleichzeitigen Entlehnung von Substantiven oder Adjektiven mit derselben Wurzel konnte -av- als verbales Ableitungssuffix identifiziert werden. Einige Sprecher verwenden dieses Suffix produktiv auch mit nichtslawischem lexikalischem Material. Strukturell ist es nicht notwendig, aber es hat einen bestimmten pragmatischen Wert: Es signalisiert eine Neubildung und eine typisch lettgallische Form in Opposition zum Standardlettischen.

Eine wohl noch stärkere Signalwirkung haben die aus dem Slawischen entlehnten Präfixe pad-/pod-, pro- und roz-, die der Gegenstand von Abschnitt 4 waren. Sie werden nahezu ausschließlich mit bereits vorhandenen Verbalstämmen verbunden, und es ist unwahrscheinlich, dass sie durch Analyse von Lehnwörtern entstanden sind. Viel eher sind sie durch eine Analyse des Modellworts direkt als Präfixe entlehnt worden. Dies wurde sicher dadurch begünstigt, dass slawische und baltische Sprachen ähnliche Verbalpräfixsysteme haben. Außerdem sind Präfixe weniger fest mit dem Stamm verbunden, was ihre Ablösung einfacher macht. In älteren oder konservativeren Varietäten des Lettgallischen begegnen die genannten Präfixe zumeist in lokaler Bedeutung und füllen dabei teilweise Lücken im System heimischer Präfixe. Wie bei den entlehnten Stämmen kann das Modell aus dem Polnischen, Belarussischen oder Russischen stammen. Heutige Autoren verwenden *pod-*, *pro-* und *roz-* hingegen in vielen verschiedenen Bedeutungen, häufig direkt nach einem slawischen (zumeist russischen) Modell. Obwohl relativ viele Verben mit einem dieser Präfixe in mündlichen und schriftlichen Texten belegt sind, enthalten Wörterbücher nur einige wenige. Bei der Verwendung in Texten ist häufig nicht zu entscheiden, ob es sich um eine Ad-hoc-Bildung nach slawischem Modell oder um ein präfigiertes Verb handelt, das bereits im Wortschatz zumindest eines Teils der Sprachgemeinschaft etabliert ist.

Die entlehnten Präfixe sorgen für Dynamik im verbalen Wortschatz. Wie das Suffix *-av-*, aber noch stärker und häufiger, signalisieren Sprecher damit die Eigenständigkeit des Lettgallischen, markieren eine Abgrenzung gegenüber dem Standardlettischen und bejahen Mehrsprachigkeit als Teil ihrer Identität. Im verbalen Bereich scheinen Wortbildungselemente diese Funktion besser erfüllen zu können als lexikalische Wurzeln und Stämme, denn die Zahl entlehnter Verben (d. h. verbaler Stämme) ist nicht groß, als Lexeme werden viel häufiger Substantive und Adverbien entlehnt. Der Vorteil entlehnter Affixe kann darin liegen, dass Neubildungen leicht verständlich sind: der lexikalische und der flexionsmorphologische Teil gehören zum lettgallischen System, das Präfix hat eine mehr oder weniger vage Bedeutung (das Suffix *-av-* hat gar keine), die im Kontext profiliert wird. Wenn auch viele der neuen Präfixbildungen ein russisches Modell haben, sind für ihr Verständnis keine guten Russischkenntnisse notwendig. Würden ganze Verben ad hoc entlehnt und integriert (d. h. mit stammbildendem Suffix und Flexionsmorphemen versehen), wäre ein höherer Grad an Zweisprachigkeit bei Sprechern und Hörern erforderlich, außerdem wäre der Aufwand des Kodierens und Dekodierens höher. Bei aktiver Zweisprachigkeit kann es stattdessen in Situationen, in denen beide Sprachen aktiviert sind, zur Ad-hoc-Entlehnung kompletter Verbformen kommen.

6 Nachweise

6.1 Sprachen und Abkürzungen in den Glossen

BEL	Belarussisch	DEM	Demonstrativpronomen	PA	Partizip aktiv
LTG	Lettgallisch			PFV	perfektiv
LVS	Standardlettisch	DIM	Diminutiv	PL	Plural
POL	Polnisch	F	feminin	PRS	Präsens
RUS	Russisch	FUT	Futur	PST	Präteritum
1, 2, 3	erste, zweite, dritte Person	GEN	Genitiv	PVB	Verbalpräfix
		IMP	Imperativ	RFL	Reflexivmarker
ACC	Akkusativ	INF	Infinitiv	SG	Singular
ADD	additive Partikel oder Konjunktion	LOC	Lokativ	ST1	stammbildende Suffixe
		M	maskulin	ST2	
CAUS	Kausativ	NEG	Negation	ST3	
DAT	Dativ	NOM	Nominativ	SUF	sonstiges Suffix
DEF	definit	NPST	non-past		

6.2 Quellen

6.2.1 Gedruckte Titel

ADT (1983), Jokubauska, N. (Hrsg.), *Augšzemnieku dialekta teksti: Latgaliskās izloksnes* [Hochlettische Dialekttexte: Lettgallische Mundarten], Riga: Zinātne.

Bērzkalns, Anatolijs (2007), *Latgaļu volūdas vōrdu krōjums* [Wortschatz der lettgallischen Sprache], Rēzekne: Latgolas Kulturas centra izdevnīceiba. (Lettgallisch-deutsches Wörterbuch.)

Evangelia toto anno (2004), *Evangelia toto anno 1753: Pirmā latgaliešu grāmata* [Das erste lettgallische Buch], Faksimile mit Wortindex und einem Nachwort von Anna Stafecka, Rīga: LU Latviešu valodas instiūts.

Jūrdžs, Andryvs (1999), *Myužeygays kalinders* [Ewiger Kalender] [1916], mit einer Einleitung und einem Glossar herausgegeben von Anna Stafecka, Rēzekne: Latgales Kultūras centra izdevniecība. (1916 handschriftlich verbreitetes Werk.)

Kursīte, Janīna / Anna **Stafecka** (2003), Hrsg., *Latgale: Valoda, literatūra, folklora* [Lettgallen: Sprache, Literatur, Folklore], Anthologie, Rēzekne: Latgales Kultūras centra izdevniecība.

Lukaševičs, Valentīns (2011), *Latgaliešu-latviešu vārdnīca* [Lettgallisch-lettisches Wörterbuch], Daugavpils: Daugavpils Universitātes akadēmiskais apgāds »Saule«.

Rēķena, Antoņina (1998), *Kalupes izloksnes vārdnīca* [Wörterbuch der Mundart von Kalupe], 2 Bde., Rīga: Latviešu valodas institūts.

Ulanowska, Stefanija (2011), »Łotysze Inflant Polskich, a w szczególności z gminy Wielońskiej powiatu Rzeżyckiego. Obraz etnograficzny przez Stefanię Ulanowską. Część III. Zbiór Wiadomości do Antropologii Krajowej, Tom XVIII, Dz. II« [Letten aus dem polnischen Livland, insbesondere aus der Gemeinde Viļāni im Bezirk Rēzekne. Ethnografisches Bild von Stefania Ulanowska. Teil 3. Sammlung von Nachrichten zur Nationalen Anthropologie, Bd. 18, Abt. 2] [Kraków 1895], in Stefanija Uļanovksa, *Pūļu Inflantejis latvīši, i sevišķi Rēzeknis apriņka Viļānu pogosta: Etnografiskys tāluojums*, hrsg. v. Aleksejs Andronovs und Lideja Leikuma, Reiga 2011, S. 232–492, auch digital zugänglich. (Latgalistikys biblioteka 2.)

6.2.2 Digitale Titel

Leikuma (2013), *Lietuviešu-latviešu-latgaliešu vārdnīca* [Litauisch-lettisch-lettgallisches Wörterbuch], erstellt 2011–2013 unter Leitung von Lidija Leikuma, . CLARIN-LV digital library at IMCS, University of Latvia, frei zugängliche digitale Publikation.

MuLa, MuLa 2012, *Mūsdienu latgaliešu tekstu korpuss (MuLa)* [Korpus lettgallischer Texte der Gegenwart »MuLa«, Version 2012], 1 Million Wortformen, frei zugängliche digitale Sammlung.

6.3 Verwendete Literatur

6.3.1 Gedruckte Titel

Alexiadou, Artemis (2017), »Building verbs in language mixing varieties«, *Zeitschrift für Sprachwissenschaft* 36:1, S. 165–192.

Arkadiev, Peter / Axel **Holvoet** / Björn **Wiemer** (2015), »Introduction: Baltic linguistics – state of the art«, in Peter Arkadiev/Axel Holvoet/Björn Wiemer (eds.), *Contemporary Approaches to Baltic Linguistics*, Berlin & Boston: De Gruyter Mouton, S. 1–109.

—, — / Kirill **Kozhanov** (Ms.), »Borrowing of morphology«, submitted to Peter Ackema/ Sabrina Bendjaballah/Eulàlia Bonet/Antonio Fábregas (eds.), *The Wiley Blackwell Companion to Morphology*, version of January 2021.

Auer, Peter (1998), *From Code-Switching via Language Mixing to Fused Lects: Toward a Dynamic Typology of Bilingual Speech*, Konstanz: Universität Konstanz. (InLiSt 6.)

Backus, Ad / Margreet **Dorleijn** (2009), »Loan translations versus codeswitching«, in Bullock, Barbara E. / Almeida Jacqueline Toribio (eds.), *The Cambridge Handbook of Linguistic Code-Switching*, Cambridge: Cambridge University Press, S. 75–94.

[**Breidaks**, Antons] Антон Брейдак (2006), »Латгальский язык« [Das Lettgallische], hrsg. v. A. V. Andronov / L. Leikuma, in Vladimir N. Toporov et al. (Hrsg.), *Языки мира: Балтийские языки*, Moskva: Academia, S. 193–213.

—, — (2007a), »Augšzemnieku dialekta latgalisko izlokšņu dialektālā leksika un tās vēsturiskie sakari« [Die dialektale Lexik der lettgalischen Mundarten des Oberlettischen und ihre historischen Zusammenhänge] [1969], in Antons Breidaks, *Darbu izlase*, Bd. 1, hrsg. v. Ilga Jansone et al., Rīga: LU Latviešu valodas institūts, S. 39–238. (Dissertation zur Erlangung des Grades eines Kandidaten der Wissenschaften, Universität Riga 1969.)

[—, —] Антон Брейдак (2007b), »Происхождение предлога *da* и приставки *da-* в балтийских языках« [Der Ursprung der Präposition *da* und der Vorsilbe *da-* in den baltischen Sprachen] [1972], in Antons Breidaks, *Darbu izlase*, Bd. 2, hrsg. v. Ilga Jansone et al., Rīga: LU Latviešu valodas institūts, S. 216–220. (Zuerst erschienen in Latvijas PSR ZA Vēstnis 1972, Nr. 4, S. 137–142.)

Bullock, Barbara E. / Almeida Jacqueline **Toribio** (2009), »Themes in the study of codeswitching«, in Barbara Bullock/Almeida J. Toribio (eds.), *The Cambridge Handbook of Linguistic Code-Switching*, Cambridge: Cambridge University Press, S. 1–17.

Dux, Ryan (2017), »Classifying language contact phenomena: English verbs in German«, *Journal of Germanic Linguistics* 29:4, S. 379–430; auch per DOI.

Endzelīns, Jānis (1971), »Латышские заимствования из славянских языков« [Lettische Entlehnungen aus slawischen Sprachen] [1899], in Jānis Endzelīns, *Darbu izlase*, Bd. 1, Rīga: Zinātne, S. 80–113.

—, — (1979), »Sīkumi / Лингвистические мелочи / Miszellen« [1927], in Jānis Endzelīns, *Darbu izlase*, Bd. 3:1, Rīga: Zinātne, S. 436–443. (Erstmals erschienen in *Filologu biedrības raksti* 7, 1927.)

Forker, Diana (2020), »The late success of Soviet language policy: the integration of Russian verbs in languages of the former Soviet Union«, *International Journal of Bilingualism* 25:1, S. 240–271; auch per DOI.

Friedman, Victor A. (2008), »Codeswitching and code integration in Romani«, in Max Bane / Juan José Bueno Holle / Thomas Grano / April Lynn Grotberg / Yaron McNabb (eds.), *Proceedings from the Annual Meeting of the Chicago Linguistic Society* 44:2, Chicago: Chicago Linguistic Society, S. 123–138.

Gardani, Francesco (2021), »On how morphology spreads«, *Word Structure* 14:2, S. 129–147; auch per DOI.

Hancock, Ian (1992), *Notes on Romani grammar.* 4th edn., London–Austin: Romanestan Publications.

Jankowiak, Mirosław (2009), *Gwary białoruskie na Łotwie w rejonie krasławskim* [Weißrussische Dialekte der Region Krāslava in Lettland], Warszawa: Slawistyczny Ośrodek Wydawniczy.

[**Kožanov**, Kirill] Кирилл Кожанов (2013), »История изучения глагольных префиксов в литовском языке, II« [Geschichte des Studiums der Verbalpräfixe des Litauischen, 2], *Славяноведение* 4, S. 96–102.

[—, —] Kirill Kozhanov (2014), »Priešdėlio *da-* semantika lietuvių kalboje« [Die Semantik des Präfixes *da-* im Litauischen], in Tatjana Civjan / Maria Zavjalova / Artūras Judžentis (eds.), *Baltai ir slavai: dvasinių kultūrų sankirtos*, Vilnius: Versmė, S. 254–274.

[—, —] Кирилл Кожанов (2015), *Балто-славянские ареальные контакты в области глагольной префиксации* [Balto-slawische areale Kontakte im Bereich der Verbalpräfixe], PhD thesis, Москва: Институт славяноведения Российской академии наук.

[—, —] Kirill Kozhanov (2016), »Verbal prefixation and argument structure in Lithuanian«, in Axel Holvoet / Nicole Nau (eds.), *Argument Realization in Baltic*, Amsterdam: John Benjamins, S. 363–402.

Kuņicka, Kristīne (2016), *Latgales poļu valoda kā poļu valodas periferiālais dialekts: paaudžu atšķirību aspekts / Polish language in Latgale as a peripheral dialect of Polish: generational differences*, Summary of PhD thesis, Daugavpils: Daugavpils Universitāte.

Lazdiņa, Sanita / Heiko F. **Marten** / Solvita **Pošeiko** (2011), »The Latgalian language as a regional language in Latvia: a characterisation and implications in the context of languages in Europe«, *Via Latgalica* 3, S. 6–18.

Leikuma, Lidija (1982), »Aizgūto verbu iekļaušanās Izvaltas izlkoksnes sistēmā« [Die Eingliederung entlehnter Verben in das System der Mundart von Izvalta], in L. Orlovska (Hrsg.), *Leksiskas un gramatikas inovācijas*, Riga: Latvijas Valsts universitāte, S. 54–60.

Marten, Heiko F. / Sanita **Lazdiņa** (2016), »Latgalian in Latvia: How a minority language community gains voice during societal negotiations about the status of two major languages«, in Martin Pütz / Neeke Mundt (eds.), *Ideological, Attitudinal and Social Identity Perspectives*, Frankfurt: Peter Lang, S. 195–222.

Matras, Yaron (2007), »The borrowability of structural categories«, in Yaron Matras / Jeanette Sakel (eds.), *Grammatical Borrowing in Cross-Linguistic Perspective*, Berlin: De Gruyter Mouton, S. 31–73.

—, — (2009), *Language contact*, Cambridge: Cambridge University Press.

—, — (2015), »Why is the borrowing of inflectional morphology dispreferred?«, in Francesco Gardani / Peter Arkadiev / Nino Amiridze (eds.), *Borrowed Morphology*, Berlin: De Gruyter Mouton, S. 47–80.

Muysken, Pieter (20139, »Two linguistic systems in contact: grammar, phonology, and lexicon«, in Tej K. Bhatia / William C. Ritchie (eds.), *The Handbook of Bilingualism and Multilingualism*, Chichester and Malden: Wiley-Blackwell, S. 192–215.

Nau, Nicole (1995), *Möglichkeiten und Mechanismen kontaktbewegten Sprachwandels: Unter besonderer Berücksichtigung des Finnischen*, München–Newcastle: Lincom Europa. (Edition Linguistik 8.)

—, — (2011), *A Short Grammar of Latgalian*, München: Lincom Europa. (Languages of the World: Materials 482).

—, — (2012), »Modality in an areal context: the case of a Latgalian dialect«, in Björn Wiemer / Bernhard Wälchli / Björn Hansen (eds.), *Grammatical Replication and Grammatical Borrowing in Language Contact*, Berlin: Mouton de Gruyter, S. 471–514.

Reķēna, Antoņina (2008), »Priedēkļa *da* un palīgvārda *da* nozīmes un lietojums augšzemnieku dialekta izloksnēs salīdzinājuma ar lietuviešu valodu un slāvu valodām« [Bedeutung und Verwendung des Präfixes *da* und des Funktionsworts *da* in den Mundarten des oberlettischen Dialekts im Vergleich zum Litauischen und zu den slawischen Sprachen] [1967], in Antoņina Reķēna, *Raksti valodniecībā, I daļa*, Liepāja: LiePa, S. 153–168. (Zuerst erschienen in *Latviešu valodas teorijas un prakses jautājumi*, Rīga: Zvaigzne, 1967, S. 81–93.)

Seifart, Frank (2015), »Direct and indirect affix borrowing«, in *Language* 91:3, S. 511–532.

—, — (2017), »Patterns of affix borrowing in a sample of 100 languages«, in *Journal of Historical Linguistics* 7:3, S. 389–431.

Smetonienė, Anželika (2015 a), *Lietuvių kalbos priesaginiai veiksmažodžiai, slavizmai ir hibridai (XVI–XVII a. LDK tekstuose)* [Suffixverben, Slavismen und Hybride im Litauischen (in Texten aus dem Großfürstentum Litauen vom 16./17. Jahrhundert)], Diss., Universität Vilnius.

—, — (2015 b), *Suffixed Slavic Loan Verbs and Hybrids of the Lithuanian Language (in the XVI–XVII C. Texts of the Grand Duchy of Lithuania)*. Summary of PhD thesis, Vilnius: Universität Vilnius.

Stolt, Birgit (1964), *Die Sprachmischung in Luthers ›Tischreden‹*, Stockholm: Almqvist & Wiksell.

Šuplinska, Ilga / Sanita **Lazdiņa** (2009), eds., *Valodas Austrumlatvijā: Pētījuma dati un rezultāti / Languages in Eastern Latvia: Data and Results of Survey*, Rēzekne: Rēzeknes Augstskola. (Via Latgalica, Supplement.)

Wichmann, Søren / Jan **Wohlgemuth** (2008), »Loan verbs in a typological perspective«, in Thomas Stolz / Dik Bakker / Rosa Salas Palomo (eds.), *Aspects of Language Contact*, Berlin–New York: De Gruyter Mouton, S. 89–122; auch per DOI.

Wiemer, Björn (2003), »Dialect and language contacts on the territory of the Grand Duchy of Lithuania from the 15th century until 1939«, in: Kurt Braunmüller / Gisella Ferraresi (eds.), *Aspects of Multilingualism in European Language History*, Amsterdam–Philadelphia: Benjamins, S. 105–143.

—, — (2004), »Population linguistics on a micro-scale: lessons to be learnt from Baltic and Slavic dialects in contact«, in Bernd Kortmann (ed.), *Dialectology Meets Typology: Dialect Grammar from a Cross-Linguistic Perspective*, Berlin–New York: Mouton de Gruyter, S. 497–526.

—, — (2009), »Zu entlehnten Präfixen und anderen morphosyntaktischen Slavismen in litauischen Insel- und Grenzmundarten«, in Lenka Scholze / Björn Wiemer (eds.), *Von Zuständen, Dynamik und Veränderung bei Pygmäen und Giganten: Festschrift für Walter Breu zu seinem 60. Geburtstag*, Bochum: Brockmeyer, S. 347–390.

—, — (2013), »Zur arealen Stufung im baltisch-slavischen Kontaktgebiet (und dabei auftretenden methodischen Desideraten)«, in Sebastian Kempgen / Monika Wingender / Norbert Franz / Miranda Jakiša (eds.), *Deutsche Beiträge zum 15. Internationalen Slavistenkongress Minsk 2013*, München: Sagner, S. 313–324.

[—, — / Kirill **Kožanov** / Aksana **Erker**] Б. Вимер / К. А. Кожанов / А. Эркер (2019), »Корпус славянских и балтийских говоров TriMCo: структура, цели и примеры примененя« [Das Korpus slawischer und baltischer Dialekte ›TriMCo‹: Struktur, Ziele und Anwendungsbeispiele], *Балто-Славянские исследования* 20, S. 122–143; auch per DOI.

—, — / Ilja **Seržant** / Aksana **Erker** (2014), »Convergence in the Baltic-Slavic Contact zone: triangulation approach«, in Juliane Besters-Dilger / Cynthia Dermarkar / Stefan Pfänder / Achim Rabus (eds.), *Congruence in Contact-Induced Language Change*, Berlin: De Gruyter, S. 15–42.

Winford, Donald (2003), *An Introduction to Contact Linguistics*, Oxford: Blackwell.

—, — (2010), »Contact and borrowing«, in Raymond Hickey (ed.), *The Handbook of Language Contact*, Oxford: Wiley-Blackwell, S. 170–187.

Wohlgemuth, Jan (2009), *A Typology of Verbal Borrowings*, Berlin–New York: De Gruyter Mouton.

6.3.2 Digitale Titel

Census (2011) = *Tautas skaitīšana 2011: Centrālās statistikas pārvaldes datubaze* [Volkszählung 2011: Datenbank des Zentralen Amtes für Statistik], digitale Ressource.

Pakerys, Jurgis (2014), »Naujųjų skolinių duomenų bazės veiksmažodžių morfologija« [Die Morphologie von Verben der ›Datenbank neuer Lehnwörter‹], in *Taikomoji kalbotyra* 3, digitale Ressource.

Der Südosten Litauens als hybrider Sprachraum? Überlegungen mit Blick auf Polszczyzna Wileńska und Po Prostu

Ein Überblick
von Anastasija Kostiučenko (Greifswald)

Outline

Southeast Lithuania is particularly suitable for researching linguistic contact phenomena in general and the Balto-Slavic contacts in particular. For this very reason, the article investigates how the concept of hybridity being applied in cultural studies can be used to describe and better understand this language area and identity issues. The focus here lies on the Polish idiom (called *polszczyzna wileńska*), a mixed polish-based urban variety commonly used by youth in Vilnius, as well as on the mixed Belarusian-based variety or idiom (called *po prostu*), both de facto showing further internal (socio-) linguistic variation. The article discusses how the idioms spoken in and around Lithuania's capital Vilnius can be sociolinguistically classified and which role both the hybrid language practices and self-attributions like 'the Locals' (called *tutejszy/tutejsi*) play herein.

Gliederung

1	Einleitung und Zielstellung	113
2	»Hybridität« und hybride Sprachpraktiken – ein interdisziplinärer Überblick	114
3	Zur Spezifik der Sprach(en)situation im Südosten Litauens	116
3.1	Wer?	117
3.2	In welcher Sprache / in welchen Sprachen?	119
4	Zusammenfassende Überlegungen zum Potenzial des Begriffs der Hybridität bezogen auf den Südosten Litauens	122
5	Fazit und Ausblick	123
6	Nachweise	124
6.1	Primärliteratur	124
6.2	Sekundärliteratur	124
	6.2.1 Gedruckte Titel ... 124 — 6.2.2 Digitale Titel ...127	

> *Gdzie nie kręć się, na majówce w Wilnie wszędzie wsie bazariat po polsku. Na te kilka dni robi się taka cipa mała Polska – prikoł taki. Szkoda, kanieszna, że turyści najczęściej takie kazły w kiedach, które ryczą na całą ulicę, jakby ich nikt nie rozumiał i zawsze nie dawolne, że cipa w Wilnie wsio drogo. Bywali młode panienki z tymi turystami, ale my ich jakoś nie kadrili, bo oni zawsze wyglądali rozumniejsze, i rozmawiali dużo ładniej niż my. Ja też jakoś wstydził się do nich zagadać, bo rozmawiał po tutejszemu i cziuju ich nie weźmisz tak prosto, bo trzeba duzo gadać pra różne „ważne" ciemy.*
> — Bartosz Połoński, *Robczik*, Kapitel »Majówka« [Maifeiertage]; eine Übersetzung des Zitats folgt in Abschnitt 3.2 meines Beitrags

1 Einleitung und Zielstellung

Das Motto dieses Beitrags ist ein Zitat aus dem Roman *Robczik*[1] des Vilniusser Autors Bartosz Połoński (*1981) und es illustriert eine der gemischten Sprechweisen bzw. Sprachpraktiken, die im Südosten Litauens und insbesondere in der Gegend von Vilnius und in der Stadt selbst in dieser oder ähnlicher Form bei den Sprecher*innen slawischer Sprachen beobachtet und insofern als ›prototypisch‹ für diesen Landstrich angesehen werden können. Inwiefern hierbei aus der Sicht der Soziolinguistik von einer hybriden Sprechweise oder einem hybriden Idiom die Rede sein kann, soll im vorliegenden Beitrag diskutiert werden. Połoński selbst meint, sein *Robczik* sei in einem »präzedenzlosen« (*neturinti precedenty*), zeitgenössischen urbanen Idiom verfasst – in »der Jugendsprache der Hiesigen« (*tuteišių jaunimo kalba*), die in der Region Vilnius entstanden sei und von den dortigen jungen Leuten gesprochen werde (Połoński 2020: 13; s. auch Robczik 2021 [digital]). Auf die Problematik der Bezeichnungen poln. *tutejszy* 'der Hiesige' bzw. *tutejsi* 'die Hiesigen', lit. *vietiniai/čionykščiai* 'die Hiesigen' in Kontext von sprachlicher Varianz gehe ich ausführlich weiter unten ein. Obwohl Połoński von Hause aus kein Sprachwissenschaftler ist, erkennt er, dass die fragliche Jugendsprache nicht einheitlich ist und dass zwei Hauptversionen bzw. Sprachvarianten zu unterscheiden seien: Eine »offizielle Version« (*oficiali tuteišių kalba*), die eine oft nicht gelungene Annäherung an das Polnische in Polen darstelle und daher für ›die Hiesigen‹ etwas »künstlich klinge« (*skamba dirbtinai*), sowie eine eher »dialektale Version« (*dialektinė kalba*), die beispielsweise im Alltag oder auf dem Schulhof gebraucht werde (Połoński 2020: 13–14). Połoński hat auf alle Fälle in dem Punkt recht, dass das gemeinte Idiom eine außergewöhnliche Kombination (system-)linguistischer Merkmale besitzt. Aber auch aus der Perspektive der Soziolinguistik stellt es ein wichtiges Untersuchungsobjekt dar, weil sein Gebrauch realiter weit über das von Połoński beschriebene Verbreitungsgebiet und die von ihm genannte Zielgruppe hinausgeht. Wie jedes andere Idiom erfüllt es für seine Sprecher*innen auch spezifische Funktionen und ist daher domänentypisch.

Aus den genannten Gründen verwundert es nicht, dass seit Jahrzehnten ein großes linguistisches Interesse an der Erforschung der sprachlichen Verhältnisse im Südosten Litauens besteht (insbesondere in der litauischen und polnischen Linguistik, aber zunehmend

---

[1] Zum Titel: Poln. *Robczik*, lit. *Robčikas* ist eine Koseform des Vornamens Robert bzw. Robertas. Zum Roman: *Robczik* befindet sich noch im Entstehungsprozess. Veröffentlicht wurden bis November 2021 acht Kapitel bzw. Auszüge. Das ist der Homepage des Autors zu entnehmen. Eine Übersetzung des Romans ins Litauische ist für 2023 angekündigt; so steht es auf der Facebookseite für *Robczik*.

auch im deutschsprachigen Raum) und dass sich die Sprachwissenschaftler*innen gerade von dem besonderen Polnisch des Landstrichs faszinieren lassen.[2] Davon zeugt die Fülle an internationaler Fachliteratur, die bis dato zu diesem Sprachraum vorliegt, auch wenn einige der Fragen, die bisher gestellt und diskutiert wurden, nicht unumstritten geblieben sind – so bspw. ausgerechnet die beiden, für Slawistik und Baltistik zentralen Fragen, wie die linguistischen Verhältnisse zwischen Balten und Slawen generell zu interpretieren seien (Kalėdienė 2017: 21) und wie die einzelnen Idiome und Varietäten, die in den mehrsprachigen Gegenden Litauens gesprochen werden, soziolinguistisch zu typologisieren seien. An die umstrittenen Fragen knüpft auch der vorliegende Beitrag an, dessen Ziel darin besteht, der Frage nachzugehen, inwiefern der Südosten Litauens als hybrider Sprachraum angesehen werden kann und welche Rolle dabei dem Vilniusser Polnisch, also der Polszczyzna Wileńska, und dem Idiom »Po Prostu« [Einfache Sprache] zukommt.[3] Bevor ich darauf näher eingehen kann, möchte ich zwei Punkte umreißen, die für das Problemfeld zentral sind, und zwar erstens das Verständnis von Hybridität und zweitens die Spezifik der Sprach(en)situation im Südosten Litauens im Hinblick auf die Idiome, mit denen gemischte Sprachpraktiken realisiert werden.

2 »Hybridität« und hybride Sprachpraktiken – ein interdisziplinärer Überblick

Vor allem seit den bahnbrechenden Arbeiten von Said (1993) und Bhabha (1994) erfreut sich die Erforschung der Hybridität in den Kultur- und Literaturwissenschaften großer Popularität. Für beide Disziplinen stellt »Hybridität« einen »postkolonialen Schlüsselbegriff« (Schwarz 2015: 163) dar, genauso wie Bhabhas Theorie vom »dritten Raum« zu den Schlüsselideen der postkolonialen Theorie gehört. Zunehmend findet der Begriff der Hybridität auch Eingang in die Sprachwissenschaft, und vor allem für die Soziolinguistik ist er von großer Relevanz geworden. So werden beispielsweise die sprachlichen Situationen in der Ukraine und in Weißrussland, wo die gemischten Idiome Suržyk und Trasjanka sozial eine große Rolle spielen,[1] zunehmend unter dem Label sprachlicher und kultureller Hybridität behandelt.[2] Mit der Frage der Identität der Russischsprachigen in der Ukraine aus der Sicht der postkolonialen Theorie und dem Phänomen der Hybridität befasst sich der Politikwissenschaftler Puleri (2020). Puleri greift in diesem Zusammenhang auf das Phänomen der Hybridität zu, weil sich dadurch »der strikte Binarismus zwischen russischer und ukrai-

---

2 Speziell zum slawisch-baltischen Kontaktgebiet siehe bspw. den Beitrag von Zielińska (2004) oder die fünfundzwanzig Beiträge von Čekmonas, welche sich mit dem Kontakt von Litauisch, Weißrussisch und Polnisch in den mehrsprachigen Gebieten Litauens befassen und welche von Kalėdienė zusammengestellt und 2017 herausgegeben wurden.

3 Zielińska (2004: 302) stellt dazu fest, dass der Terminus der Einfachen Sprache von den Informant*innen selbst stamme und von ihnen in den wissenschaftlichen Diskurs gewandert sei.

1 In diesem Zusammenhang schreibt Hentschel (2014: 1): »Millionen von Menschen in Weißrussland und der Ukraine sprechen – zumindest in gewissen Situationen – nicht Weißrussisch bzw. Ukrainisch oder eben Russisch ›in Reinform‹. Vielmehr praktizieren sie eine gemischte weißrussisch-russische bzw. ukrainisch-russische Rede. Diese deutlich gemischten Formen der Rede aus genetisch eng verwandten und strukturell sehr ähnlichen ostslawischen Sprachen werden in Weißrussland ›Trasjanka‹ und in der Ukraine ›Suržyk‹ genannt.«

2 Für den ukrainischen Kontext wären hier z. B. die Monografie von Bilaniuk (2005) zu nennen, oder ihr Seminar aus dem Jahre 2018, das sie im Rahmen des 23. Greifswalder Ukrainicums gehalten hat. Sowohl den ukrainischen als auch den weißrussischen Kontext berücksichtigt bspw. der Sammelband von Hentschel et al. (2014).

nischer Kultur überwinden« lasse (ZOiS-Interview 2020 [digital]). Im linguistischen Hybriditätsdiskurs werden bi- und multilinguale Sprachpraktiken von Jugendlichen beschrieben, deren Realisierungen weltweite Parallelen aufweisen (siehe z. B. Hinnenkamp/Meng 2005). In der slawistischen Systemlinguistik spricht man von »Hybriden«, »hybriden Strukturen« oder »hybriden Wortformen«, wenn es um Morphologie und Wortbildung geht (wie bspw. in den Arbeiten von Waszakowa 2003, Filatova 2007, Hentschel 2008 oder Tesch 2014). Somit wird der Begriff »Hybridität« je nach wissenschaftlichem Zusammenhang unterschiedlich aufgefasst, eingesetzt und operationalisiert. Mit Blick auf die Verwendung des Begriffs »Hybridität« im Bereich der Kulturwissenschaft und auf die entsprechenden Ausführungen von Garciá Canclini (1995 [1989]) konstatiert Erfurt (2003: 21): »Hybridität bezieht sich auf Phänomene, die in der Interaktion verschiedener Kulturen entstehen und auf Mischung basieren.« Damit gibt Erfurt bereits 2003 eine m. E. für die Soziolinguistik programmatische Forschungsrichtung vor, welche sich von sprachpuristischen Vorstellungen löst:

> Worum es also geht, ist danach zu fragen, was es für die Sprecher bedeutet, verschiedene Sprachen als Ressourcen für die Kommunikation zu nutzen, (Elemente von) Sprachen zu mischen und sich auf diese Weise in ein Spannungsverhältnis zu den in der Gesellschaft verbreiteten sprachlichen Ideologien, Normvorstellungen und Bewertungen zu begeben. (Erfurt 2003: 8)

Je nach Zusammenhang und Sprachraum können die Antworten auf diese komplexe Frage unterschiedlich ausfallen. So beschäftigt sich beispielsweise Hinnenkamp (2010) mit dem polykulturellen Selbstverständnis und den hybriden Sprachpraktiken, denen sich türkischstämmige Jugendliche bedienen, welche in den Großstädten und urbanen Zentren Deutschlands leben. In seinem Fazit führt Hinnenkamp den Begriff »Hybridolekt« ein, der sich an die in der Soziolinguistik üblichen -lekte anlehnen und ein Synonym zu Erfurts (2003) Begriff »Multisprech« darstellen soll (Hinnenkamp 2010: 247). Somit liegen der Forschung zwei weitere Begriffe vor, die auf das Phänomen der Hybridität abzielen: Hybridolekt und Multisprech.

Die Mehrsprachigkeitsforschung liefert inzwischen ebenfalls eine Reihe von Termini, die sich direkt oder indirekt mit der sprachlichen Hybridität im Sinne einer Sprachenmischung befassen: Die Ideen reichen von *code switching* oder *code-mixing* über *language crossing* bis hin zu *metrolingualism* und *translanguaging*. Es geht in der einschlägigen Literatur darum, die Sprachpraxis der städtischen Jugendlichen, die in Abhängigkeit von Kommunikationsraum und -situation zu sehen ist, mit angemessenen Begriffen zu erfassen (Li 2011; Androutsopoulos et al. 2013a, Androutsopoulos et al. 2013b). Insbesondere ist mit Blick auf Sprachenmischung und das oben zitierte Beispiel aus dem Roman *Robczik* der Terminus »Translanguaging« interessant, wenn man davon ausgeht, dass unter ihm »das spielerisch-kreative Kombinieren sprachlicher Elemente verstanden wird, die als nicht zusammengehörig gelten« (Busch 2017: 58). Gerade im Hinblick auf die Jugendsprache ist die spielerische Komponente zentral, denn sie gilt als einer der Motive für solche Verwendungsweisen von Sprache. Die hybriden Praktiken setzen allerdings Transkulturalität voraus, für die man annimmt, dass »moderne Gesellschaften und zeitgenössische Kulturen von internen Differenzen und externen Vernetzungen geprägt sowie von gegenseitigen Durchdringungen und Hybridisierungen durchzogen sind« (Freitag 2010: 125). Deshalb werden auch innerhalb der Soziolinguistik zunehmend Überlegungen und Vorschläge (insbesondere in der Migrationsforschung) deutlich,[3] sich vom Denken in und Beforschen von Kulturen als homogenen Gebilden oder »einheitlichen Blöcken« zu distanzieren und folg-

---

3   Auch innerhalb der Fremdsprachendidaktik wird diese Tendenz zunehmend erkennbar, bspw. bei Freitag (2010).

lich kulturelle Hybridität im Sinne einer Vermischung als »Grundmerkmal heutiger Kulturen« (Freitag 2010: 125) aufzufassen:

> Ins Blickfeld rücken dann Zwischenräume jenseits binärer Zuordnungen sowie kulturelle Überschneidungen und Verflechtungen, in denen unterschiedlichste globale und lokale Elemente miteinander kombiniert werden und neue, hybride Formen hervorbringen. Kulturelle Phänomene, die bis dahin getrennt betrachtet wurden, werden zusammengedacht. (Yildiz 2019: 23)

Aus dieser Logik ergibt sich, dass auch Sprachpraktiken in mehrsprachigen Arealen vom ›hybriden‹ Blickwinkel her gedacht und betrachtet werden sollten, um die jeweiligen sprachlichen und kulturellen Verhältnisse möglichst realitätsnah abbilden und rezipieren zu können. Im Folgenden sollen deshalb die sprachlichen und kulturellen Verhältnisse im Südosten Litauens und insbesondere in Vilnius und seiner Umgebung dargestellt werden, wobei der Fokus der Darstellung auf der Polszczyzna Wileńska und dem Po Prostu sowie auf deren Sprecher*innen liegen soll.

3 Zur Spezifik der Sprach(en)situation im Südosten Litauens

Wie eingangs erwähnt, gilt das slawisch-baltische Kontaktgebiet[1] in der einschlägigen Forschung »als ein einzigartiges ethnolinguistisches und soziolinguistisches ›Laboratorium‹« (Zielińska 2004: 297), sodass es nicht verwundert, dass es zu diesem Gebiet bereits eine Fülle an Forschungsliteratur vorliegt. Einen Überblick über die historischen Umstände, die zum Entstehen eines solch sprachlich und ethnisch besonderen Gebietes (vor allem mit dem Fokus auf der Wileńszczyzna) beigetragen haben, geben die wegweisenden soziolinguistischen Arbeiten von Turska (1995 [1939]), Čekmonas (2017 [1990]), Zinkevičius (1993) und Kurzowa (1993) – um nur einige Arbeiten zu nennen. Eine ausführlichere Darstellung in deutscher Sprache liefern die historischen Arbeiten von von Rauch (1990) und Niendorf (2006; 2012). Eine soziolinguistische Beschreibung der aktuellen sprachlichen Situation in Litauen, von ihren sprach(en)politischen Aspekten und den Einstellungen der Sprecher*innen gegenüber dem Litauischen, Polnischen und Russischen geben zum einen die beiden Bände von *Miestai ir kalbos* [Städte und Sprachen], die 2010 und 2013 von Meilutė Ramonienė herausgegeben wurden, zum anderen zwei Arbeiten der Verfasserin (Kostiučenko 2016; 2020).

Mit Blick auf die Spezifik der Sprach(en)situation im Südosten Litauens und die beiden fraglichen Idiome, die im Fokus des vorliegenden Kapitels stehen, sollte man die soziolinguistische Annäherung an den Sprachraum mit der Beschreibung seiner Sprecher*innen beginnen, bevor man den Idiomen bzw. Varietäten selbst Aufmerksamkeit widmet, gleichwohl beide Aspekte miteinander verflochten sind. In dem Zitat aus Połońskis *Robczik*, das das Motto dieses Beitrags abgibt, gesteht der Vilniusser Protagonist, dass er sich geschämt habe, die »viel schöner sprechenden« jungen Frauen aus Polen anzusprechen, denn im Gegensatz zu ihnen sprächen er und seine Umgebung ja nur »wie die Hiesigen« (*po tutejszemu*, wörtlich »nach der Art der Hiesigen«). Es stellen sich somit mehrere Fragen: Wer sind diese Hiesigen, welche Probleme bringt dieser Begriff für die Erforschung der einzelnen Idiome im Südosten Litauens mit sich und welches Idiom ist mit dem Ausdruck *po tutejszemu* eigentlich genau gemeint? Somit kehren wir theoretisch gesehen wieder zur ›klassischen‹ Frage der Soziolinguistik zurück, die Joshua Fishman ins Spiel gebracht hat: »Wer

---

[1] Das slawisch-baltische Kontaktgebiet umfasst nicht nur den Südosten Litauens, sondern auch einige andere Regionen in Litauen, dann das nordwestliche Weißrussland und Südostlettland (Zielińska 2004: 297).

spricht was und wie mit wem in welcher Sprache[2] und unter welchen sozialen Umständen mit welchen Absichten und Konsequenzen?« (hier zitiert nach der Paraphrase von Dittmar 1997: 25). Die zentralen Teilfragen sind hierbei in erster Linie die nach dem »wer?« und dem »in welcher Sprache?«.

3.1 Wer?

Rein semantisch ist die Bezeichnung »die Hiesigen« aus heutiger Sicht eindeutig: Sie referiert auf das Vorhandensein einer lokalen Identität und einer direkten Verbundenheit der Bewohner*innen der fraglichen Ort- oder Landschaft mit dieser Ort- bzw. Landschaft.[3] Somit drückt der Begriff eine Zugehörigkeit zu diesem geografischen Raum aus. Sich als »hiesig« zu bezeichnen ist eine Art Bekenntnis, und soziolinguistisch gesehen wird damit eine klare Position bezogen.[4] Das wissenschaftliche Problem der aktuellen soziolinguistischen Ein- bzw. Zuordnung in Bezug auf die Hiesigen Litauens liegt darin begründet, dass die einzelnen Sprecherinnen und Sprecher, die sich selbst mit *tutejszy* bzw. *tutejsi* bezeichnen, in Wirklichkeit unterschiedliche (Misch-)Idiome[5] sprechen, und zwar entweder Po Prostu oder das in Vilnius und seiner Umgebung gesprochene Polnisch, die Polszczyzna Wileńska. Viele beherrschen beides, und es herrscht ein klares diglossisches Verhältnis, in welchem die Varietät des Polnischen eindeutig den höheren sozialen Status genießt. In seinem einführenden Beitrag zu dem wegweisenden Werk von Turska (1995 [1939]) schreibt der in Litauen bekannte Sprachkontaktforscher Valerijus Čekmonas (1995: 9–10) von den litauischen Pol*innen, ihren Siedlungsgebieten und ihren Sprachen Folgendes:

> *Ausschließlich Polnisch* spricht die ländliche Bevölkerung auf einer kleinen [Sprach]Insel im Bezirk Trakai (rund um Rudiškės [und] in einigen Dörfern nördlich von Trakai), im nördlichen Teil des Bezirks Vilnius und im südlichen Teil des Bezirks Širvintos; [außerdem] im Südosten Litauens – in kleinen Arealen einer Zone Zarasai – Turmantas – Dorf Gaidė. / Den gesamten südlichen Teil (ab dem Fluss Vilija/Neris) des Bezirks Vilnius, den Bezirk Šalčininkai und den östlichen Teil des Bezirks Trakai wie auch den Streifen, der sich an Belarus im Bezirk Švenčionys anlehnt, besiedeln *Polen, deren Haupt- und Haussprache Belarussisch («prostaja mova») ist*.[6]

Von dem Umstand, dass es sich bei Po Prostu und Polszczyzna Wileńska um unterschiedliche (Misch-)Idiomen handelt, zeugen die empirisch basierten kontrastiven Analysen auf

---

2   Der Begriff »Sprache« ist für Fishman ein Oberbegriff, der nicht nur Standardvarietäten umfasst, sondern auch alle möglichen anderen.
3   Diese Referenz kommt auch ganz klar in der einschlägigen ethnographischen und folkloristischen Literatur zum Ausdruck, so bspw. bei Leparskienė/Baltėnas (2019). Der Titel ihres Buches lautet schlicht, aber eindeutig »Die Hiesigen« (*vietiniai*).
4   »Bekenntnis« meint, dass die Personen sich in erster Linie freiwillig als Hiesige bezeichnen; eine Zuordnung durch Dritte ist zweitrangig bzw. unnötig. Genauso wird es in der Soziolinguistik auch bei der Frage gehandhabt, ob und wer zu einer Minderheit gehört oder nicht: In erster Linie kommt es auf die Selbstzuordnung an.
5   Hier und im Folgenden: Die Schreibung mit dem eingeklammerten Teil »Misch-« soll darauf hinweisen, dass es in der Forschung umstritten ist, inwiefern es sich um einen Mix aus unterschiedlichen Sprachen handelt (vgl. z. B. Kalėdienė 2017: 22).
6   Übersetzung und Hervorhebung durch die Verfasserin. Die Bezeichnung der Ortschaften in Litauen folgt der litauischen Orthografie. Orig.: »Только по-польски сельское население говорит на небольшом островке в Тракайском районе (вокруг Рудишкес, в некоторых деревнях к северу от Тракай), в северной части Вильнюсского района, в южной части Ширвинтского; на юго-востоке Литвы – в небольших ареалах в зоне Зарасай – Турмантас – д. Гайде. / Всю южную (до р. Вилии – Нерис) часть Вильнюсского района, Шальчининкский район и восточную часть Тракайского района, а также полосу, прилегающую к Белоруссии в Швенчёнском районе, населяют поляки, для которых основным, домашним языком является белорусский («простая мова»).«

Systemebene, auch wenn es gleichzeitig berechtigte Zweifel an den Differenzen zwischen Po Prostu und Polszczyzna Wileńska gibt.[7] Zu den unterschiedlichen Positionen innerhalb der Sprachwissenschaft vgl. man die Arbeit von Koji Morita (2006: 146). Besonders wichtig in diesem Kontext ist die innerhalb der polnischsprachigen Linguistik scheinbar weniger populäre Beobachtung von Dini (2000: 377), dass sowohl die lokale Varietät des Weißrussischen in Litauen als auch die dortige Varietät des Polnischen mit dem Ausdruck *po prostu* bezeichnet würden und dass sich letztere auf dem Substrat des Litauischen und Weißrussischen formte. Mit Blick auf diese Positionierung erscheint auch die Schlussfolgerung von Morita (2006: 144–145) plausibel, dass die Bezeichnung eines Idioms als »einfach« nicht mit einem konkreten Idiom in Verbindung stehe, sondern nur seinen niedrigeren Status in Augen der Sprecher*innen markiere.

Aus meiner Sicht sorgt also ausgerechnet die Laienbezeichnung und Selbstzuordnung *tutejszy* bzw. *tutejsi* für die meisten Verwirrungen, die leider auch im wissenschaftlichen Diskurs noch vereinzelt anzutreffen sind. Zum Teil könnte die Verwirrung damit erklärt werden, dass die jeweiligen Forscher*innen ihren Fokus nur auf ein bestimmtes Idiom richten und die Daten mithilfe qualitativer Methoden erheben (z. B. Sprachbiografien), wobei die Aussagen der Betroffenen, dass sie zu den Tutejsi gehörten, und die Tatsache, dass sie sich häufig ethnisch als Pol*innen bezeichnen, zweifellos wahrheitsgemäß widergegeben werden. So hält Kalėdienė (2017: 22) zu den älteren Sprecher*innen von Po Prostu Folgendes fest: »Sie bezeichnen sich selbst als ›Hiesige‹, obwohl sie offiziell ethnische Pol*innen[8] sind" (*Save vadina »vietiniais« (tuteišiais), nors oficiali jų tautybė yra lenkų*; Kalėdienė 2017: 22). Im Endeffekt wird deutlich, dass sich dadurch, dass die lokalen Mehrsprachigen in Litauen sich selbst als Tutejsi bezeichnen, gleichzeitig das Problem ergibt, deren Idiome wissenschaftlich auseinanderzuhalten, solange es nicht um rein systemlinguistische Studien geht. Im internationalen wissenschaftlichen Diskurs herrscht deshalb auch Uneinigkeit darüber, wie die beiden fraglichen Idiome soziolinguistisch einzuordnen seien. Das Ganze wird zusätzlich nicht zuletzt dadurch erschwert, dass innerhalb des in Litauen gesprochenen Polnischen und Weißrussischen sowieso noch weitere Varianz besteht, was unbestritten ist, wenn auch noch nicht genügend erforscht (mehr dazu gleich unter 3.2).

Hinzu kommt auch noch ein weiterer, die Forschung erschwerender Umstand: die Gestalt der affektiven und der kognitiven Einstellungskomponenten sowie etablierter Sprachideologien. Denn die Hiesigen sprechen (Misch-) Idiome, die wenig Prestige besitzen, was den meisten von ihnen auch bewusst ist: »Sie erklären selbst, dass dies [Po Prostu] eine Haussprache sei, die dazu diene, sich mit Tieren zu unterhalten, und nicht mit Fremden oder in der Kirche, wo man Polnisch zu sprechen habe« (*Jie patys aiškina, kad tai esanti namų kalba, skirta bendrauti su gyvuliais, o ne su svetimaisiais ir ne bažnyčioje, kur reikia kalbėti lenkiškai*; Kalėdienė 2017: 22). So meinen bspw. auch die Proband*innen der Studie von Rutkowska (2019: 191), dass das in Litauen gesprochene Polnisch – ihr eigenes Polnisch! – nicht richtig und nicht sauber sei. Dieselbe Einstellung kommt auch im Zitat aus

---

7   So schreibt Wiemer (2003: 235): »Bereits diese wenigen Fälle lassen den folgenden Schluß zu: Merkmale, die häufig als typisch für die PolKres [Polszczyzna Kresowa] angeführt werden, eignen sich oft gar nicht als unterscheidende Kriterien gegenüber der MP [Mowa Prosta] (sowie evtl. auch anderer Varietäten des Kontaktareals), oder sie zeugen davon, daß die PolKres ein starkes ostslavisches (speziell weißrussisches) Substrat aufweist und sich in diesem Sinne von der MP gerade nicht unterscheidet.«

8   Anders als die deutschen Behörden unterscheidet der litauische Staat die Kategorien von Ethnie und Staatsbürgerschaft. Die Bewohner*innen Litauens besitzen in der Regel die litauische Staatsbürgerschaft, können sich aber zusätzlich durch ihre Ethnie differenzieren lassen.

dem Roman *Robczik* (s. Motto) zum Ausdruck, denn es handelt sich in den betreffenden Kreisen um eine geläufige Überzeugung. Allerdings lässt sich ein allmählicher Wandel dieser Einstellungen ins Positive verzeichnen; s. bspw. ein Interview mit Karolina Słotwińska (Prie Smetonos, vom 04.04.2022 [digital]), die stolz auf ihre vilnius-polnische Herkunft und lokale Varietät ist.

3.2 In welcher Sprache / in welchen Sprachen?

Von der nicht unproblematischen Selbstbezeichnung der Sprecher*innen, die Hiesigen zu sein, und von ihrer ethnischen Zuordnung haben wir gesprochen. Nun sollen die fraglichen (Misch-) Idiome, die diese Sprecher*innen im Alltag gebrauchen, genauer unter die Lupe genommen werden. Ohne Anspruch auf Vollständigkeit möchte ich zunächst einige Bezeichnungen präsentieren, die für das in Litauen und insbesondere in Vilnius und Umgegend gesprochene Polnisch ›im Volk‹ wie im wissenschaftlichen Diskurs zirkulieren. In einem auf YouTube veröffentlichten Interview aus dem Jahre 2010 erklärt Krystyna Rutkowska, Polonistin an der Universität Vilnius, dass die jüngere Generation, die aus den Dörfern nach Vilnius gezogen sei, von Zuhause »eine mundartliche Variante des Polnischen« (*gwarową odmianę języka polskiego*) mitgebracht habe. Während des Studiums an litauischen Bildungseinrichtungen würden die Studierenden aber nicht nur Polnisch, sondern auch andere Sprachen verwenden, insbesondere Litauisch und Russisch. Und die gemischten Mundarten, die daraus entstünden, seien mit Elementen des Litauischen und Russischen gefüllt und »verschmutzt«. Für Rutkowska handelt es sich auch gar nicht mehr um Mundarten (*gwary*), sondern um ein »Sprachmischmasch« (*język kisz-misz*). Sie vertritt also eine puristische Ansicht, wobei sie meint, dass es doch wohl beschämend sei, so falsch Polnisch zu sprechen, zumal man sowohl in den Schulen als auch an den Hochschulen auf Hochpolnisch unterrichtet werde (Rutkowska 2010: WilnotekaLT, Minuten 0:30–1:07 und 3:23–3:44). Im selben Video hört man übrigens aus dem Off die Bezeichnung »Sprache von Vilnius« (*język wileński*; op. cit.: Minute 4:23). Der Autor des Romans *Robczik*, Bartosz Połoński, dessen Interviewausschnitt im selben YouTube-Video gezeigt wird, unterscheidet hingegen das Sprechen »nach Art von Warschau« (*po warszawsku*) vom Sprechen »nach Art von Vilnius« (*po wileńsku*; op. cit.: Minuten 1:45–2:00); letzteres bezeichnet er dann synonym mit »die hiesige Sprache« (*tutejszy język*; op. cit.: Minute 4:45).

In einer späteren Arbeit dokumentiert Rutkowska (2019: 191), welche Bezeichnungen die im Südosten Litauens lebenden Pol*innen für die in ihrer Region gesprochenen Sprachen gebrauchen: Nicht nur neutrales *język* 'Sprache' sondern auch Bezeichnungen wie *gwara* 'Mundart', *mowa* 'Sprache, Rede, Sprechweise', *rozmowa* 'Gespräch', *gadanie* 'Gerede, Geplapper' und *gawęda* 'Geplauder'. Das Polnische wird zwar neutral mit *język polski* oder *polszczyzna* bezeichnet,[9] aber auch negativ konnotierte Bezeichnungen werden verwendet: *gwara, gwara wileńska, wioskowy język, prosty język, prosta rozmowa, prosta gawęda, po prostemu, żargonskaja (mowa), nieczysta polska rozmowa, gruba rozmowa* (Rutkowska 2019: 191). Die lokale, dialektale Varietät des Weissrussischen[10] werde von litauischen Pol*innen ähnlich wie das Polnische bezeichnet, nämlich mit *prosty język, po prostu, po*

---

9 Für Bezeichnungen, die in früheren akademischen Werken für das Polnische in Litauen gebraucht bzw. dort erwähnt werden, siehe bspw. die Arbeit von Kurzowa (1993: 62–64).

10 Dass die Mowa Prosta alias Po Prostu, deren Verbreitungsgebiet sich zum größten Teil mit der Verbreitungszone des in Litauen gesprochenen Polnischen deckt, eine ostslavische Grundlage und somit »eine weißrussische grammatische und phonetische Basis« aufweist, wird detailliert und überzeugend im Aufsatz von Wiemer (2003; Zitat von S. 227) nachgewiesen.

prostemu (loc. cit.; auch Dini 2000: 377). Rutkowska (2019: 206) ist allerdings der Meinung, dass die Bezeichnung *tutejsza mowa* für das in Litauen gesprochene Polnisch nicht gebraucht werde und dass es eigentlich falsch sei, aus wissenschaftlicher Sicht das Polnisch mit Adjektiven wie *tutejszy* oder »einfach« zu bezeichnen (bernardinai.lt 2017 [digital]). Dagegen wird die *mowa prosta* mit ihren weißrussischen Basis durchaus als *język tutejszy* bezeichnet (Wiemer 2003: 227).

Im Kontext dieser terminologischen Auseinandersetzung schreibt Karaś (2017: 48):

> Meine Informant*innen haben oft gesagt, dass ihre Sprache »einfach« (sie würden *po prostu/po prostemu* sprechen), »gemischt«, »verheddert« sei, wobei sie das interferierte Polnisch mit einer großen Anzahl von Wörtern aus dem Weißrussischen, Russischen oder aus dem alten Kresy-Slawischen litauisch-ruthenischen Ursprungs meinten, und nicht die Art von »einfacher« Sprache (einer weißrussischen Mundart), die im Süden des Vilniusser Gebiets bekannt ist. Ähnlich bezeichneten die Informant*innen die dort gesprochenen weißrussischen Mundarten ebenfalls als ein Sprechen »po prostemu« (ed. Smułkowa 2011). Die Bezeichnung *język prosty* [einfache Sprache] steht in diesen Gebieten entweder für Mundarten des Weißrussischen im Allgemeinen oder für das lokale Polnisch.[11]

Somit können wir festhalten, dass die terminologischen und sachlichen Verwirrungen, von denen oben die Rede war, auf den Umstand zurückzuführen sind, dass sich die Sprecher*innen des Polnischen in Litauen gelegentlich genauso mit *tutejsi* und ihr Idiom mit *język prosty* bezeichnen, wie sich auch die Sprecher*innen eines Idioms, das dem Weißrussischen nahesteht, *tutejsi* nennen und von ihrer *prosta mowa* sprechen. Wichtig ist der Vorschlag von Geben (2019), die ein Lehrwerk für Studierende der Geisteswissenschaften an der Universität Vilnius geschrieben hat und den Versuch unternimmt, die Varietäten des Polnischen, das in Litauen gesprochen wird, zu charakterisieren und zugleich zu typologisieren. Sie differenziert aus: eine *odmiana standardowa* 'Standardvarietät' für das geschriebene wie gesprochene Hochpolnisch, eine *odmiana kulturalna* 'Kulturvarietät', eine *odmiana regionalno-gwarowa* 'regional-mundartliche Varietät' und schließlich *odmiany mieszane* 'Mischvarietäten', wobei die *kulturalna* und die *regionalno-gwarowa* zur gemischten Varietät gehören (Geben 2019: 21). Diese Varietäten beziehen sich auf gesprochene Sprache. In aller Kürze zusammengefasst, unterscheiden sie sich im Hinblick auf den Grad ihrer Interferenz durch andere Kontaktsprachen der Region (Geben 2019: 20–22): Die Kulturvarietät des Polnischen sprechen in der Regel diejenigen, die polnischsprachigen Schulunterricht genossen haben oder Hochschulbildung besitzen; die regional-mundartliche Varietät[12] sprechen Menschen polnischer Herkunft, die auf dem Lande leben oder keinen hohen Bildungsgrad besitzen, sowie diejenigen Jugendlichen, die in der Schule auf Russisch oder Litauisch unterrichtet wurden; und schließlich werden die beiden Mischvarietäten gesprochen, die aber nach Geben keiner Ausdifferenzierung unterliegen könnten, da es ihnen an Merkmalen der Regionalität oder Dialektalität fehlte. Auch Irena Masoit, Soziolinguistin und Expertin für polnisch-litauischen Sprachkontakt, äußerte in einem Interview, dass das Polnische in Litauen nicht einheitlich sei, was von seinem Reichtum zeuge,[13] und

---

11 Orig.: »Moi informatorzy często stwierdzali, że ich język jest „prosty" (mówią „po prostu"/„po prostemu"), „mieszany", „splątany", mając na myśli jednak polszczyznę zinterferowaną, z dużą liczbą białorutenizmów, rusycyzmów czy starych kresowizmów o genezie litewsko-ruskiej, a nie typ języka „prostego" (gwary białoruskiej), znany z południa Wileńszczyzny. Podobnie używane tam gwary białoruskie informatorzy również określali jako mówienie „po prostemu" (Smułkowa red. 2011). Określenie „język prosty" na tych terenach oznacza albo ogólnie gwary białoruskie, albo polszczyznę lokalną.«

12 Sie wird seitens der Sprachwissenschaftler*innen auch noch weiter ausdifferenziert (Geben 2019: 22, in Anlehnung an Masojć 2001: 33).

13 2016 veröffentlichten Rutkowska und ihr Team eine interaktive Karte, die die Verbreitung der unterschiedlichen Varietäten, die die Pol*innen in Litauen sprechen, visualisiert und mit deren Hilfe man auch Hörbeispiele samt ihren Transkripten aufrufen kann (Rutkovska 2016 [digital]).

dass die fragliche Jugendsprache kein Dialekt sei, sondern eine Mischsprache, die keine Entsprechung in Polen habe; zugleich handele es sich um einen Slang (bernardinai.lt 2017 [digital]).

Der von Masoit gemeinten (Misch-) Varietät bzw. dem Jugendslang hat Bartosz Połoński in seinem Roman ein Denkmal gesetzt. Schauen wir uns daher den im Motto zitierten Ausschnitt seines Werks etwas genauer an und suchen wir dabei nach Elementen, die der Interferenz auf lexikalischer Ebene unterliegen bzw. ad hoc aus dem Russischen transferiert wurden (s. Erklärungen in eckigen Klammern) und die auch dem Standardpolnischen fremd sind. Denn ohne diesen Analyseschritt ist auch die Übersetzung des Abschintts aus dem ›Polnischen‹ ins Deutsche kaum möglich.[14]

(1) Gdzie nie kręć się, na majówce w Wilnie wszędzie **wsie bazariat** po polsku.

Wohin du auch hingehst, zu Majówka [Maifeiertage in Polen] **unterhalten sich** [russ. *базарить* (Jargon, просторечие), umgs. für *разговаривать*, hier an Stelle von poln. *rozmawiać*] in Vilnius **alle** [russ. *все*, an Stelle von poln. *wszyscy*] und überall auf Polnisch.

(2) Na te kilka dni robi się taka **cipa** mała Polska – **prikoł** taki.

Für diese wenigen Tage entsteht hier **quasi** [russ. *типа* (umgs.), steht im Russ. für *вроде, как будто*, hier an Stelle von poln. *jakby, chyba*] ein kleines Polen – so ein **Gag** [russ. *прикол* (umgs.) 'Scherz, Witz'].

(3) Szkoda, **kanieszna**, że turyści najczęściej takie **kazły** w **kiedach**, które ryczą na całą ulicę, jakby ich nikt nie rozumiał i zawsze **nie dawolne**, że **cipa** w Wilnie **wsio** drogo.

Schade, **natürlich** [russ. *конечно*, hier an Stelle von poln. *oczywiście*], dass Touristen, meist solche **Idioten** [russ. *козлы* (umgs.), ein Schimpfwort in der Art von »Dummköpfe«] in **Sneakers** [russ. *кеды*] sind, die über die ganze Straße brüllen, als würde sie niemand verstehen, und die immer **unzufrieden** [russ. *недовольный*] sind, dass es in Vilnius **halt** [russ. *типа*] **alles** [russ. *всё*, hier an Stelle von poln. *wszystko*] teuer sei.

(4) Bywali młode panienki z tymi turystami, ale my ich jakoś nie **kadrili**, bo oni zawsze wyglądali rozumniejsze, i rozmawiali dużo ładniej niż my.

Zusammen mit diesen Touristen pflegten auch junge Damen unterwegs zu sein, aber irgendwie haben wir sie nicht **angemacht** [russ. *кадрить* (umgs.) 'eine Person umwerben'], denn sie sahen immer klüger aus als wir und redeten auch viel schöner.

(5) Ja też jakoś wstydził się do nich zagadać, bo rozmawiał po tutejszemu i **cziuju** ich nie weźmisz tak prosto, bo trzeba dużo gadać pra różne „ważne" **ciemy**.

Ich schämte mich auch irgendwie, sie anzusprechen, denn ich sprach in der Art eines Hiesigen und ich **ahnte** [russ. *чую* (umgs.) zu *чуять*, hier metaphorisch 'etwas erraten'], die kriegst du nicht so einfach rum, denn da musst du viel über verschiedene »wichtige« **Themen** [russ. *темы*, hier an Stelle von poln. *temat*] quatschen.

In diesem kurzen Abschnitt treffen wir also auf zahlreiche Worte und Formen, die es im Standardpolnischen nicht gibt, wie bspw. *ciemy* [ˈtsʲemɨ], *cipa* [ˈtsipə], *wsie* [ˈfʃʲe], *wsio* [ˈfʃʲɵ], welche phonetisch an das Polnische angepasst wurden bzw. die ›polnische‹ Aussprache der russischen Wörter *темы, типа, все* und *всё* darstellen. Darunter ist *cipa*, das aus dem russ. umgs. *типа* 'quasi' herzuleiten ist und ›korrekt‹ als Partikel gebraucht wird, besonders missverständlich, da es leicht mit poln. *cipa* 'Fotze' verwechselt werden kann. Einige Ad-hoc-Transfers aus dem Russischen wie bspw. **nie dawolne* sind grammatikalisiert. Durch den hohen Grad an Mischung lässt sich jedoch nicht immer eindeutig erkennen, welche Sprache die Matrixsprache und welche die eingebettete Sprache darstellt; beim Lesen entsteht der Eindruck, dass die Rollen immer wieder wechseln. Obwohl manche syntaktische Konstruktion relativ eindeutig ist, wie bspw. im Satz: *w Wilnie wszędzie wsie ba-*

---

14 Einige Fragmente aus *Robczik* wurden bereits ins Hochpolnische übertragen (s. Ha!art 2014 [digital]). Interessanterweise finden sich dazu die folgenden Überschriften, deren Humor sicherlich beabsichtigt ist: »Wersja polska« [die polnische Version] für den Originaltext und »Wersja też polska« [auch die polnische Version] für die Übersetzung ins Standardpolnische.

zariat po polsku. Der grammatische Kern dieses Satzes, *wsie bazariat* zu russ. *все базарят*, entstammt aufgrund der Verbform eindeutig dem Russischen. Auf lexikalischer Ebene gibt es im Textzitat zahlreiche Transfers aus dem Russischen, die allerdings auch im Russischen selbst nicht zum Standard bzw. zur Literatursprache gehören, sondern Elemente der russischen Umgangssprache, des Jargons und des Jugendslangs sind. Im zitierten Abschnitt des Romans kommen litauische Lexeme nicht vor, dennoch gibt es andere Textstellen, an denen auch zahlreiche Elemente aus dem Litauischen auftreten, wobei es sich im Unterschied zum Russischen meist um standardsprachlichen Wortschatz handelt.

Auf den ersten Blick handelt es sich bei dem analysierten Beispiel um eine chaotische, spontane und kreative Ad-hoc-Mischung, die keinen klaren Regeln zu unterliegen scheint. Jedoch lassen sich durchaus bestimmte Regelmäßigkeiten beobachten, wie bspw. die phonetische Anpassung russischer Wörter an das Polnische. Die vom Autor des Romans beabsichtigte und verschriftlichte Anpassung ruft beim Lesen eindeutige Assoziationen mit der Aussprache, die für die lokalen Polnischsprecher*innen charakteristisch ist, hervor. Um mehr über solche ›Regelmäßigkeiten‹ sagen zu können, bedürfte es einer umfangreichen Analyse von Korpora auf allen sprachlichen Ebenen. Eine solche stellt bis dato noch ein Desiderat dar. Da allerdings das zitierte (Misch-) Idiom außer in *Robczik* bisher kaum verschriftlicht wurde, könnte eine solche Analyse nur auf zahlreiche Sprachaufnahmen und Transkripte Bezug nehmen. Zweifelsohne würde auch die Analyse der sprachlichen Beiträge und Kommentare in sozialen Netzwerken Aufschluss über die linguistischen Besonderheiten des Idioms und seines Gebrauchs geben.

Unabhängig von noch fehlenden Analysen lässt sich jedoch sagen, dass einer Mischsprache wie dem ›lokalen‹ Polnisch die kommunikative Mindestbedingung zu eigen ist, dass Produzent*innen und Rezipient*innen eine entsprechende ›erweiterte‹ Sprachenkompetenz besitzen. Denn wie auch Peterson (2015: 49) treffend sagt, »Wörter aus einer anderen Sprache ad hoc verwenden zu können, setzt voraus, dass man sich in dieser anderen Sprache auskennt«. Solche Mehrfachkompetenzen setzen zudem ein hybrides Kulturverständnis voraus, im Rahmen dessen eine bestimmte ethnische, kulturelle Identität nicht nur mit einer einzigen Sprache, einem singulären Idiom oder Register gleichgesetzt wird. Daher erscheint es sinnvoll, sich den sprachlichen Verhältnissen im Südosten Litauens aus der Perspektive der Hybridität zu nähern, was im nächsten Kapitel erfolgt.

4 Zusammenfassende Überlegungen zum Potenzial des Begriffs der Hybridität bezogen auf den Südosten Litauens

Die ersten wissenschaftlichen Annäherungen an das Phänomen der Hybridität, auf denen auch der vorliegende Beitrag bereits aufbaut, erfolgten durch die vereinzelten Versuche, im Südosten Litauens eine Sprachensituation der Heteroglossie zu sehen; und zwar sprach man konkret von der »Vilniusser Heteroglossie« (*Vilnietiškoji heteroglosija*; s. den Beitrag auf »sociologai.lt 2012« [digital]). Der Begriff »Heteroglossie« geht auf Bachtin und etwa auf das Jahr 1935 zurück, und er steht heute für »Vielstimmigkeit« (Sutherland 2012: 140) bzw. für die Kreuzung von Sprachen und Kulturen. Den Unterschied zwichen Heteroglossie und Polyphonie, beides von Bachtin verwendet, erklärt Sutherland (2012: 141) folgendermaßen: »Heteroglossie unterscheidet sich von Polyphonie insofern, als sie über die Stimme an sich hinausgeht und auch deren soziale Herkunft analysiert. In der Sprache und in den Wörtern, die Sprache bilden, erkannte Bachtin faszinierende soziale Mischungen.« Briedis (2012: 177) vermutet, dass interessanterweise gerade die Sprachensituation von Vilnius und seine Alltagserfahrungen in dieser bereits damals multinationalen Stadt Bachtin veranlasste, die Idee der Heteroglossie zu entwickeln. An »faszinierenden Mischungen« von sozialer Relevanz fehlt es, wie aufgezeigt, in Vilnius bis heute nicht. Die Termini »Hybridität« und »Heteroglossie« schließen m. E. einander nicht aus – im Gegenteil, sie lassen sich sogar als komplementär erachten, wenn man davon ausgeht, dass kulturelle und sprachliche Hybridität eine notwendige Voraussetzung für Heteroglossie ist oder zumindest ihr basaler Hintergrund. In den mehrsprachigen Arealen im Südosten Litauens haben wir es durchaus mit einer hybriden Sprachpraxis zu tun, und ein Beispiel für solche Praxis wurde im Roman *Robczik* niedergelegt.

Auch die innerhalb der germanistischen Forschung erarbeiteten Begriffe »Hybridolekt« und »Multisprech« sind für die hier betrachteten gemischten Idiome produktiv, denn mit den üblichen Analysekategorien und den üblichen Theorien der Sprachkontaktforschung und Soziolinguistik lassen sich Mischvarietäten de facto kaum greifen. Allerdings stellen die beiden Begriffe aus meiner Sicht keine Synonyme dar: Während »Hybridolekt« die soziolinguistische Zuordnung eines Idioms in einem konkreten Varietätenraum erlaubt, zielt »Multisprech« eher auf alle möglichen Sprachpraktiken, die mithilfe von Sprach(en)mischungen realisiert werden. Somit lässt sich sagen, dass ein Multisprech theoretisch mithilfe sowohl von Hybridolekten wie auch anderen *-lekten* ausgeführt werden kann. Übertragen auf die im Beitrag diskutierten Idiome der Polszczyzna Wileńska und des Po Prostu bedeutet dies, dass die ›vermischende‹ Sprachpraxis, die auf Grundlage der lokalen polnischen Varietät oder dem Po Prostu unter Einbeziehung von Elementen aus den Litauischen, Russischen und ihrer Varietäten erfolgen, Multisprechpraktiken darstellen und eine hybride Identität ihrer Sprecher*innen nicht nur befördern, sondern auch aufrechterhalten und weitertradieren. Dadurch steigt das Covert-Prestige dieser Idiome innerhalb der lokalen Sprachgemeinschaft. Mit Blick auf die Diskussion rund um den Begriff *tutejszy* bzw. *tutejsi* und seine feste Verankerung im Bewusstsein der in Litauen lebenden Sprecher*innen erscheint es sinnvoll, für die Bezeichnung der dortigen gemischten slawischsprachigen Idiome das für das Deutsche und Englische neutrale Adjektiv »lokal« bzw. *local* zu gebrauchen und somit von »lokalen Idiomen«, von einem »lokalen Multisprech« oder auch von »lokalen Sprachpraktiken« im slawisch-baltischen Kontaktgebiet zu sprechen. Dabei darf nicht aus den Augen verloren werden, dass die lokalen Idiome eine Binnendifferenzierung in Varietäten, die sich u. a. durch eine Vermischung verschiedener Sprachen auf allen Sprachebenen auszeichnen, und in welche, die bestimmten Standardvarietäten näherstehen, aufweisen.

5 Fazit und Ausblick

Der Südosten Litauens ist ein Traumland für die Erforschung von Sprachkontaktphänomenen und insbesondere für die Erforschung der slawisch-baltischen Sprachkontakte. Die Anzahl der dort gesprochenen Sprachen und Idiome und ihrer soziolinguistischen Profile sind ein wichtiges Forschungsfeld, das weitergeführt und zudem ausgebaut werden sollte. Die zahlreichen Bezeichnungen, die für die Idiome vor Ort zirkulieren, geben nicht nur Aufschluss über ihre Beschaffenheit, sondern markieren unmissverständlich ihr soziales Prestige. Es lässt sich beobachten, dass die präskriptiv, puristisch orientierte Sprachauffassung, die im litauischen wissenschaftlichen Diskurs in Bezug auf das Litauische dominiert, auch auf das in Litauen gesprochene Polnisch übertragen wird. So gelten alle Idiome, so sie Elemente anderer Sprachen enthalten, als fehlerhaft und ›verschmutzt‹. Da die Soziolinguistik keine präskriptive, sondern eine deskriptive Sicht auf die gesamte Problematik einnimmt, kann sie die sprachlichen Entwicklungen und Verhältnisse nur weiter beobachten. Faszinierend bleibt, dass das lokale Polnisch in Vilnius und Umgegend sowie Po Prostu trotz ihrer überwiegend negativen Fremd- und Eigenbewertung weiterhin aktiv in privaten und halböffentlichen Domänen verwendet werden und dass man sich mit ihnen durchaus auch identifiziert. Dabei handelt es sich um eine hybride Identität.

Im Falle der Polszczyzna Wileńska und des Po Prostu haben wir es mit (Misch-) Idiomen zu tun, die seit Jahrzehnten unter Mehrsprachigkeitsbedingungen existieren, sich daraus speisen und diese auch weitertradieren. Für ihre Sprecher*innen haben sie eine besondere soziale Relevanz und fungieren als Kompromisssprachen. Dieser Terminus, der auf Jespersen (2003 [1925]) zurückgeht, eignet sich meines Erachtens besonders gut, um die lokalen gemischten Idiome im Südosten Litauens zu charakterisieren. Eine Kompromisssprache übernimmt eine Vermittlerrolle zwischen den beteiligten Varietäten und trägt zu ihrer Annäherung bei. Entscheidend ist dabei, wie man spricht, und nicht, welches Idiom man spricht. Durch die Wahl eines ›einfacheren‹ Registers erfolgt ein Kompromiss, der es allen Beteiligten erlaubt, sich unabhängig vom sozialen Status und Bildungsgrad zu verständigen. Dass eine Kompromisssprache sich aus hybriden Praktiken speist, ist evident. Insofern haben wir im Südosten Litauens eine komplexe Sprach(en)situation mit besonderen Sprecher*innen.

Mein Beitrag ging deshalb der Frage nach, inwiefern der Begriff der Hybridität sinnvoll zur Beschreibung dieses Sprachraums herangezogen werden kann. Im Ergebnis lässt sich sagen, dass es durchaus sinnvoll ist, sich den beiden umstrittenen Idiomen und dem sprachlichen Alltag aus dem Blickwinkel der kulturellen und sprachlichen Hybridität zu nähern, zumal solche Mischcodes kein Alleinstellungsmerkmal Litauens sind, sondern weltweit beobachtet werden können, sodass Analysen unter Anwendung der Kategorie der Hybridität zu länderübergreifenden Vergleichen führen können. So könnte die Anwendung des Begriffs auf die Beschreibung der sprachlichen Verhältnisse im Südosten Litauens nicht nur zu einem besseren, tieferen Verständnis dieses Sprachraums beitragen, sondern auch seinen Eingang in die internationale Soziolinguistik als Modellregion beschleunigen. Die soziolinguistische Forschung zur Hybridität würde aus meiner Sicht einen gemeinsamen Nenner herbeiführen, der in zahlreichen einschlägigen Arbeiten zu Kontaktarealen bemängelt wird.

6 Nachweise

6.1 Primärliteratur

Robczik, Homepage des Romans, per URL.

6.2 Sekundärliteratur

6.2.1 Gedruckte Titel

Androutsopoulos, Jannis / Ingrid **Breckner** / Bernhard **Brehmer** / Kristin **Bührig** / Roland **Kießling** / Julia **Pauli** / Angelika **Redder** (2013a), »Facetten gesellschaftlicher Mehrsprachigkeit in der Stadt – kurze Einleitung«, in Angelika Redder et al. (Hrsg.), *Mehr-*

sprachige Kommunikation in der Stadt: Das Beispiel Hamburg, Münster et al.: Waxmann, S. 13–27.

—, — / Yin Feng **Hsieh** / Joanna **Kouzina** / Reyhan **Şahin** (2013 b), »Vernetzte Mehrsprachigkeit auf Facebook: Drei Hamburger Fallstudien«, in Angelika Redder et al. (Hrsg.), *Mehrsprachige Kommunikation in der Stadt: Das Beispiel Hamburg*, Münster et al.: Waxmann, S. 161–197.

Bhabha, Homi K. (1994), *The Location of Culture*, London–New York: Routledge.

Bilaniuk, Laada (2005), *Contested Tongues: Language Politics and Cultural Correction in Ukraine*, Ithaka–London: Cornell University Press.

Briedis, Laimonas (2012), *Vilnius: Savas ir svetimas* [Vilnius: Heimisch und fremd], Vilnius: Baltos lankos.

Busch, Brigitta (^{2}2017), *Mehrsprachigkeit*, Wien: Facultas.

[**Čekmonas**, Valerijus] Валерий Чекмонас (1995), »Поляки Литвы в настоящее время (Вступительная статья)« [Die Polen Litauens in der Gegenwart (ein einführender Beitrag)], in Halina Turska (Галина Турска), *O powstaniu polskich obszarów językowych na Wileńszczyźnie / О происхождении польскоязычных ареалов в Вильнюсском крае*, Vilnius: Mintis, S. 5–58.

[—, —] Walery Czekmonas (2017), »O etapach socjolingwistycznej historii wileńszczyzny i rozwoju polskiej świadomości narodowej na Litwie« [1990] [Zu den Etappen der soziolinguistischen Geschichte der Region Vilnius und zur Entwicklung des polnischen nationalen Selbstbewusstseins in Litauen], in *Valerijus Čekmonas: kalbų kontaktai ir sociolingvistika*, hrsg. von Laima Kalėdienė, Vilnius: Lietuvių kalbos institutas, S. 127–135.

Dini, Pietro Umberto (2000), *Baltų kalbos: Lyginamoji istorija* [Die baltischen Sprachen: Eine vergleichende Geschichte], Vilnius: Mokslo ir enciklopedijų leidybos institutas.

Dittmar, Norbert (1997), *Grundlagen der Soziolinguistik: Ein Arbeitsbuch mit Aufgaben*, Tübingen: Max Niemeyer.

Erfurt, Jürgen (2003), »›Multisprech‹: Migration und Hybridisierung und ihre Folgen für die Sprachwissenschaft«, in Jürgen Erfurt (Hrsg.), *»Multisprech«: Hybridität, Variation, Identität*, Duisburg: Universitätsverlag Rhein-Ruhr, S. 5–33. (Osnabrücker Beiträge zur Sprachtheorie 65.)

Filatova, Nataliya (2007), *Ukrainisch im Kontakt mit anderen europäischen Sprachen: Englische, deutsche, russische Entlehnungen im Bereich der Politik*. Universität Erlangen-Nürnberg: Dissertation, auch digital.

Freitag, Britta (2010), »Transkulturelles Lernen«, in Wolfgang Hallet / Frank G. Königs (Hrsg.), *Handbuch Fremdsprachendidaktik*, Seelze-Velber (Hannover): Klett & Kallmeyer, S. 125–129.

Garciá Canclini, Néstor (1995), *Hybrid Cultures: Strategies for Entering and Leaving Modernity*. Minneapolis–London: University of Minnesota Press. (Übersetzung aus dem Spanischen; das Original erschien 1989.)

Geben, Kinga (2019), *Współczesny język polski: Swoistość języka polskiego na Litwie: Skrypt dla studentów I stopnia kierunków humanistycznych* [Gegenwartspolnisch: Die Besonderheit des Polnischen in Litauen: Unterrichtsmaterial], Vilnius: Vilniaus universiteto leidykla.

Hentschel, Gerd (2008), »Zur weißrussisch-russischen Hybridität in der weißrussischen ›Trasjanka‹«, in Peter Kosta / Daniel Weiss (Hrsg.), *Slavistische Linguistik 2006/2007: Referate des 32. Konstanzer Slavistischen Arbeitstreffens, Männedorf bei Zürich, 18.–20.*

September 2006, und Referate des 33. Konstanzer Slavistischen Arbeitstreffens, Potsdam, 4.–6. September 2007, München: Sagner, S. 169–219. (Slavistische Beiträge 464.)

—, — / Oleksandr **Taranenko** / Sjarhej **Zaprudski** (2014), Hrsg., *Trasjanka und Suržyk – gemischte weißrussisch-russische und ukrainisch-russische Rede: Sprachlicher Inzest in Weißrussland und der Ukraine?*, Frankfurt/Main et al.: Peter Lang.

Hinnenkamp, Volker (²2010), »Sprachliche Hybridität, polykulturelle Selbstverständnisse und ›Parallelgesellschaft‹«, in Gudrun Hentges / Volker Hinnenkamp / Almut Zwengel (Hrsg.), *Migrations- und Integrationsforschung in der Diskussion: Biografie, Sprache und Bildung als zentrale Bezugspunkte*, Wiesbaden: VS Verlag für Sozialwissenschaften, S. 231–254.

—, — / Katharina **Meng** (2005), *Sprachgrenzen überspringen: Sprachliche Hybridität und polykulturelles Selbstverständnis*, Tübingen: Narr Francke Attempto.

Jespersen, Otto (2003), *Die Sprache: Ihre Natur, Entwicklung und Entstehung* [1925], Hildesheim–Zürich–New York: Georg Olms Verlag. (Reprint der Ausg. v. 1925.)

Kalėdienė, Laima (2017): »Įžanga« [Einleitung], in *Valerijus Čekmonas: kalbų kontaktai ir sociolingvistika*, hrsg. von Laima Kalėdienė, Vilnius: Lietuvių kalbos institutas, S. 21–37.

Kostiučenko, Anastasija (2016), *Sprachen und ihre Sprecher in Litauen: Eine soziolinguistische Untersuchung zum sozialen Status des Litauischen, Polnischen und Russischen*, Berlin: Logos. (Zugl. Universität Greifswald: Dissertation 2015.)

—, — (2020), »Language situation in Lithuania — is there anything to worry about?« in Stephan Kessler / Marko Pantermöller (Hrsg.), *The Social Status of Languages in Finland and Lithuania — A Plurimethodological Empirical Survey on Language Climate Change*, Berlin et al.: Peter Lang, S. 107–197. (Sprachkönnen und Sprachbewusstheit in Europa / Language Competence and Language Awareness in Europe 11).

Kurzowa, Zofia (1993), *Język polski Wileńszczyzny i kresów północno-wschodnich XVI–XX w.* [Das Polnisch der Region Vilnius und der nordöstlichen Grenzlande des 16.–20. Jhs.], Warszawa–Kraków: PWN.

Leparskienė, Lina / Arūnas Baltėnas (2019): *Vietiniai: Nepaprasta kelionė į Trakų kraštą* [Die Hiesigen: Eine außergewöhnliche Reise in die Region von Trakai], Vilnius: Lietuvių literatūros ir tautosakos institutas.

Li, Wei (2011), »Moment analysis and translanguaging space: discursive construction of identities by multilingual chinese youth in Britain«, *Journal of Pragmatics* 43, S. 1222–1235.

Morita, Koji (2006), *Przemiany socjolingwistyczne w polskich społecznościach na Litwie (region Trocki) i Białorusi (region Iwieniecki): Studium porównawcze* [Soziolinguistischer Wandel in den polnischen Gemeinschaften Litauens (Region Trakai) und Weißrusslands (Region Iwjanez): Eine vergleichende Studie], Warszawa: Slawistyczny ośrodek wydawniczy.

Niendorf, Mathias (2006), *Das Großfürstentum Litauen: Studien zur Nationsbildung in der Frühen Neuzeit (1569–1795)*, Wiesbaden: Harrassowitz.

—, — (2012), »Zwischen historischer und ethnischer Nation: Die litauische Nationalbewegung und die Rolle der Sprache«, in Konrad Maier (Hrsg.), *Nation und Sprache in Nordosteuropa im 19. Jahrhundert*, Wiesbaden: Harrassowitz, S. 294–312.

Peterson, John (2015), *Sprache und Migration*, Heidelberg: Winter.

Puleri, Marco (2020), *Ukrainian, Russophone, (Other) Russian: Hybrid Identities and Narratives in Post-Soviet Culture and Politics*, Frankfurt/Main et al.: Peter Lang.

Ramonienė, Meilutė (2010), Hrsg., *Miestai ir kalbos* [Städte und Sprachen], Vilnius: Vilniaus universiteto leidykla.

—, — (2013), Hrsg., *Miestai ir kalbos II: Sociolingvistinis Lietuvos žemėlapis*. [Städte und Sprachen II: Die soziolinguistische Karte Litauens], Vilnius: Vilniaus universiteto leidykla.

von Rauch, Georg (³1990), *Geschichte der baltischen Staaten*, München: Deutscher Taschenbuch-Verlag.

[Rutkowska, Krystyna] Kristina Rutkovska (2019), »Kalbos, tautybės ir valstybingumo sąsajos pietryčių Lietuvos lenkų naratyvuose« [Die Beziehungen zwischen Sprache, Nationalität und Staatlichkeit in den Darstellungen von Polen aus Südostlitauen], in Irena Smetonienė / Marius Smetona / Kristina Rutkovska (Hrsg.), *Kalba: Tauta: Valstybė*, Vilnius: Vilniaus universiteto leidykla, S. 179–251.

Said, Edward (1993), *Culture and Imperialism*, London: Vintage Books.

Schwarz, Thomas (2015), »Hybridität: Ein begriffsgeschichtlicher Aufriss«, *Zeitschrift für interkulturelle Germanistik* 6:1, S. 163–180.

Sutherland, John (2012), »Heteroglossie«, in John Sutherland, *50 Schlüsselideen Literatur*, übers. v. Martina Wiese, Heidelberg: Spektrum, S. 140–143.

Tesch, Sviatlana (2014), »Morphological hybrids: Belarusian-Russian word forms in Belarusian Trasjanka«, in Gerd Hentschel / Oleksandr Taranenko / Sjarhej Zaprudski, Hrsg., *Trasjanka und Suržyk – gemischte weißrussisch-russische und ukrainisch-russische Rede: Sprachlicher Inzest in Weißrussland und der Ukraine?*, Frankfurt/Main et al.: Peter Lang, S. 219–231.

Turska, Halina (Галина Турска) (1995), *O powstaniu polskich obszarów językowych na Wileńszczyźnie / О происхождении польскоязычных ареалов в Вильнюсском крае* [1939] [Zur Entstehung der polnischen Sprachgebiete in der Region Vilnius], Vilnius: Mintis. (Verwendet wurde der Reprint der Ausg. v. 1939, der in die genannte Ausgabe eingebunden ist.)

Waszakowa, Krystyna (2003), »Czy w słowotwórstwie pojęcie hybryda jest przydatne?« [Ist der Begriff »Hybrid« in der Wortbildung nützlich?], *Poradnik językowy* 10, S. 3–11.

Wiemer, Björn (2003), »›Mowa prosta‹ – Präliminaria zu einer strukturellen Beschreibung«, in Renate Blankenhorn / Joanna Błaszczak / Robert Marzari (Hrsg.), *Beiträge der Europäischen Slavistischen Linguistik (POLYSLAV)*, Band 6, München: Verlag Otto Sagner, S. 227–237.

Yildiz, Erol (2019), »Postmigrantische Lebensentwürfe jenseits der Parallelgesellschaft«, in Alexander Böttcher / Marc Hill / Anita Rotter / Frauke Schacht / Maria A. Wolf / Erol Yildiz (Hrsg.), *Migration bewegt und bildet: Kontrapunktische Betrachtungen*, Innsbruck: Innsbruck university press, S. 13–27.

Zielińska, Anna (2004), »Mowa Prosta und andere Begriffe aus dem Vokabular des Forschers in der slavisch-baltischen Kontaktzone«, *Zeitschrift für Slawistik* 49, S. 297–307.

Zinkevičius, Zigmas (1993), *Rytų Lietuva praeityje ir dabar* [Ostlitauen in der Vergangenheit und heute], Vilnius: Mokslo ir enciklopedijų leidykla.

6.2.2 Digitale Titel

 Bernardinai.lt (2017), »Tarmę turime puoselėti, bet ir su slengu nepakovosime« [Wir müssen den Dialekt pflegen, aber lasst uns den Slang auch nicht bekämpfen], Infoportal.

Bilaniuk, Laada (2018), »The politics of hybridity and purity in Ukrainian language and identity«, Seminarreihe im Rahmen des 23. Greifswalder Ukrainicums, Archivseite.

Ha!art (2014), »Fantomy Europy Środkowo-Wschodniej« [Die Phantome Mittel- und Osteuropas], *Kelet* 48:4, Internetmagazin.

Polonskis, Bartošas (2020), »Romanas ›Robčikas‹: seksas, narkotikai ir šaltanosiai tuteišiškiai«, *Kalbų vakaras* 13: *Kalbų vakaro kalbos*, S. 13–15, digitale Zeitschrift der Universität Vilnius.

Prie Smetonos (2022), »Kalba tuteišiškai ir tuo didžiuojasi« [Spricht auf ›Hiesig‹ und ist stolz darauf], *Žinių radijas*, Sendung vom 04.04.22, Videointerview.

[Rutkowska, Krystyna] Kristina Rutkovska (2016), Hrsg., *Lietuvos lenkų tarmės* [Die Mundarten der Polen in Litauen], interaktive Karte, Universität Vilnius.

Sociologai.lt (2012), »Vilnietiškoji heteroglosija: Vilniaus lenkų kalbiniai ypatumai šiandien« [Die Vilniusser Heteroglossie: Sprachliche Besonderheiten der Vilniusser Polen heute], Infoportal.

WilnotekaLT (2010), »Rozmówki polsko-wileńskie« [Polnisch-Vilniusser Gespräche], You-Tube-Kanal.

ZOiS-Interview (2020), »Meet the Author – Marco Puleri ›Die Identität russischsprachiger Menschen in der Ukraine wurde sozial und politisch vereinnahmt‹««, Archivseite des ZOiS Berlin.